1964 Democratic National Convention

The Winner

Miss America of 1964, Donna Axum, won America's heart at her own convention last September at Atlantic City. And, fittingly, Donna refreshes with the drink that's always the winner—light, bracing Pepsi-Cola. You'll love the way Pepsi's sparkling-light taste drenches your thirst, refreshes like no other. So think young . . . say "Pepsi, please!"

Now it's Pepsi for those who think young

"PEPSI-COLA" AND "PEPSI" ARE TRADEMARKS OF PEPSI-COLA COMPANY, REG. U.S. PAT. OFF. © 1964, PEPSI-COLA COMPANY

UNIVERSAL AMERICAN
CORPORATION
200 PARK AVENUE, NEW YORK, N. Y. 10017

MAJOR SUBSIDIARIES AND DIVISIONS

THE AMERICAN PULLEY COMPANY, PHILADELPHIA, PA.
    HARDIE SPRAYING PRODUCTS, PHILADELPHIA, PA.

AMRON CORPORATION, WAUKESHA, WIS.

BINGHAM STAMPING, TOLEDO, OHIO

BOHN ALUMINUM & BRASS COMPANY, DETROIT, MICH.
    BEARING AND BUSHING DIVISION, GREENSBURG, IND.
    HEAT TRANSFER DIVISION, DANVILLE AND BEARDSTOWN, ILLINOIS
    FOUNDRY DIVISION, SOUTH HAVEN, MICH. & BUTLER, IND.
    EXTRUSION, BRASS AND FABRICATION DIVISIONS, ADRIAN & HOLLAND, MICH.

PAUL HARDEMAN, INC., DETROIT, MICH.; STANTON, CALIF.; NEW YORK, NEW YORK
    YOUNG SPRING & WIRE COMPANY, DETROIT, MICH.
    AUTOMOTIVE PRODUCTS DIVISIONS, DETROIT, MICH.; CHICAGO, ILL.; ECORSE, MICH.; ARCHBOLD, OHIO; LOS ANGELES, CALIF.
    YOUNG SPRING & WIRE CORPORATION OF CANADA, LTD., WINDSOR, ONTARIO; AJAX, ONTARIO, (TORONTO)
    CANADIAN AUTOMOTIVE TRIM DIVISION, AJAX, ONTARIO

CLIMATE CONDITIONING COMPANY, STANTON, CALIF.
TRUCK & CONSTRUCTION EQUIPMENT DIVISION, BOWLING GREEN, OHIO; UPPER SANDUSKY, OHIO; OTTAWA, KANSAS; DETROIT, MICH.
UTILITY METAL PRODUCTS DIVISION, PASADENA, CALIF.
PAUL HARDEMAN INTERNATIONAL, S.A., STANTON, CALIF.

HUBBARD SPOOL, GARRETT, IND.

LIVINGSTON ROCK & GRAVEL CO., INC.
    LIVINGSTON-GRAHAM INC., EL MONTE, CALIF.
    JONES CONCRETE COMPANY, SANTA MONICA, CALIF.

MORSE TWIST DRILL & MACHINE COMPANY, NEW BEDFORD, MASS.

NORMA-HOFFMANN BEARINGS COMPANY, STAMFORD, CONN.

SUPER TOOL COMPANY, ELK RAPIDS, MICH.

VAN NORMAN MACHINE COMPANY, SPRINGFIELD, MASS.

VON KOHORN-UNIVERSAL CORPORATION, STANTON, CALIF.
    BUTTERWORTH MANUFACTURING COMPANY, DIVISION, BETHAYRES, PA.

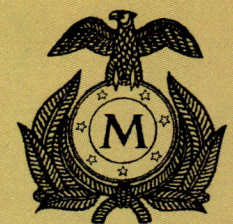

Enjoy The Grand Manner of Matson to Hawaii

Come aboard luxurious SS Lurline. Here, on Matson's Pacific between the Mainland and Hawaii, discover regal comforts, lavish considerations—the pleasure and leisure of ocean travel. For 4½ days and 5 nights each way charms and graces that have all but disappeared from life on land surround you every moment. It's so much more enjoyable to go to and from Hawaii in the Grand Manner of Matson.

Yet a Matson cruise is not costly. Economy staterooms with bath nearby are priced from $414 round trip. Staterooms with private bath start at $567 round trip. And the price of your ticket includes all of the countless niceties for which Matson's exclusively First Class liners are renowned. To select your stateroom and sailing date see your travel agent. Or write Matson Lines, 215 Market Street, San Francisco 5, California.

THE VACATION WAY TO AND FROM HAWAII

Consider paper.
Used with imagination, its power to

notify, beautify, glorify,

is incalculable.
We offer the world's largest selection of commercial printing papers. And we can help you use them with great imagination.
Champion Papers

Here's a car built to support any population explosion. It's a Ford Country Squire looking young all over.

More brawn in the body puts more life in today's Ford Motor Company cars

Young bodies grow strong with exercise. But a car body has to be born rugged. Especially with a flock of husky youngsters in the family.

How long a life your car body has depends on how solidly it's built. If it's not strong—wear and tear, squeaks and rattles. That's why all Ford-built cars give you so much extra reinforcing.

Take the roof those youngsters are perched on. Three separate steel braces make it super-solid to sit on (or ride under). Doors are built like a safe. Steel inside and out. That means stronger, safer, quieter doors. Slam one—you can tell by the sound they're solidly built. Underneath, too, extra heavy construction keeps the body more solid and silent, even over washboard roads.

Engineering excellence like this puts more value into Ford Motor Company cars wherever you look. It's all part of a plan to give you today's best-built cars. A plan where engineering designs the quality for the car. Manufacturing precision puts it there. Severe testing sees that it stays.

RIDE WALT DISNEY'S MAGIC SKYWAY AT THE FORD MOTOR COMPANY WONDER ROTUNDA, NEW YORK WORLD'S FAIR

Ford-built means better built  MUSTANG · FALCON · FAIRLANE · FORD · THUNDERBIRD
COMET · MERCURY · LINCOLN CONTINENTAL

MOTOR COMPANY

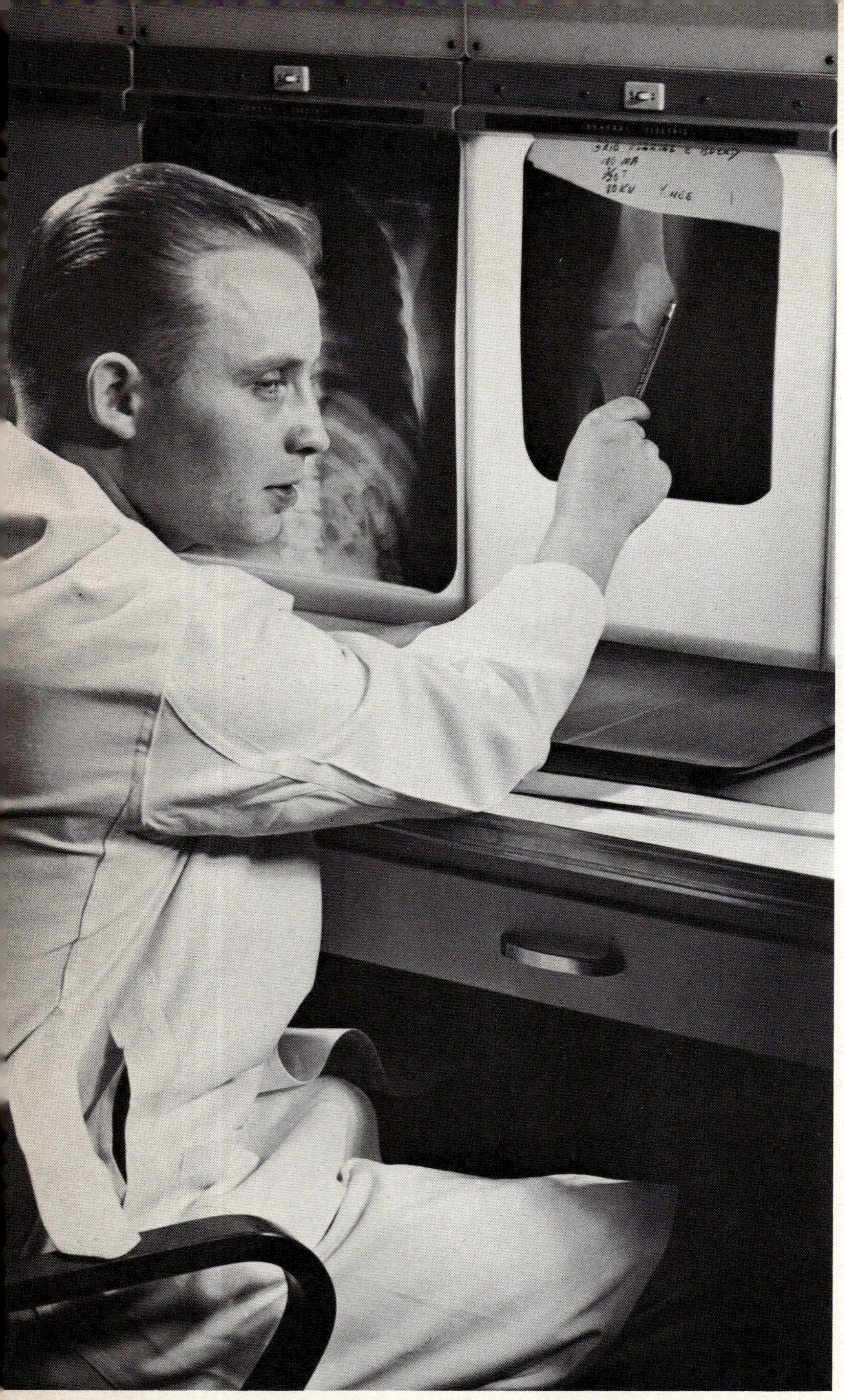

cenco ferrania

Working together for America's good health

Great advances in the use of radiological techniques for diagnosing disease are helping to save thousands of lives each year.

The development and increasing use of these techniques has created a growing demand for exceptionally high quality X-ray film and chemicals. High quality supplies, at low cost, help make a better level of diagnosis available to greater numbers of people, including those benefitting through federal, state and private medical assistance programs.

To meet this growing need, Cenco Instruments Corporation an important manufacturer of scientific instruments and supplies to the research and medical communities, has joined forces with Ferrania of Italy, one of the world's highly regarded makers of X-ray film and chemicals.

Cenco's more than three-quarters of a century's experience serving the American scientific and medical communities has resulted in an expert knowledge of the technical problems and needs of hospitals and researchers. Cenco provides Ferrania with production guidance in line with their knowledge of market requirements.

Ferrania provides Cenco with the manufacturing capability for producing low cost, premium quality radiographic supplies for normal requirements as well as new types to meet advanced requirements.

Cenco X-Ray Company, an entirely new division of Cenco Instruments Corporation, and Ferrania are helping the American medical community to provide the finest medical care available anywhere in the world.

CIC-4-211

cenco X-RAY U.S. DISTRIBUTOR OF **ferrania** RADIOGRAPHIC MATERIALS

a division of Cenco Instruments Corporation
Chicago, Illinois

How to make perfect copies from colors, objects, pages in books, pencil writing, ball point pen signatures in seconds. Automatically. On ordinary paper. For about a nickel a copy.

The Xerox 914 below is shown in actual operation. The green light you see is the 914 scanning light. The light passes under the original document on the scanning plate making a perfect copy. Every time. You borrow the 914. You pay Xerox only for the copies you make. (Based on a minimum number of copies per month.) This all figures to be about 5¢ a copy. **XEROX**

Watch General Eisenhower, Senators Humphrey and Ervin on ABC-TV and XEROX convention coverage and election night returns.

XEROX CORPORATION, ROCHESTER, N.Y. 14603. OFFICES IN MAJOR U.S. CITIES. CANADA: XEROX OF CANADA LIMITED, TORONTO. OVERSEAS: RANK XEROX LTD., LONDON; FUJI-XEROX CO., LTD., TOKYO, BOTH JOINTLY OWNED WITH RANK ORGANISATION, LTD.

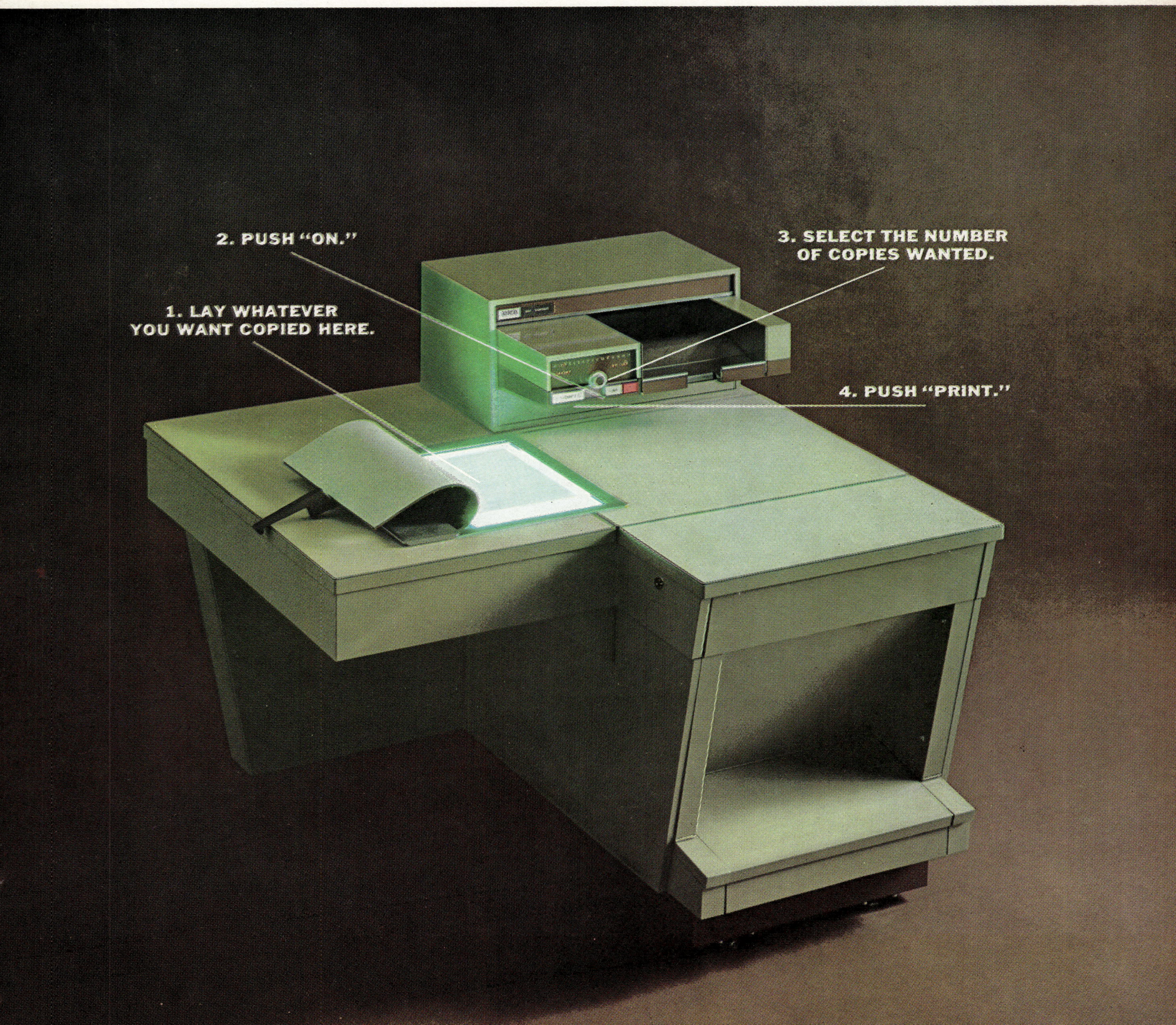

1. LAY WHATEVER YOU WANT COPIED HERE.
2. PUSH "ON."
3. SELECT THE NUMBER OF COPIES WANTED.
4. PUSH "PRINT."

You can read character all over its face!

Large capitals.......... demonstrate pride

Simplicity of style.... shows maturity

Even spacing............ reveals consistency

.....Large loops point to pleasure

.....Easy flow reveals excellent taste

.....Slanting script shows individualit[y]

6 YEARS OLD. IMPORTED IN BOTTLE FROM CANADA. BLENDED CANADIAN WHISKY. 86.8 PROOF. IMPORTED BY HIRAM WALKER IMPORTERS, INC., DETROIT, MICHIGAN

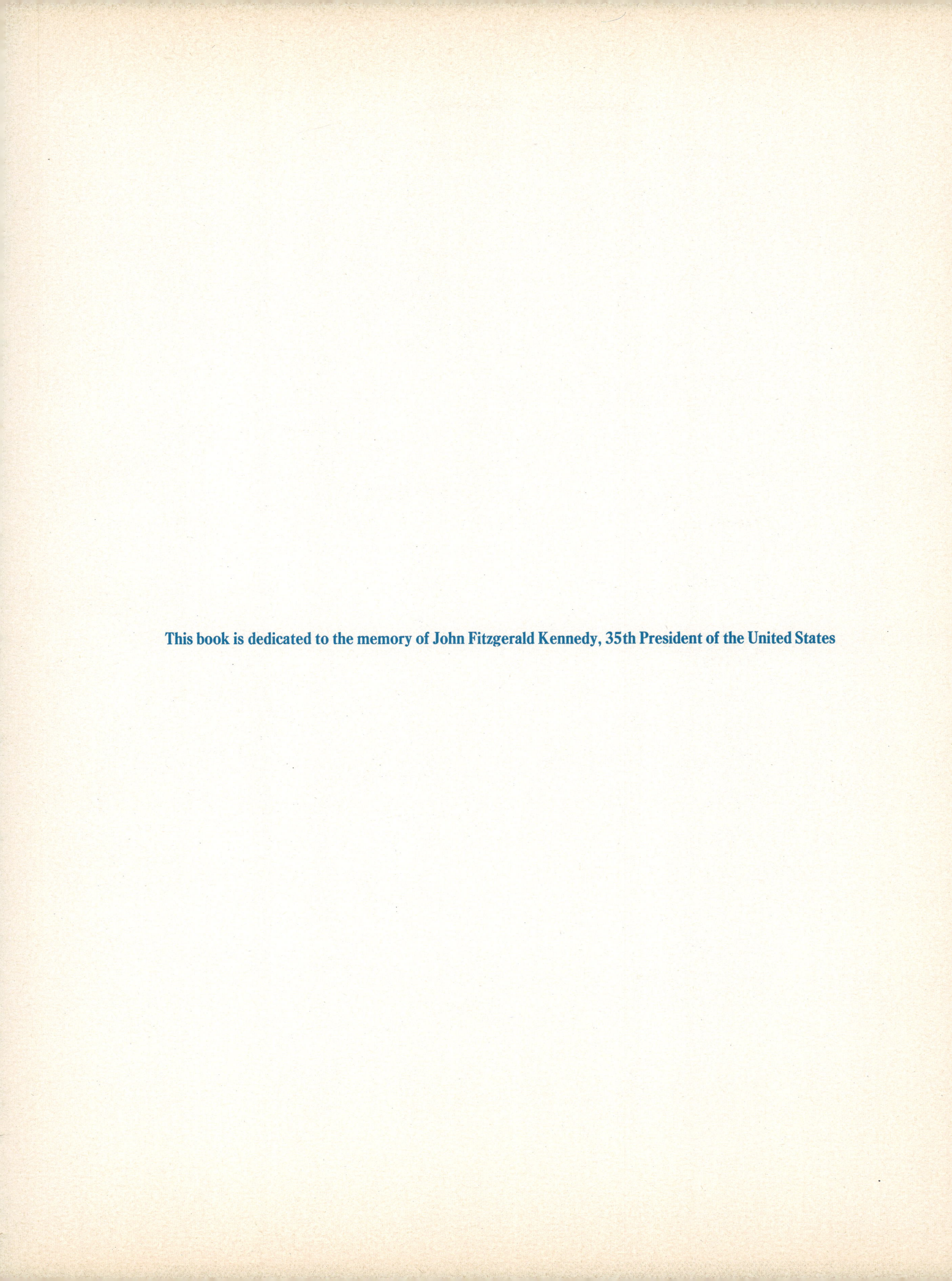

This book is dedicated to the memory of John Fitzgerald Kennedy, 35th President of the United States

PUBLISHED BY 1964 DEMOCRATIC CONVENTION PROGRAM BOOK COMMITTEE: 1625 "I" STREET, N. W., WASHINGTON, D. C.: COPYRIGHT 1964 BY THE DEMOCRATIC NATIONAL CONVENTION PROGRAM BOOK COMMITTEE. ALL RIGHTS RESERVED.: PRINTED IN THE UNITED STATES OF AMERICA BY JUDD & DETWEILER, INC., WASHINGTON, D. C.: DESIGNED BY DOYLE DANE BERNBACH, INC., NEW YORK, N. Y.

contents

Part I
THE DEMOCRATIC PARTY
The Democratic Party and
American Leadership in the World
by William Attwood
Page 18
"The Great Collaboration"
by Sidney Hyman
Page 34

Part II
JOHN FITZGERALD KENNEDY
John Fitzgerald Kennedy
by Arthur Schlesinger, Jr.
Page 72
The Kennedy Record
by John Bartlow Martin
Page 78

Part III
LYNDON BAINES JOHNSON
'A President—Not a Candidate'
by John Steinbeck
Page 94
"The Great Society"
by President Lyndon Baines Johnson
Page 98

Part IV
PRESIDENTS' LADIES
Presidents' Ladies
by Marianne Means
Page 115

Part V
BUILDING THE GREAT SOCIETY
Education For The Great Society
Page 130
Space —
"A Position of Pre-eminence"
Page 142
The Peaceful Role
of Atomic Energy
Page 146

Part VI
NOW...ABOUT "POLITICS"
Conventions And Communications
by Sidney Hyman
Page 157
In The Beginning Is The Word
by Sidney Hyman
Page 160
A History Lesson About
Dark Horses
by Sidney Hyman
Page 166

The
Democratic
Party

THE DEMOCRATIC PARTY AND AMERICA'S LEADERSHIP IN THE WORLD

by William Attwood. Former Foreign Editor of Look Magazine...European correspondent for Collier's Magazine...Writer, New York Herald Tribune...Former Ambassador to Guinea ...Now Ambassador to Kenya.

Thomas Jefferson, who used to say that the American Revolution was intended for all mankind, would be proud to be a Democrat today. He would be proud of the role America has played in our time, under Democratic leadership, in shaping the history of mankind's most revolutionary era. And he would be proud of the way the world has responded to the leaders—and the leadership—of the Party he founded 166 years ago.

When Jefferson was President, America was a defenseless confederation standing at the mercy of great world powers, a debtor nation with an agricultural economy. Yet Jefferson proclaimed that our nation was the strongest on earth, not because of our military might or our productive capacity—for we had neither—but because of our revolutionary ideals and our high moral purpose.

Today the United States is no longer poor and defenseless. Our military might and productive capacity are second to none. But the real roots of America's present strength and influence in the world are still the ideals and principles enunciated by Jefferson and carried out at home and abroad by Democratic Presidents in our own century.

It is no accident that a global traveller today can easily find streets and avenues and monuments in the capital cities of every continent honoring the name and memory of Woodrow Wilson, of Franklin

Roosevelt, of Harry Truman and now of John F. Kennedy; nor that he will have to look long and hard and usually in vain for any such tributes to Presidents Taft, Harding, Coolidge or even Eisenhower. For the Democratic party and its policies have been in tune with the times in which we live, and its leaders have stirred the hearts of all mankind. But in this era of violent and unprecedented change, the basic Republican policy has been to fight change—both at home and abroad, to deny that it is happening and to be unready for it when it comes.

Time and again the Republicans have looked back and sought ways to avoid the burdens of world leadership and to take it easy; time and again the Democrats have looked ahead and sought ways to shoulder the burdens and to get things done. That is why American leadership has not always been effective in this century; for periods of action and achievement under Democratic Presidents have been interrupted by periods of drift and stagnation each time the Republicans came to power.

Our emergence as a world power is a comparatively recent event. Up until World War I United States foreign policy was essentially continental: its objectives were to acquire and develop new land in North America and keep the European powers

out of the Western Hemisphere. At the end of the 19th century we had achieved these objectives. The West was won, the frontier had disappeared and the Monroe Doctrine, enforced in part by the British fleet, had kept us secure from European imperialism.

World War I ended our comfortable isolation. With British sea power threatened by Germany, our Atlantic moat suddenly became a defenseless plain. We entered the war to meet that threat, and in the process became a world power.

Woodrow Wilson, our wartime leader, had a vision, like Franklin Roosevelt a generation later, of a better world order emerging from the agony of war—a world order in which America would have to play a leading part. Wilson's social and economic programs, called the New Freedom, had already strengthened and invigorated American society and laid the foundation for Roosevelt's New Deal. Now he saw that America's youthful vigor and idealism were needed to lay the foundation for a stable peace on the ruins of dynastic Europe.

Wilson's Fourteen Points and his dream of a League of Nations to enforce peace made him a hero among the people of Europe. In 1919, when he became the first American President to go abroad, cheering crowds everywhere turned his trip into a triumphal tour. Because of Wilson and what he stood for, America's prestige and influence in the world had never been higher.

But Wilson's hopes were shattered back home by what Dean Acheson has called a "ferocious" attack on him and his policies by the Republican Party. Hungry for victory in 1920, the Republicans in effect told the voters what they wanted to hear —that it was time to relax, make money and forget about the world beyond our shores.

Governor Cox, the Democratic candidate, spoke of the vigorous leadership that America was going to have to exert if we were to win the peace. He developed Wilson's idea of "creative statesmanship" and said, as Democrats say today, that America must always be pressing onward toward what Wilson called the New Freedom—and what John F. Kennedy called the New Frontier.

But America listened instead to the soft and reassuring words of Warren Harding who said the country needed "...not heroism but healing, not nostrums but normalcy...not submergence in internationality but sustainment in triumphant nationality."

That is what the country was offered, what it voted for and what it got. Wilson said, after the election, "We will see the tragedy of it all." We did. In ten years the tragedy was economic disaster for America. A decade later the tragedy was a holocaust of war that engulfed the world.

Meanwhile, under Harding, Coolidge, and Hoover, America in the twenties reverted to a now archaic isolationism. In Europe, the League of Nations limped along without us, while Hitler and Mussolini flexed their muscles. In Latin America, dollar diplomacy dispatched U. S. Marines to make the continent safe, not for American ideals, but for American business—and the scars have barely healed today. The United States became more or less irrelevant in international politics. And small wonder. For timid, unimaginative and conservative government is bound to develop a timid, unimaginative and conservative foreign policy.

It was Roosevelt and the New Deal that finally restored the image of a vital, progressive America concerned for the welfare of its own citizens and sympathetic to its neighbors' problems.

For foreign and domestic policies cannot be separated. When Franklin Roosevelt and George Norris built the TVA in the 1930's, the story of its remarkable success reached the people of the world, and visitors from everywhere came to marvel at these mighty dams and the flowering of a richer and fuller life for millions of people. As John F. Kennedy said in the 1960 campaign, "The reason that the people of the world believed in the Good Neighbor Policy of Franklin Roosevelt was that Franklin Roosevelt was a good neighbor here at home."

In short, when we are on the move in America we are respected for it abroad. But when the story of America is a story of apathy, neglect and indifference, no amount of propaganda can hide the truth from people in other countries. When a Negro child is denied admission to a school, or an unemployed miner faces grim poverty, the image of America is defaced and our capacity for leadership is eroded. We Democrats have known this truth for a long time, but the Republicans, with their view of the Federal Government as a necessary evil, seem oblivious to it even today.

Like Wilson, Roosevelt was a fighting leader—in peace, against poverty and despair at home; and in war, against the new worldwide menace of fascism. His foreign policy reversed years of Republican isolationism and chauvinism. The Good Neighbor Policy and the Reciprocal Trade Agreement opened up a new era of cooperation and understanding with our friends. And his famous "quarantine the aggressors" speech, his call for a peacetime Selective Service Act and his support for lend-lease when World War II broke out made it plain to the world where America stood in the fight against Nazi and Japanese imperialism.

The war mobilized American power as never before. Our servicemen and equipment found their way to every corner of the globe. And with victory in 1945, America became the hope and salvation of a battered and impoverished Europe and Japan now threatened by the agents of a new imperialism. A return to Harding's "normalcy" this time would have been truly fatal to the cause of freedom in the world. Fortunately, though the Republicans captured the Congress in 1946, a great Democratic President, Harry S. Truman, was in the White House.

Under his leadership, the Fair Deal succeeded the New Deal, free world unity was forged and the Soviet threat to Western Europe turned back. U. S. firmness stopped the Russians in Iran and Turkey in 1946. U. S. aid saved Greece in 1947. The Marshall Plan restored Europe's economy.

And it was under Democratic leadership that America provided the impetus for the United Nations, the North Atlantic Treaty and the Organization of American States. Between 1947 and 1950 alone hardly six months passed without new and audacious policies for peace being evolved and set in motion. We were the unchallenged leaders of the free world and we acted the part. We proclaimed the Truman Doctrine, we launched the Point Four Program, we defeated the Berlin Blockade and we stopped Communist aggression in Korea.

These bold and decisive actions won the respect of friend and foe alike and constituted a revolution in American foreign policy. And thanks to the momentum which they generated, America was able to coast through the eight fumbling years that followed.

The prevailing attitude was reflected in the budget message of 1955, of which Walter Lippmann wrote, "In this budget, the exigencies of the cold war receive no more than token recognition."

Yet these were the years when the Soviet Union, under Nikita Khrushchev, launched a major propaganda and economic effort to win the allegiance of the restless masses in the poor and newly independent nations. These were the years when the Soviets beat us into space and beat us to the punch in posing as the champions of peace in a war-weary world.

And these were the years when the image of the United States, as the nation which gave birth to the Declaration of Independence and the Four Freedoms, was tarnished and discredited by rampant McCarthyism at home and by smugness and saber-rattling abroad.

While our Foreign Service was being demoralized by witch-hunts, John Foster Dulles demoralized our friends and allies with loud and hollow pronouncements about "unleashing Chiang" and "massive retaliation." He threatened Europe with "an agonizing reappraisal" of our policies, which never took place, frightened the world with talk of "brinkmanship" and antagonized India and other potential friends by denouncing neutralism as "immoral."

Madison Avenue catchwords replaced meaningful consultation and hardheaded diplomacy to the point that our two oldest allies, France and Britain, launched their attack on Suez without even informing us. In response to Communist propaganda that trumpeted peace, independence and trade, we stressed the kind of security pacts and military missions which once stopped Stalin's soldiers but no longer worked against Khrushchev's salesmen. Instead of educating the American people to the facts of life in a changing world, the Republicans clung to the stale slogans of the past and replied to any criticism by accusing Democrats of being soft on Communism—and worse.

In 1954, Richard Nixon scorned the decision to stop Communist aggression in Korea as the "fruitless and unnecessary" result of a "Truman-Acheson stumblebum program" and accused Adlai Stevenson of "spreading pro-Communist propaganda" for calling attention to the alarming rate of Soviet economic growth.

What the Democrats were saying during this period was that we could not afford to rest on our oars. As Lyndon Johnson told a Washington audience in 1958: "We need the marshalling of our resources, physical and mental, such as we have never had before. We need imagination and freshness. We need force and boldness in our leadership." What the Republicans were saying in effect is that if we balanced the budget and produced more consumer goods, the Soviet challenge would somehow disappear.

President Eisenhower was in no mood to rally the country to achieve a greater tempo in our development of national power. To do so, he said, "...we would have to take our country and make it an armed camp and regiment it and get people steamed up like you did in wars." Finally, in 1960, Walter Lippmann was moved to write: "Mr. Eisenhower...has resigned himself to an attitude of defeatism in which there is no faith that our people have the will, the energy, the resourcefulness and the capacity to close ranks, if they are summoned to a greater effort. Mr. Eisenhower is talking like a tired old man who has lost touch with the springs of our national vitality."

Thus, by 1960, we had lost much of the esteem and confidence that we had earned in the world during the Roosevelt and Truman years. McCarthyism did fade away, largely because of the Senate censure vote in which Lyndon Johnson, as Majority Leader, played a key role; but the inaction and indecision in high places that permitted its excesses did not disappear. As Adlai Stevenson said in 1960, the Eisenhower Administration "...did not produce a single new idea or policy that will stand the test of time or the scrutiny of history."

The American people had discovered that the "modern Republicans" of the fifties were little different from the Old Guard Republicans of the twenties. The difference, as Mort Sahl once put it, was that the Old Guard thought that nothing should be done for the first time, while the modern Republicans felt it should, but not now.

In 1960, the nation was ready to move again—and it did by electing John Fitzgerald Kennedy President. He expressed America's mood early in the campaign out in California when he said: "We can better unite the free world in an aggressive battle against poverty and disease and illiteracy when we have successfully eliminated those same features from our own system—when we have demonstrated that we are on the move in this country—when we have demonstrated that we are capable of leadership at home as well as abroad."

While Nixon proclaimed that American prestige was never higher (despite the fact that Eisenhower had just cancelled a trip to Japan because of anti-American riots), Kennedy hammered at the need for U. S. action and initiative in foreign affairs.

He said he was tired of reading every day what Mr. Khrushchev was doing—he wanted to read what the President of the United States was doing. He sought the Presidency, he said, "...because I want to get things done."

In November, the voters gave Kennedy that chance; and in January, on the Capitol steps, he delivered an inaugural address that echoed around the world:

"Let the word go forth from this time and place, to friend and foe alike, that the torch has been passed to a new generation of Americans, born in this century, tempered by war, disciplined by a hard and bitter peace, proud of our ancient heritage and unwilling to witness or permit the slow undoing of those human rights to which this nation has always been committed, and to which we are committed today at home and around the world."

Friend and foe alike quickly sensed the power and purpose of the new Administration.

And those of us who were privileged to represent our country abroad in 1961 could say with pride, "This is what President Kennedy believes. This is what America stands for."

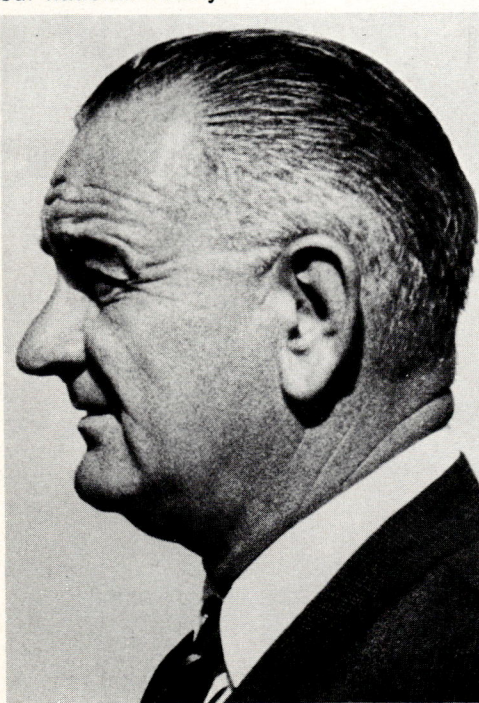

John F. Kennedy was trusted and respected by the young leaders of our revolutionary world because he could speak their language: he understood their problems and could make them understand ours. They thought of him as a friend. It was because of him that the leaders of black Africa have been so understanding of the torment and violence of our own struggle for equality at home.

And our adversaries respected him too. During the Cuban crisis, the Russians discovered they were up against the kind of man who spoke softly but could not be bluffed or pushed around. Kennedy's handling of that crisis was a turning point in the cold war. His firmness, coupled with restraint, paved the way for last year's nuclear test treaty—the first significant step in the long road towards a lasting peace.

A few months later, the President who had done so much in so short a time to restore American prestige was shot in Dallas. And the world mourned with us. For he had captured the affection as well as the imagination of people in every corner of the globe.

Fortunately, the momentum that John F. Kennedy gave our country will continue in the years ahead. As Adlai Stevenson wrote a few months ago, "The drive, the convictions, the principles and programs that were a part of the New Frontier will never be lost so long as Lyndon Johnson is President."

In this election year, Democrats can be confident that he will be President for a long time to come. And the country can be thankful. For President Johnson, like his Democratic predecessors, is an authentic leader. He knows that leadership that would rather drift than make tough decisions will not keep the initiative in the cold war. He knows that leadership that cares more about interest rates than the public interest will never hear the voice of humanity. He knows that leadership that does not understand the needs of our own people will never understand the needs of mankind.

Franklin Roosevelt once said that his generation had "a rendezvous with destiny." So does ours. And the destiny of our generation is to save peace and freedom, not only for America, but for the whole family of man. The destiny of this generation of Americans is to make history again.

We have made history only under strong Presidents. We have one today. Like Thomas Jefferson, who used the power of the Presidency on behalf of the people, Lyndon Johnson has been and will be giving all of his vitality, his courage and his intelligence to the service of his country.

And like Jefferson, who believed the American Revolution belonged to all mankind, President Johnson spoke of America's role in building a safer, saner world when he addressed the representatives of 113 countries at the United Nations last December:

"Man's age-old hopes remain our goal: that this world, under God, can be safe for diversity, and free from hostility, and a better place for our children and all generations in the years to come. And therefore, any man and any nation that seeks peace, and hates war, and is willing to fight the good fight against hunger and disease and ignorance and misery, will find the United States of America by their side, willing to walk with them, walk with them every step of the way."

Words like these coming from the President of the United States are heard and read around the world. And their echoes tell us that with Lyndon Johnson in the White House, we can rest secure that America's revitalized prestige and moral leadership in the world will continue to serve the cause of peace and freedom in the years ahead.

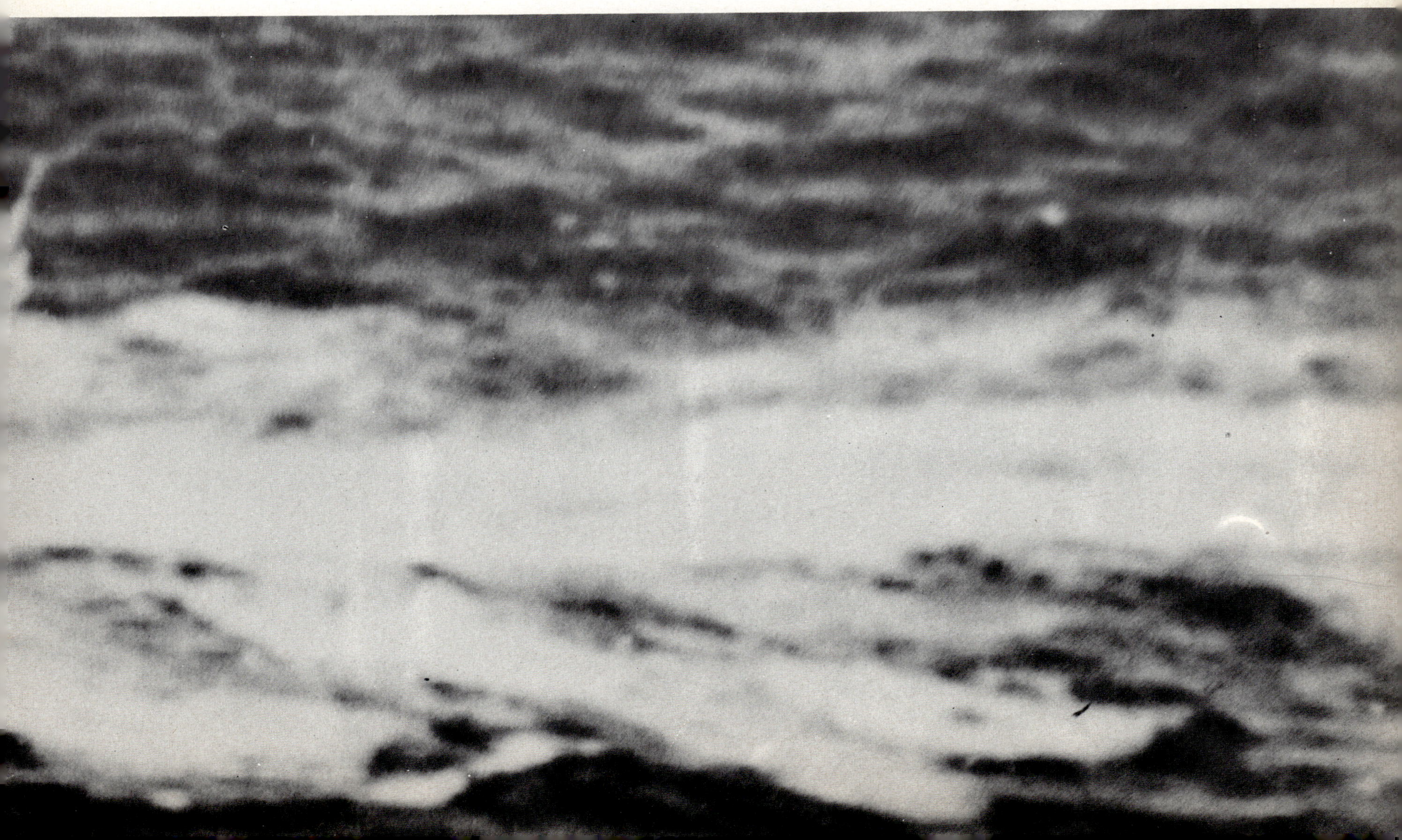

On the move with America

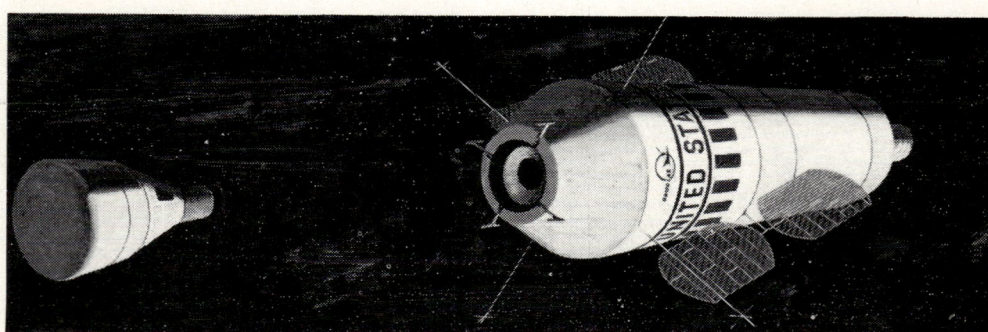

Douglas has undertaken advanced planning studies for a National Aeronautics and Space Administration 6 man orbiting space laboratory.

The Douglas DC-9 will offer 565 mile per hour jetliner service to thousands of communities which the bigger jets now overpass.

The Douglas royal family of jet transports, DC-8s, DC-8Fs and DC-9s, add up to an incomparable airline team.

The new Douglas Space Systems Center, one of the world's finest, will help maintain U.S. space leadership.

PAUL HARDEMAN, INC.

PAUL HARDEMAN, INC., STANTON, CALIF.; DETROIT, MICH.; NEW YORK, NEW YORK
    YOUNG SPRING & WIRE COMPANY, DETROIT, MICH.
        AUTOMOTIVE PRODUCTS DIVISIONS, DETROIT, MICH.; CHICAGO, ILL.; ECORSE, MICH.; ARCHBOLD, OHIO; LOS ANGELES, CALIF.
        YOUNG SPRING & WIRE CORPORATION OF CANADA, LTD., WINDSOR, ONTARIO; AJAX, ONTARIO, (TORONTO)
        CANADIAN AUTOMOTIVE TRIM DIVISION, AJAX, ONTARIO
    CLIMATE CONDITIONING COMPANY, STANTON, CALIF.
    TRUCK & CONSTRUCTION EQUIPMENT DIVISION, BOWLING GREEN, OHIO; UPPER SANDUSKY, OHIO; OTTAWA, KANSAS; DETROIT, MICH.
    UTILITY METAL PRODUCTS DIVISION, PASADENA, CALIF.
    PAUL HARDEMAN INTERNATIONAL, S.A., STANTON, CALIF.

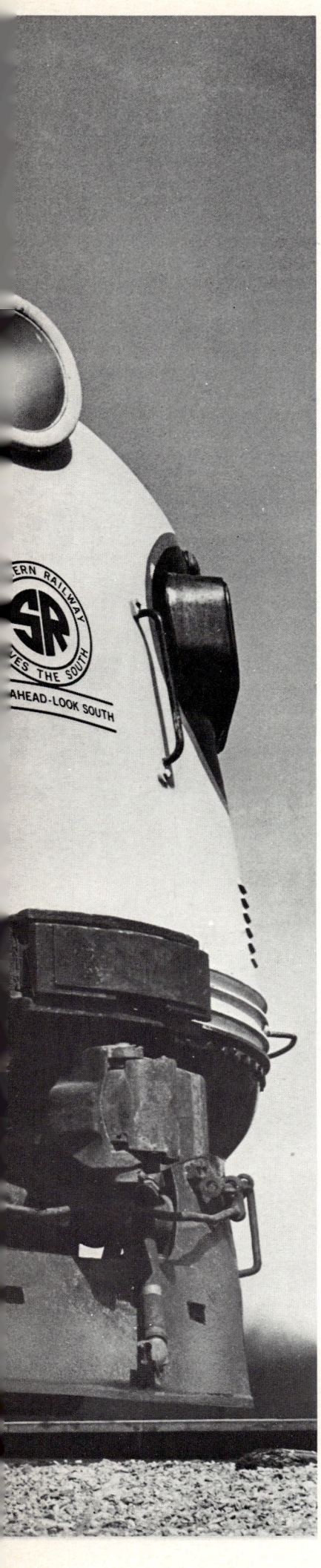

think BIG!

OUR FOREFATHERS DID. And from their dreams grew the strongest, most prosperous country the world has ever known. One big reason for this was railroad transportation — vital then, as now, to America's growth, economy and defense.

Now for the big thought! Today, *your constituents* are being cheated out of several billion dollars annually by artificially high freight rates. Rates kept high by regulation which kills off real competition. As lawmakers, you can put this money in their pockets. How? By passing legislation recommended to Congress by President Kennedy and President Johnson to substitute competition for unnecessary regulation of *reductions* in freight rates on agricultural and bulk commodities. This also will improve the competitiveness of American products against foreign products, at home and abroad.

It's a big thought, all right — as big as all of America's consumers. The lawmakers of our country should have the foresight and courage to correct this sorry situation.

D.W. Brosnan
PRESIDENT

SOUTHERN RAILWAY SYSTEM
WASHINGTON, D.C.

CONVENTION HALL
ATLANTIC CITY, N.J.

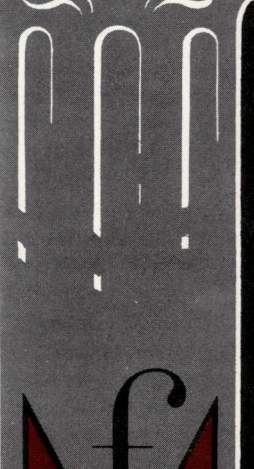

HALLS OF FAME

Wherever and whenever structures with great public appeal are created, Fischbach and Moore is on the job. Our roster of noteworthy electrical installations in this field includes the Convention Hall in Atlantic City—erected in 1928—and other auditoriums in leading cities throughout the nation. For every conceivable type of electrical installation, call on Fischbach and Moore.

"who we serve proves how we serve"

DALLAS MUNICIPAL AUDITORIUM
DALLAS, TEX.

METROPOLITAN OPERA HOUSE
IN THE LINCOLN CENTER FOR THE PERFORMING ARTS
NEW YORK, N.Y.

McCORMICK PLACE EXPOSITION CENTER
CHICAGO, ILL.

FISCHBACH AND MOORE
INCORPORATED
ELECTRICAL CONTRACTORS

COMPLETE ORGANIZATIONS AT: NEW YORK • ATLANTA • CHICAGO • COCOA • DALLAS • DENVER • DETROIT • FLINT • GARY-EAST CHICAGO
HOUSTON • KANSAS CITY • LOS ANGELES • PITTSBURGH • SAN DIEGO • SAN FRANCISCO • SEATTLE • WASHINGTON, D.C.
IN CANADA: FISCHBACH AND MOORE OF CANADA, LTD., MONTREAL • TORONTO **IN AUSTRALIA:** O'DONNELL, GRIFFIN, FISCHBACH & MOORE PTY. LTD., MELBOURNE

The rest of the world will hear what happens here through ITT Communication Systems and Equipment

worldwide electronics and telecommunications **ITT**

Fastest—between Chicago and the Pacific Northwest!

WE SHAVED A DAY OFF THE
CHICAGO-SEATTLE RUN, THANKS TO OUR

CREATIVE CREWS

THE MILWAUKEE ROAD

America's resourceful railroad

Put this one in the record book! Oct. 26, 1963. The Milwaukee Road's new XL-Special fast freight train No. 261 pulls out of Chicago. In 55½ hours the XL is in Seattle. That's a whole day faster than the old running time. Its eastbound counterpart, The Thunderhawk, train No. 262, is the pace setter from the Pacific Northwest to Chicago. *No other railroad matches this service!*

Lopping a day off the schedule was a challenge to our famous Creative Crews. Skilled engineering and operating crews set changes in speed—from mile post to mile post—to establish what seemed like an almost impossible schedule. But the schedules are solid—and the service dependable.

Shipper response has been enthusiastic. Important time and important money are saved when a shipment arrives a whole day sooner—faster than any other rail or truck service.

Fast-freight service is another dramatic example of how the Creative Crews of The Milwaukee Road develop new ways for doing better what the railroads do best. Let your Milwaukee Road representative give you the facts about this fast-freight service. *The Milwaukee Road, Union Station Bldg., Chicago, Illinois 60606*

The Great Collaboration
by Sidney Hyman

by Sydney Hyman. Assistant to Chairman, Encyclopedia Britannica...Associated with Robert Sherwood in the Pulitzer Prize-winning biography, *Roosevelt and Hopkins*...Author, *The American President* and *Beckoning Frontiers*...Contributing writer to New York Times Magazine, Harper's, The Reporter, The Saturday Review, Look.

He was eighty-three years old, his hand could barely hold a pen, and an impatient ambassador of death was at his door. Yet the vital idea that shaped his life's work gave him strength and time for a last task. He was writing a letter due to be read ten days later at a Jubilee celebration in Washington, D. C. It would also be read in the limitless future wherever men dreamt of winning back their right to be human.

> All eyes are opened, or opening, to the rights of man (he wrote.) The general spread of the light of science has already laid open to every view the palpable truth, that the mass of mankind has not been born with saddles on their backs, nor a favored few booted and spurred, ready to ride them legitimately, by the grace of God. These are grounds of hope for others. For ourselves, let the annual return of this day, forever refresh our recollections of these rights, and an undiminished devotion to them.

In other matters, the old man sometimes changed his mind.

There was a time when he was for a "strict construction" of the Constitution, and a time when he construed it liberally; a time when he felt that local government was the real citadel of individual liberty, and a time when he used the full powers of the central government to make America "an empire of liberty;" a time when he argued that America must stay an agricultural nation, and a time when he urged its industrialization; a time when France was the second home of his heart, and a time when he was prepared to turn his back on France and "marry America to the British fleet and nation."

"No maxim," he explained as he drew the moral of his own story, "can be laid down as being wise and expedient for all times and circumstances." The maxim to be applied to a concrete case "... must depend on the circumstances which shall then govern." Was everything, then, changeable? Yes, said he, everything "... except the inherent, unalienable rights of man." These he had steadily served throughout most of his titanic career. Now, however, that career was at its terminal point.

In the dark of a night ten days after the Jubilee letter was sent off, the old man awoke from a fitful sleep. "Is it the Fourth?" he asked the watchers at his bedside. They nodded yes. He murmured, "Ah." Then he serenely closed his eyes.

So died Thomas Jefferson at Monticello, fifty minutes past meridian on July 4, 1826, a half century after the Declaration of Independence he had written was proclaimed to the world.

He had no son to carry on his name. But he had founded a political party, and it carried his seed within its body from one generation to the next.

* * * *

The party twice changed its name. First it was the Republican party (to distinguish it from Monarchists.) Next it was the Democratic-Republican party. Then in the third decade of the 19th century, there was a split in the connecting hyphen, and the name chosen remains what it is today — the Democratic party. The party also changed its views about transient political questions and explained itself as Jefferson did when he wrote:

> Laws and institutions must go hand in hand with the progress of the human mind. As that becomes more developed, more enlightened, as new discoveries are made, new truths disclosed, and manners and opinions change with the change of circumstances, institutions must advance also, and keep pace with the times. We might as well require a man to wear still the coat which fitted him when a boy, as civilized society to remain ever under the regime of their barbarous ancestors.

There was, however, an internal unity in the career of the Democratic party, and the factor making it so was its collaboration with the idea about the rights of man.

The idea turned a loose alliance of local units, first assembled in 1791-3, into a national party. It gave the party the emblem on the banner it unfurled in 1796 when it staged its first campaign for the Presidency. It made the party a force born to have no rest itself, and to allow no rest to the cozy. It compelled the party to see that each success it won was but a down payment on tasks to be done. It bound the party to the proposition that merely to be an American is to live in a kind of moral condition and to have a full-time career.

A list of the more specific achievements that were born of the collaboration between the Democratic party and the idea about the rights of man, reads like a textbook on American government itself. Thus, among other things, the Democratic party made the right to vote a right based on citizenship instead of property. It broke the monopoly of political power by the gentry, and made public posts an attainable goal for qualified men of any origin. It democratized access to knowledge by laying the foundations for a free and universal system of public education. It built new institutions to catch the tone of public opinion, to educate and organize it, and to bring it to bear on the acts of the government. It won for the people the right to choose the President directly, developed the case for a strong President, made the Presidency the special office of the people — and the special servant of the national interest when that interest is something far more than the sum of its component parts.

Democrats were also the first to persuade Americans that a political party could act as an agent of responsible power, and could itself brace the Constitutional system for responsible power. It could screen men for major elective and appointive posts, give a boost to humane men and stand in the way of the bigoted and the intransigent. It could make the party machinery a bridge over the Constitutional chasm between the Executive and the Legislature so that both could march together toward great national objectives. It could forestall violent changes outside the Constitution by working for orderly change within the Constitution.

Then, again, the Democratic party ventured to make itself a school where the native born and the immigrant, the leaders and the led alike were taught the ways of freedom. They were taught specifically that American freedom moves by checks and mutual concessions; that its inner spirit is chivalry and human fraternity; that its shape is like a cathedral on which successive ages have worked, each in its own style—but with a shared love that gives the different parts a unity all the more profound because no one mind conceived of the edifice as a whole.

Nor was this all that was taught in the great Americanization school of the Democratic party. It taught that the first duty of leaders is to explain themselves; that in their proper rivalries with each other, they must always take care not to break the social contract; that any fair political proposal is an invitation to a discussion project; that even after a decision about it is reached, the discussion must go on until dissent is dissolved and a natural consensus is reached.

It taught, further, that no one interest in the land is large enough to form a majority by itself; that each, measured by the aggregate of the others in the nation, is a minority interest; that a majority is formed only through a concurrence of views among many minorities; that even a numerical majority of 50 plus a fraction of 1 percent of the electorate has no autonomous power to act as though anything it does is self-justified; that the numerical majority to be right, must also be just; that the numerical minority of 50 less a fraction of 1 percent may in certain cases have a suspensive political veto over the legal majority, provided it places itself under a self-denying ordinance in its use of that veto.

Again, in the great Americanization school, a line of Presidential and legislative leaders trained by the Democratic party, carried the rights of man beyond the point where the case stood in Jefferson's day. They began, as he did, with political rights, to shield the individual against any strong-arm tactics by the central government. To this they then added the idea of economic rights, to shield the individual from any strong-arm tactics by concentrated private economic power; and in this connection made the central government an ally of the imperiled individual. To the idea of political and economic rights, they added the idea of social and cultural rights, and again made the central government an ally of the individual who was being denied those rights through no fault of his own. More that that, they actively fostered the conditions of material abundance which went far toward eliminating "class conflicts" in American life—since under conditions of material abundance, the grant of one man's wants no longer entailed a curtailment of another man's goods. Lastly, in the 20th century, in the great Americanization school of the Democratic party, Americans first learned of the need, decided on the choice of means, and then embarked on the work of making the rights of man the common property of deprived humanity around the globe.

* * * *

We know that the collaboration between the Democratic party and the idea about the rights of man did not always sound with the spontaneous harmony of the heavenly choir. From time to time, it was broken into by bitter internal quarrels, by wilful not seeing, and by rending ordeals when the particular "rights" of one set of men clashed with the particular "rights" claimed by a second set. Yet to speak this truth is not to speak the whole truth.

The whole truth is that if the Democratic party were a sectional or one-interest party, it could have been spared many of its tormented hours. But after its founding days, it became a national, multi-interest party embracing every legitimate interest, value and point of view in the nation at large. It embraced agricultural and manufacturing interests, rural and metropolitan man, "old" natives and "new" immigrants, capital and labor, producers of raw materials and producers of finished goods, men of the professions and those who shaped things with their hands, men nostalgic for the past and men afire with hopes for the future, white people and colored people, Christians and Jews, Protestants and Catholics, the advocates of a Small America and the advocates of a world-girdling Big America.

History affords no comparable example of a political party so constituted. If there is a cause for wonder, therefore, it is not that the Democrats now and again have known internal storms. The wonder is that the late 1850's was the sole time when the party could not contain the storms within itself. In fact, that one failure paradoxically underlines the historic mission of the party as the binding hoop of the Union. For it was only when the Democrats of the North and South at last went their separate ways after the 1860 convention in Charleston, that the Union itself fell apart —there being no alternative national political force that could still hold it together.

With that one exception, the diverse national interests and values Democrats embody, has never permitted the party to indulge itself in the luxury of weak national leadership. It is not entirely true that the Democrats, historically, have been a large group of second class roughnecks led by a small group of first class aristocrats, while the Republicans have been a small group of second class aristocrats led by a large group of first-class roughnecks. But it is entirely true that with the exception just noted, only strong men gifted in the arts of group diplomacy—men who could make their own political consciousness the source of consciousness in others—rose to national pre-eminence in the Democratic party. Here, within the party, they were tested and trained in dealing with the kind of problems that are the daily fare of government itself. They were all the better prepared, therefore, to be strong Presidents when they were raised to the White House.

A final point. Despite the storms in the collaboration between Democrats and the idea about the rights of man, on the scales of history, the stunning performance record of Democrats in advancing those rights explains as nothing else does so well, why they are now the oldest political party in the world and still the only national political party America has. It is worth remembering that since the 1791-3 founding years of the Democratic party, hundreds of other political parties have come into being on American soil and around the world—only to die from a variety of maladies. Yet all the while, from epoch to epoch, amid swift and revolutionary changes in political climates, the Democratic party—"Old Indestructible"—has lived on and on as a vital agent of American destiny.

The strategic moments in the history of the Democratic party begin with a negative fact—namely, that the Constitutional authors made no provision for political parties as an organic part of the government. But they were not blind to the prospect of their future rise. They had seen the nation split into court and country factions during colonial days. They had seen it split again into Whig and Tory factions before the Revolution, during the Revolutionary War, and in the years before the Constitutional Convention was framed. The prospect that similar division would occur in the future found its classical statement in the tenth number of the Federalist, where James Madison catalogued the different interests which grow up in any society, and divide its people into parties.

"The regulation of these various and interfering interests," he wrote, "forms the principal task of modern legislation, and involves the spirit of party and faction in the necessary and ordinary operation of government." Meanwhile, Union pure and simple would help keep "the spirit of party and faction" within proper bounds. "The smaller the society," Madison wrote, "the fewer probably will be the distinct parties and interests composing it; the fewer the distinct parties and interests, the more frequently will a majority be found in the same party; and the smaller the number of individuals composing a majority, and the smaller the compass within which they are placed, the more easily will they concert and execute their plans of oppression." But if the sphere were extended, he continued prophetically, a greater variety of parties and interests are necessarily embraced, and this would make it "less probable that a majority of the whole will have a common motive to invade the rights of other citizens."

The prophet was among the first to provide the proof that what he said was true. In 1791, James Madison joined Thomas Jefferson on a "botanizing excursion" from their native Virginia into the North and up the Hudson River. Besides the picking of a few flowers, the two men hoped to form an intersectional political entente, based on New York and Virginia, and drawing its main strength from urban mechanics and small farmers, backwoodsmen and small tradesmen.

The visiting Virginians soon got pledges of support from assorted New York leaders. They got further pledges when they extended their "botanizing excursion" into New England. The motive differed from person to person. Some leaders shared Jefferson's views on Constitutional questions, or shared his worry over the signs of aristocratic affectations among Federalists who then managed the government. Some shared his sympathy with the aims of the French Revolution, or agreed that Secretary of the Treasury Alexander Hamilton was wrong in trying to make the small farmer and worker pay the costs of his plan to turn America into a commercial and industrial nation. Other leaders disagreed with Jefferson on one or another of these points. Still others were indifferent to what he thought or said about anything, but for private reasons felt they had more to gain than to lose in a partnership with Jefferson. In any case, what the trip led to was little more than a loose federation of local units.

The work of establishing local units elsewhere and welding them into a national party under the name "Republican" began in earnest in 1793. The time was marked by Jefferson's resignation from the Washington Cabinet as Secretary of State because of his differences with Treasury Secretary Alexander Hamilton. It was also marked by the fact that increasing thunder of the Revolution within France, along with the increasing thunder of the war between France and England, split American opinion into two camps.

England and France, in their war on each other, both interfered with American commerce on the high seas. But the Federalists wished to place America on England's side — and saw in the Jeffersonian Republicans an American counterpart to the French Jacobins. The Jeffersonian Republicans, on their part, wished to place America on the side of France—and saw in the Federalists a body of men who were hostile to the "Rights of Man" proclaimed by the French Revolution in its first days, and wished instead to fasten on America the discredited practices of the English monarchy. President George Washington, on his part, tried to steer a course between the contending forces at home and overseas, and went on to issue a proclamation of American neutrality in the war between England and France.

The stage was thus set for the 1796 election where there would be chosen a successor to Washington. Jefferson, as the "understood" candidate of the Republicans, affirmed his aims by choosing "the Rights of Man" as his "campaign slogan." John Adams, as the "understood" candidate of the Federalists, chose "Peace and Prosperity" as his slogan, though there was no peace or prosperity to boast about.

Under the prevailing Presidential election system, a handful of people—not more than 5 percent of the total population met the property qualification for the right to vote—first elected state legislatures. Next, a majority of the members of a state legislature then chose the state's Electors in the Electoral College. After that, the candidates standing first and second in the count of the "independent" votes cast in the Electoral College, became respectively the President and the Vice President. In this way, Adams emerged as the President and Jefferson as the Vice President.

Two years later, the pro-French Republicans were profoundly embarrassed when President Adams submitted to Congress the report of the American commissioners sent to France in connection with the sensational XYZ Affair. The commissioners meant to compose differences between the United States and France and to restore diplomatic relations broken off by France because of the Jay Treaty negotiated between the United States and England. Now, however, the country learned that the French Directory had required a bribe as a preliminary to opening negotiations, and Americans almost unanimously became anti-French. In the autumn elections of 1798, the Federalists made marked gains in the congressional and state elections at the expense of the Republicans.

In their inflamed state of mind, the Federalists now embarked on a punitive expedition in which they used every repressive weapon at hand against the Jeffersonian Republicans. One of their weapons—the Alien and Sedition Laws they enacted—turned out to be a boomerang. The Alien portion was aimed at "the foreign vote," principally of Scottish-Irish origin, which was gravitating in increasing numbers to Jefferson's party of the underdog as it took possession of the Western wilderness. To curb the political power of these "foreign liars" and "savages"—as the Federalists called them—the period of residence for naturalization was raised from five to fourteen years. During this interval, moreover, the President could deport any alien he judged to be "dangerous to the peace and safety of the United States." The Sedition portion of the Laws, on the other hand, struck at the native-born Jeffersonian Republicans. They could be fined and imprisoned as penalties for seditious utterances or writings against the President or Congress.

Such latitude did this afford for vengeance, that the Federal courts then under Federalist control—as were the Executive and the Congress—could apply the law with savage severity against Jeffersonian Republicans for relatively innocent things. On the eve of the 1800 elections, for example, Federalist agents reached deep into Republican territory in upper New York to seize a Jedediah Peck who had circulated a petition for the repeal of the Sedition Laws. The offender was then carried through two hundred miles of Republican territory so that he could be brought to trial in New York. "A hundred missionaries, in the cause of democracy," wrote a contemporary New Yorker, "stationed between New York and Cooperstown, could not have done so much for the Republican cause as this journey of Jedediah Peck from Otsego to the capital of the State." All along the route of the procession, onlookers had graphic proof of what Jefferson and Madison had previously written when they framed the Virginia and Kentucky Resolutions in reply to the Alien and Sedition Laws:

> That if the acts before specified should stand, these conclusions would flow from them; that the general government may place any act they think proper on the list of crimes and punish it themselves, whether enumerated by the Constitution as cognizable by them; that they may transfer its cognizance to the President or any other person, who may himself be the accuser, counsel, judge, and jury, whose suspicions may be the evidence, his order the sentence, his officer the executioner, and his breast the sole record of the transactions; that a very numerous and valuable descriptions of these states being by this precedent reduced as outlaws to the absolute dominion of one man, and the barrier of the Constitution thus swept away from us all, no rampart now remains against the passions and the power of a majority of Congress, to protect from a like exportation or other more grievous punishment the ... peaceable inhabitants who may venture to reclaim their constitutional rights and liberties of the state and people, or who for other causes, good or bad, may be obnoxious to the views or marked by the suspicions of the President, or be thought dangerous to his or their elections or other interests, public or personal; that the friendless alien has indeed been selected as the safest subject of the first experiment, but the citizen will soon follow, or rather has already followed; for, already has a sedition act marked him as its prey.

The text here became the Bible of the Jeffersonian Republicans as they prepared themselves for the 1800 Presidential election. They had agreed among themselves beforehand that a firm effort should be made, first, to win party majorities in state legislatures, and second, to have them appoint electors who would presumably vote for Thomas Jefferson as President, and Aaron Burr as Vice President. The effort was so successful that the result was a near disaster. Since there was still no way an elector could designate which of the two men he explicitly preferred for the first and the second office, the disciplined Republican electors all voted for Jefferson and Burr as their Presidential choice. The result was a tie and the House of Representatives was then called to elect the President as the Constitution provided.

In February 1801, the House contained a number of lame-duck Federalists, members of "the class of 1798" who had first won their seats at the height of the anti-French, anti-Republican hysteria caused by the "XYZ Affair." Along with other Federalists who survived the defeat of their party in 1800, these men saw two glittering prospects in the tie. They could prevent any decision from being reached; and in this way they could force a call for a new election. Or, as one of them expressed it, they could elect Aaron Burr "... to cover the opposition with chagrin and to sow among them the seeds of morbid division." The day was saved for Jefferson only by the margin of strength Alexander Hamilton won for him among a handful of Federalists who had not gone mad. At the end of thirty-six ballots the House cast in the week between February 11-17, Jefferson was elected President by a count of ten states to four, and Burr became the Vice President. Immediately afterward, Hamilton drafted what was to become the Twelfth Amendment to the Constitution upon its adoption four years later. It provided that electors were to state distinctly which of the two men they voted for was preferred as President, and which was Vice President.

With the Inauguration of Jefferson as President, the party he founded — now increasingly called the Democratic-Republican party—entered a twenty-four-year period when it totally eclipsed the narrow-based Federalist party to become America's only national political party. The salient thing to be said about its performance during this period, is that it laid the basis for a major turn in the nature of the Presidency, and for a democratic revolution in the whole order of American politics and society.

"It is not true, as is alleged," Hamilton wrote of Jefferson at the time the House was balloting on the choice of a President, "that he is an enemy to the power of the Executive . . . while we were in the (Washington) Administration together, he was generally for a large construction of the executive authority and not backward to act upon it in cases which coincided with his views." The estimate proved correct, but the choice of means through which Jefferson brought "executive energy" into full play, was not fully foreseen by Hamilton. What it entailed in practice was Jefferson's direct assumption as President of the functions of a party leader standing outside the Congress, but directing the work of his party lieutenants within the Congress to put through his legislative program. President Washington had left some such function to Hamilton. President Adams was seemingly incapable of grasping the first principles of the function. It was thus left to Jefferson to explore, invent, and consolidate for future imitation, the ways and means through which a President could best act as a party leader.

Meanwhile, in the long period of the Democratic-Republican ascendancy, the vestiges of "aristocratic privilege" were everywhere brought under siege. The acquisition of the Louisiana Territory—approved by the Congress after Jefferson urged his party members in the Congress to "lay aside their metaphysical subleties"

about Constitutional questions—vastly enlarged the national patrimony. After a domestically costly effort to win through pacific means the right of freedom of the seas for American commerce, the means were won at the end of a desultory war with England.

At the end of that same war, the path was cleared for a virtually unimpeded expansion of the nation's dominion from the Atlantic to the Pacific Oceans. Then again, in the Monroe Doctrine, there was the marriage "to the British fleet and nation," which enabled the American writ to run throughout the length of Latin America. And lastly, there was the attempt in 1820 to contain the spread of slavery into the Louisiana Territory when the Northern and Southern branches of the Democratic-Republican party, both agreed to the Missouri Compromise.

* * * *

Meanwhile, on the Presidential front, there was a special institutional problem to be solved by the Democratic-Republican party. Specifically, since Presidential electors—as the 1800 contest made plain —no longer cast "independent votes" but voted the preferences of their political party, some means had to be found for a party to agree internally on its presidential nominees.

The first solution, the Congressional caucus, spanned the period between the fifth and tenth elections (1804-24). Since the man nominated in this way was certain of election—given the ascendancy of the Democratic-Republican party—by indirection it was the Congress that picked the President, contrary to the express wishes of the Constitutional convention. Yet the Congressional caucus, despite its seemingly autocratic ways, had its virtues. It produced a greater degree of party responsibility for the choice of a President and for his actions afterward. It corrected the provincialism fostered by poor physical communications and by the rule which required the electors to meet in their separate states when they chose a President. It provided a logical forum where party members in the Congress—who alone were then in a position to know and judge the range of national talent—could consult together and agree on the sort of individual who might win over a majority of the state electors.

The first major protest against "King Caucus" was heard as early as 1808 when Thomas Jefferson prepared the grounds for the impending choice of James Madison instead of James Monroe as his successor. However, it was not until fourteen years later, when Monroe himself was entering the last two years of his two terms as President, that the protests were amplified to a shriek. Sixteen Democratic-Republicans, later reduced to six, wanted the party nomination as Monroe's successor. When it became known in late 1822 that Monroe favored William H. Crawford, his Secretary of the Treasury, past experience indicated that this support would weigh heavily in Crawford's interest if a Congressional Caucus was held. Adherents to the other candidates—Henry Clay, Andrew Jackson, John Quincy Adams, John C. Calhoun, De Witt Clinton—lost no time in getting their favorites into the race by different means, primarily by nominations made by party members in state legislatures. But the question debated on all sides was whether a Democratic-Republican Congressional caucus should be held at all.

The Congressional caucus was eventually held in the House of Representatives chamber on the evening of February 14, 1824—only to advertise the imminent rupture of the party and the end of a system of Presidential selection used for two decades. Democratic-Republicans from sixteen states were present at the meeting, but the heaviest concentrations came from four states—New York, Virginia, North Carolina and Georgia. Four states furnished but one member each, while eight states were not represented at all. As was expected, a first ballot recommended the nomination of William H. Crawford as President; a further ballot recommended Albert Gallatin as Vice President. Though the formal proceedings had been frictionless, the caucus was apprehensive over the national reaction to its work. "We will not conceal our anxiety," declared a committee which had been authorized to prepare an address to the country. "To our minds, the course of recent events points to the entire dismemberment of the party to which it is our pride to be attached."

* * * *

Behind the party skirmishing, and in a sense the cause of it, was a far more important human drama, nationwide in its scope. By now, two generations since 1776 had been born as American citizens instead of British subjects, and old political alignments, old methods and old values could not contain the new juices coursing through American veins.

In the South, the tobacco economy that had sustained men like Washington, Jefferson, Madison and Monroe, approached exhaustion—and with it, the power of such men to command the nation also waned.

Nor was the cotton economy of the South much better off. In the North, the industrial and commercial interests of the seaboard, spurred to increased activity by the needs of the War of 1812, had accumulated enough capital to accelerate their own efforts. The self-employed artisan could not compete with production thus concentrated in factories; as he lost his market, he was forced to turn himself into a wage worker who serviced the new machines. But at the point where he brushed up against those who shared his fate, there were new-style Democratic-Republican leaders on the scene to remind him that through united action he could retain his self-respect and restore what he had lost in his social status.

Meanwhile, the Western hinterland formed a theatre for events even more important in their political implications. With the end of serious harassment by the English, French, Spanish and Indians, empty regions filled up with the tide of immigrants turned grain growers. Paper money and borrowing from Eastern quarters for local capital needs led to recurrent panics and to deep-seated emnities against those who alone seemed to benefit when others went bankrupt—besides which, the existing tariff system seemed to favor Eastern commercial and industrial interests at the expense of the Westerner.

One result of the interaction of these many forces was a joint lunge by the frontiersman and the urban worker for the right of universal manhood suffrage, the frontiersman being the first to win it with the help of a new generation of Democratic-Republican party leaders. But the older states along the Eastern seaboard of necessity soon moved in the same direction. To help check the loss of their population to the frontier, they gradually enlarged the base of politics by granting voting rights to those who had been denied them. Then as the suffrage movement headed by young Democratic-Republicans picked up momentum—it ran parallel with mounting pressures for free and universal education—there followed a demand from the newly enfranchised for the right to vote directly for presidential electors, and not merely for state legislators who themselves chose the Electors. By 1824, this point, too, had been won in eighteen out of twenty-four states. Next in the line of change was the Congressional caucus. The select circle of party leaders who alone passed on the virtues and talents of a presidential aspirant would have to step aside for the opinions of the "average man," expressed directly in his franchise.

* * * *

Things stood at this juncture when the 1824 Presidential contest was waged nationally within the Democratic-Republican party and when the popular vote for election was published for the first time. It showed that Jackson had 152,899 votes; Adams 105,321; Crawford 47,265; and Clay 47,087. None won a clear majority of the Electoral College vote, and for a variety of reasons, the tabulated popular vote was not itself a fair test of how any of these Democratic-Republicans stood in the nation. The Jackson supporters nonetheless felt that their man had clearly emerged as the national favorite, and when the choice of a President devolved upon the House of Representatives where John Quincy Adams was finally elected with the support of Henry Clay—the friends of Jackson were quick to detect a "corrupt bargain" that frustrated the true will of the people.

A four-year internal quarrel on this point split the Democratic-Republican party down the middle into two distinct parties. The Adams men thereupon took the Republican half of the name, in an effort to identify themselves with the Jeffersonian origins of the party. The Jackson men took the Democratic half of the name, in an effort to identify themselves with the new impulses on the march throughout the land.

With the simultaneous overthrow of "King Caucus," it was no longer possible for a Presidential aspirant to entrust his chance for success to the impact of his personality on Congressional circles alone. His stand on issues, formerly obscured by the inner discipline of one-party government and the Congressional caucus, once again weighed heavily for or against him. Thus, almost imperceptably, the gravitational center for Presidential politics shifted from the Congress to the nation at large. "Those who have wrought great changes in the world," wrote Martin Van Buren at this time, "never succeeded in gaining over chiefs; but always by exciting the multitude. The first produces only secondary results; the second is the resort of genius and transforms the face of the universe." The technical skills of oratory, he said, while important, were meaningless in the end without the "deep-seated and habitual confidence" of a majority of the assembly and of the people in general. So much was this the case that he advised against any "overtures to leaders to gain over parties." The new leader, he said, should concentrate on winning over "... the mass of the parties that he might be in a situation to displace the leaders."

As the 1828 Presidential contest approached, and with "King Caucus" dead, Presidential nominations were made principally by state legislatures. Andrew Jackson in this way was nominated by the Democrats, and his rival in the contest, John Quincy Adams, was also nominated in this way by the Republicans. This time around, Jackson won both the popular vote and the Electoral vote—the total popular vote cast was 1,156,328, or more than three times the 1824 total—and he became the first President in almost a generation who won his post without obligation to the Congress as a collective body. His strength lay in the country at large, and he used that strength to usher in a democratic revolution in the Presidential office, in party politics, in the operations of government, and in the whole tone of American life.

Perceiving that the day of the "common man" had dawned, Jackson boldly proclaimed that his chief function was that of a "tribune of the people," thereby setting the pattern to be followed ever since by outstanding Democratic Presidents. The party he directed, meanwhile, was a well-balanced alliance of North, South and West — of Southern yeomen and small planters, of pioneer farmers in the Northwest, of German and Irish immigrants in the Northern states, of urban workers, of plain country folk in New England and New York, and small capitalists yearning to be a little bigger. The party would soon become identified in theory with states' rights, though the practice of the matter was something else again. Nonetheless, in Jackson's time, the motif of the party was equality of opportunity for the individual in all matters—from education to the management of the government, from economic activities to social dignity. The tendency of the party was westward expansion. The spirit of the party was a sturdy nationalism in the service of a Big America, and the common aim of the party was to serve all these values with equal devotion.

Historians may disagree about the economic wisdom of Jackson's action in vetoing the rechartering of the National Bank. But his use of the Presidential office as a "tribune of the people" is authentically signalled in the language of the veto:

> In the full enjoyment of the gifts of heaven and the fruits of superior industry, economy, and virtue, every man is equally entitled to protection by law. But when the laws undertake to add to these natural and just advantages, artificial distinctions ... to make the rich richer and the potent more powerful, the humbler members of society, the farmers, mechanics, and laborers, who have neither the time nor the means of securing like favors to themselves, have a right to complain of the injustice of their government.... There are no necessary evils in government. Its evils exist only in its abuses. If it would confine itself to equal protection, and, as heaven does its rains, shower its favors alike on the high and the low, the rich and the poor, it would be an unqualified blessing. In the act before me, there seems to be wide and unnecessary departure from these just principles.

As the Jacksonians consolidated their strength in victory, there were those who called for a new national medium through which party members in the future could choose their standard-bearers. A prototype of the medium to be adopted was found by one of the "third parties."

In September 1830, ninety-six delegates from ten states and the territory of Michigan met at Philadelphia for a national convention of the Antimason party. Here they considered ways and means to serve the party cause across the nation. Arrangements presently were made for a second national convention to be held at Baltimore in September of the following year. Each state was allotted a number of delegates equal to its combined representation in both Congressional chambers, to be chosen by people who were opposed to secret societies. The whole of this call to arms to fight secret societies was part of an elaborate political masquerade. Its true aim was to select a Presidential candidate who could unite all elements in the nation who were opposed to a second term for Andrew Jackson. In their convention held in September 1831, the Antimasons eventually gave their Presidential nomination to William Wirt, a former Attorney General in the Cabinets of Monroe and John Quincy Adams. In due course, the party itself passed into the historical limbo filled with wraith-like causes on the order of the

Locofocos, the Know-Nothings, the Barnburners and the Hunkers.

Meanwhile, however, the new-styled Republicans saw some merit in the convention system and resorted to it in a loose way when 167 delegates from seventeen states met at Baltimore in December 1831 to choose the party candidates for President and Vice President. The meeting, at bottom, was the old Congressional Caucus with a face lifting job. There was a credentials committee which passed on the legitimacy of each delegate's presence. There was a temporary chairman and a permanent chairman. Each delegate rose as his name was called and announced his vote for a candidate. In this case, it proved to be an unanimous chorus in favor of Henry Clay for President. Each state also chose a member from its own delegation to serve on the committee which notified Clay by letter of his selection. There was a hint here, of a National Committee in the process of gestation. No party platform was adopted. But the convention, in an "address to the country," sharply criticized the Jackson Administration "for its corruption, partisanship, and abuse of power; for the hostility it had manifested to internal improvements, for treachery on the tariff question, for the war on the Bank," etc.

Meanwhile, in Democratic quarters it was assumed that Jackson would be the candidate to succeed himself. Countless bodies had already placed him in nomination. But Jackson's wish to have Van Buren as a running mate met with fierce opposition. In casting about for ways and means to circumvent the objectors, the men around Jackson soon agreed that if the party leaders met in one place they would be more amenable to reason. Thus the New Hampshire Democrats, under White House prompting came forward with the suggestion that a party convention be held. In the end, an official call was issued; the convention was held in May 1832, in the Salon of Baltimore's Atheneum; and with every state represented except Missouri, the delegates endorsed Jackson's candidacy for a second term and picked Martin Van Buren as the Vice-Presidential nominee.

It was this convention, incidentally, which adoped a rule that was fated to be a source of conflict inside the Democratic party for the next 104 years. It provided that "... two-thirds of the whole number of the votes in the convention shall be necessary to constitute a choice." The rule later enabled Southern Democrats to exert an indirect veto on any party candidate they felt was obnoxious to Southern interests. But the original motive appears to have been a desire either to hamstring Van Buren's opposition or to show the nation that he was massively supported by his party. Since he was expected to run ahead from the outset of any balloting, those who opposed him would yield when they saw no hope of mustering a two-thirds vote in their own right.

The 1832 contest, which resulted in a Democratic victory, enabled the major parties to gain first-hand experience with the device of a nominating convention. But the device might have died of atrophy were it not for the fact that the Democrats used it in preparation for the 1836 election. Jackson's determination to be succeeded in the Presidency by Martin Van Buren once again ran into opposition, and Jackson urged that a call be sent out for a national convention to be composed of delegates "fresh from the people." It is true that a great number of the delegates who met in the Democratic convention held in Baltimore in May 1835, were fresh from the government jobs they held through Jackson's patronage. Yet the same men were generally the leaders of the party's local rank and file across the nation, and to this degree, the 1836 Democratic Convention which unanimously nominated Van Buren for the Presidency, more directly represented the people in party matters than did anyone else.

* * * *

Preceding these events in the Democratic camp, a large segment of the opposition Republicans began to call itself the Whig Party in an evocation of the party name once used to identify the makers of the American Revolution. Now, however, the name stood for no more than a hope in conservative quarters that Jackson could be prevented from securing the election of his hand-picked successor. All malcontents in reach were gathered together to form the barricades. Politically, the Whigs included Republicans who had supported John Adams and Henry Clay; state's rights Democrats who had turned away from Jackson when he threatened to use arms against South Carolina in the nullification threat of 1832; former Antimasons; former Jackson men, outraged by what they called his executive usurpations; and independents who had never taken part in politics but who were persuaded that the Jacksonian course led to "... the imminent peril of our whole fabric of constitutional liberty and national prosperity."

The Whig leaders had enough contact with each other to know that if they called a nomination convention, it would never agree on the one man to oppose Van Buren in the 1836 contest. So they decided to place five Whig leaders in the race, the theory being that if each of these men in his own sphere won enough electoral votes to deny Van Buren a clear-cut majority, the House of Representatives would then convene to pick the President. If this could be managed, a little luck with a few "great blockheads" and some not "uncorruptible" men might lead to the triumph of the Whig case. William Henry Harrison, Hugh L. White, Daniel Webster, W. P. Mangum and John McLean eventually were selected to carry the banner of different Whig factions. But Van Buren won a clear electoral majority after a bitter battle.

The climax to the evolutionary line so far traced, occurred in the next election. Following their 1836 defeat, the Whigs mulled over their tactical problem and decided that their chance for success in 1840 lay in a union of forces behind a single person. Accordingly, the call went out for a great "union and harmony" convention to meet at Harrisburg, Pennsylvania, on December 4, 1839.

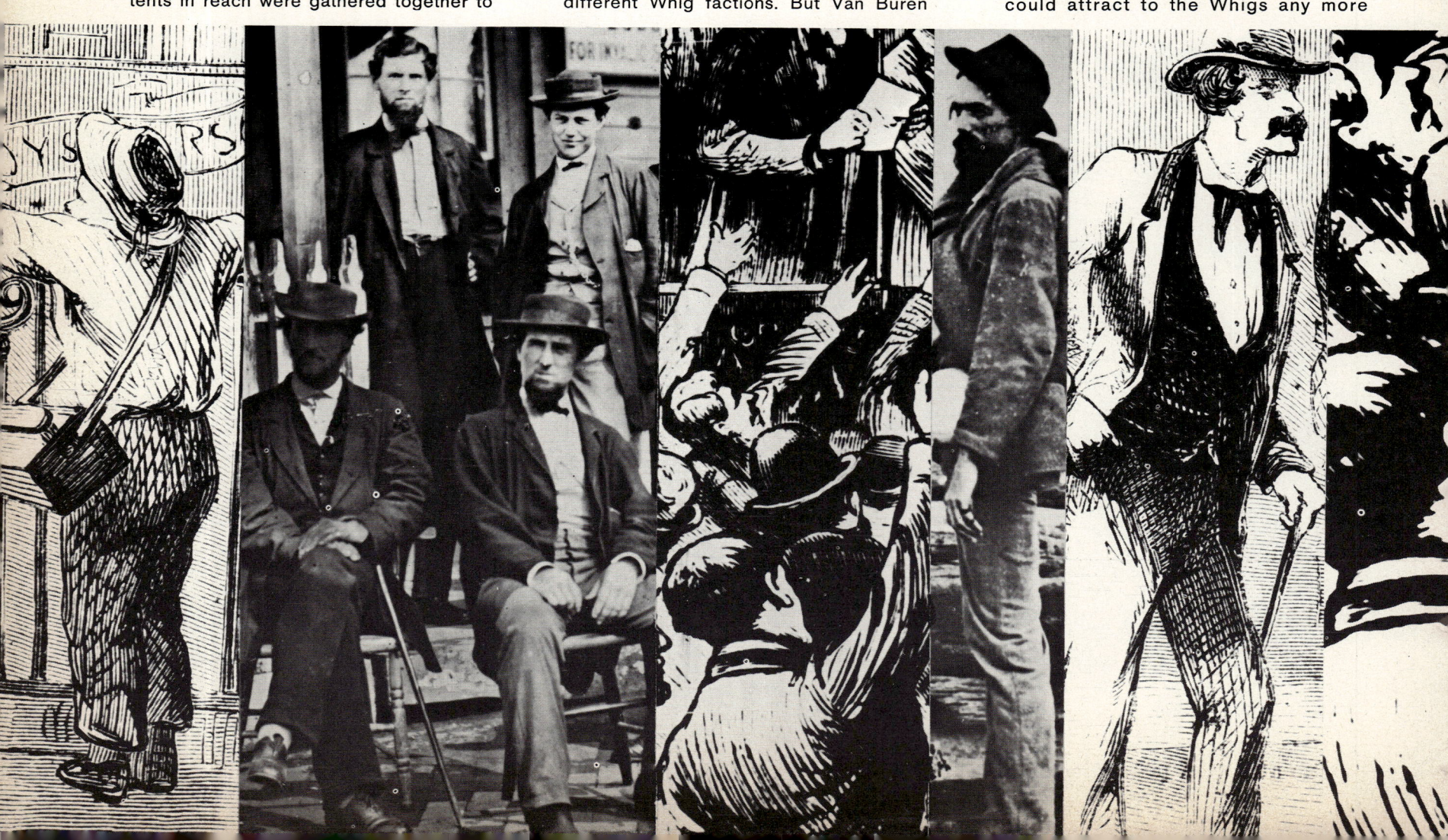

At Harrisburg the contest narrowed down to a choice between Henry Clay, the work-a-day party chieftain and William Henry Harrison, the once-forgotten military hero, who, to the surprise of many, had led the Whig field in the 1836 race against Van Buren. The decision between them was based on the straightforward principle of "availability," the first of its sort to rule a convention. Clay had made too many enemies to serve as the central peg around which the dissident Whigs could unite. On the national scene, moreover, he had been closely identified with so many "aristocratic" and unpopular causes that it was doubted whether he could attract to the Whigs any more strength than the conservative forces they already had nailed down. Harrison, on the other hand, suggested a kind of venerable neutralism that could serve as a point of union for all Whig factions. Besides, some of the more enlightened Whigs felt that the time had come to raid and displace the Jacksonians at their source of strength.

"Those may sneer who choose at appeals to popular sympathies," observed the Boston Atlas, the voice of a new breed of practical Whig politicians,... "But it is only by means like these, that masses of men, whether great or small, are ever brought to act together." Life in a democracy is such, the Atlas continued, that "in the long run those will always have the ascendancy in it, who take the most pains to secure the favour and good will, and to gain the ear of the people. Those who would have votes must descend into the forum and take the voters by the hand."

The political climate was favourable. Countless numbers of people, once loyal to the Democratic party, had grown restive when Van Buren failed to bring them the easy economic relief they wanted in hard times. If a Western Whig, dressed as another Andrew Jackson and free of any doctrinaire loyalties to suspect Whig causes, was offered to them as an alternative, he could draw to himself and the party the victorious margin of strength only disaffected Democrats could provide. Under the influence of this reasoning, the Whig Convention extolled Clay in extravagant terms for his services to the party. But it settled on Harrison as the Presidential candidate.

The delegates at Harrisburg had adjourned without writing a platform or a statement of principles. They had none to offer on which the party could agree. But an indiscreet comment of a Democratic newspaper in Baltimore provided a theme for songs, slogans, symbols, slander and buffoonery which served them far better than any lofty professions of party doctrine. The newspaper observed that Harrison would be quite content on his backwoods farm if he were limited to a pension, a log cabin and a barrel of hard cider. His need of a pension was real. But the rest of the slur was miles wide of the mark. Harrison, descended from Virginia aristocrats, had been born in a mansion. His own home in Ohio was one of the finest in the region; and his economic difficulties, far from being those of a backwoods farmer, were due in part to his expensive and ruinous speculations in land. Finally, instead of dipping into hard cider, his immersions were more often in the classics that lined the walls of his extensive private library. Nevertheless, the Whigs seized on the image of hard cider and a log cabin. They raised it as their standard and presently appeared on the political stage as the champions of all that was rustic and plebeian.

The Democratic forces in the land, brought to a quickened sense of self-awareness by the Jacksonian revolution, were treated to a caricature of themselves. Yet they embraced it and were seduced by it in an exotic political performance unparalleled even by the Republicans in their 1952 success. Whigs everywhere slipped out of broadcloth and into homespun, out of silk hats and into coonskin caps, turned from august meetings and toward barbecues and clambakes. The virtues of the poor and the rights of the workingman were vigorously blared by a range of orators from fledglings on soap-boxes to Daniel Webster, who shouted: "The man that says I am an aristocrat is a liar!" It was the Whig log cabin against the Democratic "palace," the Whig hard cider, available to all, against the champagne and the gold plates used by privileged Democrats. On lantern slides, on medallions, on lithographs and wood engravings, from watch chains and earrings, in pendants, on wheels, in windows, in town squares, in forest clearings, in rolling balls of tin or cowhide, in marching choruses, to the tune of fife and drums, in the spluttering glare of torchlight parades, in bonfires—by these and other means, the young, the middle-aged and the decrepit shouted their love for the hero of Tippecanoe—though the battle had been fought by a scrub team of nine hundred men some thirty years before against the blundering brother of Tecumseh.

"We have been sung down, drunk down, and lied down," one Democrat bitterly complained. "Are the Whigs contending for the privilege of living in log cabins?" another one asked. "Is there any despot in the land who prevents them from pulling down their mansions of bricks, of granite and of marble, and putting up log cabins in their place?" William Cullen Bryant, the Democratic editor and poet, tried his best to be reasonable. "The question," he said, "is not whether Harrison drinks hard cider . . . The question is what he and his party will do if they obtain power." The Whigs saw no need to reply. Wrong men, standing for the right thing for the wrong reason, saw their tactic succeed as, one by one, the states went to the polls. The Whigs had embraced the people, and the people carried them to victory. "They have at least learned from defeat the very art of victory!" the Democratic Review protested. "We have taught them how to conquer us!"

With a simultaneous resort in 1840 to the convention system by the two major parties then in being, the system became a permanent feature of Presidential politics. It was, moreover, a politics that bore the permanent imprint of the great work of the Jackson age in democratizing American life—and in setting the stage in its own way, for the revival of the Democratic party as a national political force after the tragic divisions that lead up to the Civil War.

* * * *

Slavery, as Stephan A. Douglas said, was a ". . . curse beyond computation to both black and white." But beyond that clear-cut fact, historians disagree on whether the Civil War itself could have been avoided. Beforehand in the North and in the South, there were violent men and men of good will. There were blind men and far-seeing men, timid men and brave men. There were men who worked to dismember the Union, and those who worked to keep it whole. There were men who called for a stand to arms either to protect or to end the institution of slavery, and those who tried through peaceful means either to stop the spread of slavery or to ease it out of existence. The hurricane rising from these differences on the eve of the Civil War killed the Whigs as a national party soon after the Compromise of 1850; and the new-born Republican party that fell heir to part of the Whig estate (temporarily seized by the Know-Nothing party), was but a sectional party. The Democrats, therefore, stood alone in the field as the only national party that still tried to contain the rising storm.

Indeed, Stephan A. Douglas' efforts to find a formula that could hold the national Democratic party together despite the national forces clashing within it, was indivisibly bound up with his larger aim to preserve the Union and to liquidate the slavery issue without secession and civil war. His ultimate failure must not black out the qualities Douglas brought to his task—energy, courage, and a political versatility through which he combined in a single personal following big business, workers, and farmers. Nor can Douglas' failure be allowed to obscure the fact that Lincoln also failed in <u>his</u> own effort to preserve the Union and to liquidate the slavery issue <u>without</u> secession and civil war.

Once the irrevocable decision was made by the firing on Fort Sumter, rank-and-file Union Democrats, taking their cue from Douglas, rallied to Lincoln's side—though they tried desperately to defend the civil liberties he suspended in the name of war needs. At the same time, state governors who were Union Democrats proved themselves among the most reliable aides Lincoln had. So much so, that Lincoln himself went out of his way to underline the extent of his dependence on rank-and-file Union Democrats and their leaders. First he dropped the name Republican as his party identity. Then he went into the 1864 Presidential contest as the candidate of the Union party, and chose as his Vice Presidential running mate, Governor Andrew Johnson of Tennessee, a Union Democrat.

After the Civil War—as on its eve—in the North and in the South alike, there were men aflame with hate and men ready to forgive. There were men who scorned the Negro and men who were eager to help prepare the Negro for a new way of life. There were hard-nosed men who felt they could get what they coveted only if the nation remained split along class and sectional lines. There were also selfless men who knew that only if these lines were bridged could the nation use its full strength in promoting the general welfare for all people equally.

In this hour, the post-Lincoln Republican party had an historic chance to make itself a national party by making itself an agent for the formulation and execution of equitable national solutions to national problems. It did the opposite. It paid lip service to Lincoln's memory, but lost his vision and his values. It settled into the mould of a sectional party, with a sectional agenda, and with sectional leaders picked on a sectional basis to work for sectional interests that lived in, by, and for themselves alone.

The whole of this narrowing process began when control of the post-Lincoln Republican party was seized by the radical Republicans in the Congress. Hostile to Lincoln in his own lifetime as President, after his death they scrapped his policy for reunion and reconciliation and crucified President Andrew Johnson for adhering to that policy. Then they usurped the commander-in-chief powers of the Presidency, took control of the army, and made military force instead of politics the heart of their approach to the South—all in the name of friendship for the emancipated Negro.

The Negro desperately needed help of every kind. He needed schools to acquire the education and the skills that had been denied him. He needed land of his own to support himself. He needed protection against the outrages of extremists who were deaf to Lee's plea for Southerners to prepare themselves for a new future instead of trying to win back the lost past. These and other needs were real and urgent. Some people saw things in this light. Some, like various radical Republican Negro leaders, helped write progressive new constitutions for Southern states that laid the basis, among other matters, for public school systems. But the main body of white radical Republicans of the North embarked on a course that left a trail of affliction behind it.

It was a course that sharpened in the South that most tragic of all conflicts—the struggle of the poor against the poor. It created material and psychological conditions where a new class of rich Southern whites played the poor whites off against the poor Negroes, and thereby denied both a chance to better themselves. It led to the loss by the Negro of the civil rights pledged him on paper by the post-Civil War amendments to the Constitution. It fostered a segregation pattern of a kind that had not existed in the South beforehand—a pattern where state and local laws made rich and poor white alike the prisoner of their own fears about the segregated Negro.

Once the basis for these afflictions was laid during the Reconstruction period and the regime of the radical Republicans, the full effect became clear after 1876 when the new policy of the Republicans toward the Negro was to have no policy at all. It was simply to abandon him to whatever fate awaited him in the South and in the North alike. In both regions, the Negro who previously could not get out of the walls a white society had built around him, now found that he could not get into the walls a white society had built around itself. He was free all right—free to wander like a displaced person over dusty roads that led to dead ends, free to be an alien in the homeland he had helped build with his labor, free to numb his senses against the deep bite of the here and now, free to dream of a somewhere and sometime when he could exchange the wrongs he suffered for the rights of man.

What of the Democrats while all this was underway?

After the surrender of Lee, those Confederates who had been Democrats before the Civil War were Democrats still. Now they extended their hand to the outstretched hand of the Union Democrats, to re-form themselves into a national party that bridged the disrupted sections of the Republic. Thus, just as the national Democratic party had been the last remaining force in the land that tried to hold the Union together on the eve of the Civil War, it now emerged as the only political force that could and did weld together the broken parts of the Union.

Its success in this respect is all the more remarkable when one takes into account the fact that in the forty-four years between the 1868 and 1912 Presidential elections, the national power of the Presidency was in Republican hands for thirty-six years. In that same period, the Democrats were often victorious in Congressional elections. Moreover, they four times won the popular vote for the Presidency, only to be counted out once (in the disputed 1876 election) by a tricky decision respecting the Electoral vote, and once (in the 1888 election) by the pattern of the Electoral vote. The eight years in all when the national power of the Presidency was in Democratic hands, between 1868 and 1912, were represented by the two but non-consecutive Administrations of Grover Cleveland. Thus the burden of national reconciliation and reunion in the other thirty-six years fell squarely on the institution of the Democratic party and on Democrats who sat in the Congress.

One would wish it were possible to say that the Democratic success at a rebuilding task where the Republicans had failed was matched by a Democratic success in preparing the Negro for full participation in American life—the other great task at which the Republicans had failed. But this cannot honestly be said. Though the Democratic party befriended the many tens of millions of white immigrants who came to the United States from Europe in the decades between 1868 and 1912, and though it spurred their assimilation in American life, the case of the Negro was by-passed. Until the northernly migration of the Negro began in earnest at the time of the First World War, Northern Democrats tacitly agreed not to challenge seriously the pattern of race relations in the South—while Southern Democrats tacitly agreed not to embarrass Northerners by highlighting the abandoned state of the relatively few Negroes who lived in their midst.

Symbolic of this mutual commitment to silence was the fact that the Democratic party platforms from the end of the Civil War until near the end of the 19th century omitted the mention of Jefferson's name—as if to avoid the thundering call that name always sounded for work on behalf of the rights of <u>all</u> men, and not white men alone.

Still, there could be no permanent silencing or denying of an outlet for the liberating and purifying powers first Jefferson and then Jackson had made into a heritage for the Democratic party.

*For, while the tired waves, vainly breaking,
Seem here no painful inch to gain,
Far back, through creeks and inlets making,
Comes silent, flooding in, the main.*

The idea about the rights of man, silently reviving its strength, would presently rise all around the beached vessel of the Democratic party's social conscience, to lift it up and over the shoals and rocks, and to enable it to resume its work as the carrier of America's best purposes. The need for this revival was urgent.

* * * *

Toward the end of the 19th century, the whole order of American life was rent from within by conflicts incident to the industrialization and urbanization of the nation. Wherever one looked there was a gathering darkness, broken only by the fire of flint shown by President Grover Cleveland in preventing the total collapse of the social frame at home, and in reasserting the strength of the Monroe Doctrine as the cornerstone of American foreign policy in the Western Hemisphere. Indeed, save for this shaft of light, European political theorists who were the apostles of anarchism, saw in the picture of dissension that greeted them in the United States, the coming Great Day for the triumph of Anarchism as the American way of life. Other European political theorists who were the apostles of Marxism concluded from the picture of violence and unrest they saw on the farms and in the cities, in the mine pits and at the factory gates, that the United States was saying yes to the prophecy Marx voiced in the Communist Manifesto. Soon — so they said — America would be the place where the Great Revolution Marx envisioned would begin.

The national picture itself looked something like this. Railroads had been pushed into the West at a rate that far outstripped the physical possibility of filling empty regions with the people who could make the roads profitable. It was not long, therefore, before all the western roads were bankrupt, ruining tens of thousands of small investors. At the same time, the immigrants the railroad builders had brought over in boatloads, had been settled near the roads without regard either to the suitability of the lands for farming purposes, or to the existence of an adequate credit mechanism that could sustain them until they sunk deep roots into their homesteads. Here and in the nation generally, available farm credit meant a tight-fisted mortgage system at high interest rates, and inflexible foreclosures for delinquent payments. Here, too, as in the nation generally, a protective tariff that favored the manufacturing interests meant that farmers were trapped in the gap between the lower prices paid them for the agricultural products they sold, and the higher prices they had to pay for the finished goods they bought. Thus a drop in farm prices, a drought, or an arbitrary increase in freight rates, could spread a contagion of distress that wiped out whole farm counties.

On the industrial front, meanwhile, the drive to pre-empt and exploit the natural resources of the nation without regard to the future, went hand in hand with the arrival of tens of thousands of immigrants to work the mines and the forests under conditions where they—and the native dispossessed farmers turned into miners and lumberjacks—became the immobilized captives of "company towns." The case was duplicated on an even larger scale where the immigrant and the native-born laborer were being assembled and then chained to the giant new industrial enterprises that were taking shape.

Then again, as the lion took from the lamb on the farming and industrial front, the fox took from the lion on the financial front. Here clever men knowledgeable in the tricks of stocks and bonds did one or both of two things. Either they lived directly off the plunder of the innocent, or they used their grip on one corporation to win a controlling grip on a second to merge them, stifle competition, annihilate the small independent producer, drive prices up and lock out the laborer who tried to bargain for better conditions.

At the same time, a short supply of capital and an inflexible monetary system led to recurrent money panics. It also enabled European private banks to wield arbitrary powers over the American economy through the mechanism of the loans they made at the beginning of the agricultural cycle to the big city banks of the Eastern seaboard—who reloaned the money to the interior banks—who reloaned it to the country banks, and so on down to the farmer. Europe's private banks consequently were in a position at any time to upset the internal balance of American economy by turning off their loans at the start of the agricultural season or by calling them before the harvest and marketing of crops enabled farmers to repay country banks to start the orderly flow of funds all the way back to their European point of origin.

These many realities—plus the fact that American governmental offices at every level seemed to swim in a great sea of corruption—squarely challenged the Democratic and the Republican parties alike. Could they act as agents of responsible power? Could they lead the work of orderly change that was necessary? Both parties for a while floundered in the face of the challenge. But this much, at least, can fairly be said of the agrarian Democrats in both the West and the South. Along with their Populist allies, they were the first to admit the reality of the challenge, and the first who tried to educate themselves—and the country—about the ways for meeting it.

* * *

It is easy enough to scoff now at some of their simplistic solutions, such as the abolition of the gold standard and the "free and unlimited" coinage of both silver and gold at the legal ratio of 16 to 1. What cannot be scoffed at is their return to Jefferson and Jackson as the sources of their inspiration, and the assertion of their programs of political, economic and social reform in the name of the rights of man. "I come to speak to you," said the 36-year-old William Jennings Bryan of Nebraska to the 1896 Democratic Convention, "in defense of a cause as holy as the cause of liberty—the cause of humanity." He told how he and his friends had fought in every state and county of the nation to get control of the Democratic party. This, said he, had invited the accusation that he and his friends were thereby disturbing the business interests of the great cities. And to this accusation he now answered:

The man who is employed for wages is as much a businessman as his employer; the attorney in a country town is as much a businessman as the corporation counsel in a great metropolis; the merchant at the crossroads store is as much a businessman as the merchant of New York; the farmer who goes forth in the morning and toils all day... and who by the application of brain and muscle to the natural resources of the country creates wealth, is as much a businessman as the man who goes upon the Board of Trade and bets on the price of grain...

We do not come as aggressors. Our war is not a war of conquest; we are fighting in defense of our homes, our families, and posterity. We have petitioned, and our petitions have been scorned; we have entreated, and our entreaties have been disregarded; we have begged and they have mocked when our calamity came. We beg no longer; we entreat no more; we petition no more. We defy them!

You come to us and tell us that the great cities are in favor of the gold standard; we reply that the great cities rest upon our broad and fertile prairies. Burn down your cities and leave our farms, and your cities will spring up again as if by magic; but destroy our farms and the grass will grow in the streets of every city in the country.

If they dare come out in the open field and defend the gold standard as a good thing, we will fight them to the uttermost. Having behind us the producing mass of this nation and the world, supported by the commercial interests, the laboring interests and the toilers everywhere, we will answer their demand for a gold standard by saying to them: You shall not press down upon the brow of labor this crown of thorns, you shall not crucify mankind upon a cross of gold.

Bryan, as the Democratic nominee for the Presidency in 1896, in 1900, and in 1908, went down to defeat. Was he right or wrong in the particular solutions he proposed to the ills of the day? Did he speak too much for a rural America and not enough for an urban America that was displacing it? Too much for the nativist American and not enough for the new immigrant? Too much for an isolated America and not enough for an America in increasing contact with Europe's great powers? Did he clearly see or was he blind to the way mass production made possible by the new industrial corporation could, if joined to effective mass purchasing power for mass consumption, multiply the wealth of the nation and raise living standards everywhere? The questions can be answered by a yes or a no, without touching the transcendent truth that his three candidacies even in defeat, had enormous positive results for the Democratic party and the nation—as did Governor Al Smith's nomination and defeat in 1928, and Governor Adlai E. Stevenson's nomination and defeat in 1952 and 1956.

Bryan focused attention on the problems of the day and forced into being a great national debate about them. He injected into American politics a fresh strain of Jeffersonian and Jacksonian values. He generated kinetic energies that forced President Theodore Roosevelt, as a Republican, to move away from a stand-pat position to the right of President William McKinley, to a new position where he bid for the leadership of the new progressive forces on the march in the land. He forced Governor Woodrow Wilson to move beyond the narrow concerns of a civil service reformer and to ride at the head of troops committed to battle for social policies. He provided the margin of support that won for Wilson the 1912 Democratic Presidential nomination. And then, when Wilson emerged as the victor in the Presidential contest following a split in the Republican party, Bryan's work in all the preceding years came to its flowering hour. For the program of reform and orderly change immediately launched by Woodrow Wilson, while the echo of his Inaugural Address still hung in the air, retained the best of what Bryan had argued for, shelved its simplicities, and added mature dimensions in line with the needs of an industrial society.

Said Wilson in his Inaugural Address:
No one can mistake the purpose for which the nation now seeks to use the Democratic party. It seeks to use it to interpret a change in its own plans and point of view... We have been refreshed by a new insight into our own life... We have made up our minds to square every process of our national life again with the standards we so proudly set up at the beginning and have always carried in our hearts.

Then he listed some of the things that ought to be altered.
A tariff which cuts us off from our proper part in the commerce of the world... and makes the government a facile instrument in the hands of private interests; a banking and currency system... perfectly adapted to concentrating cash and restricting credits; an industrial system which... holds capital in lending strings, restricts the liberties and limits the opportunities of labor, and exploits without

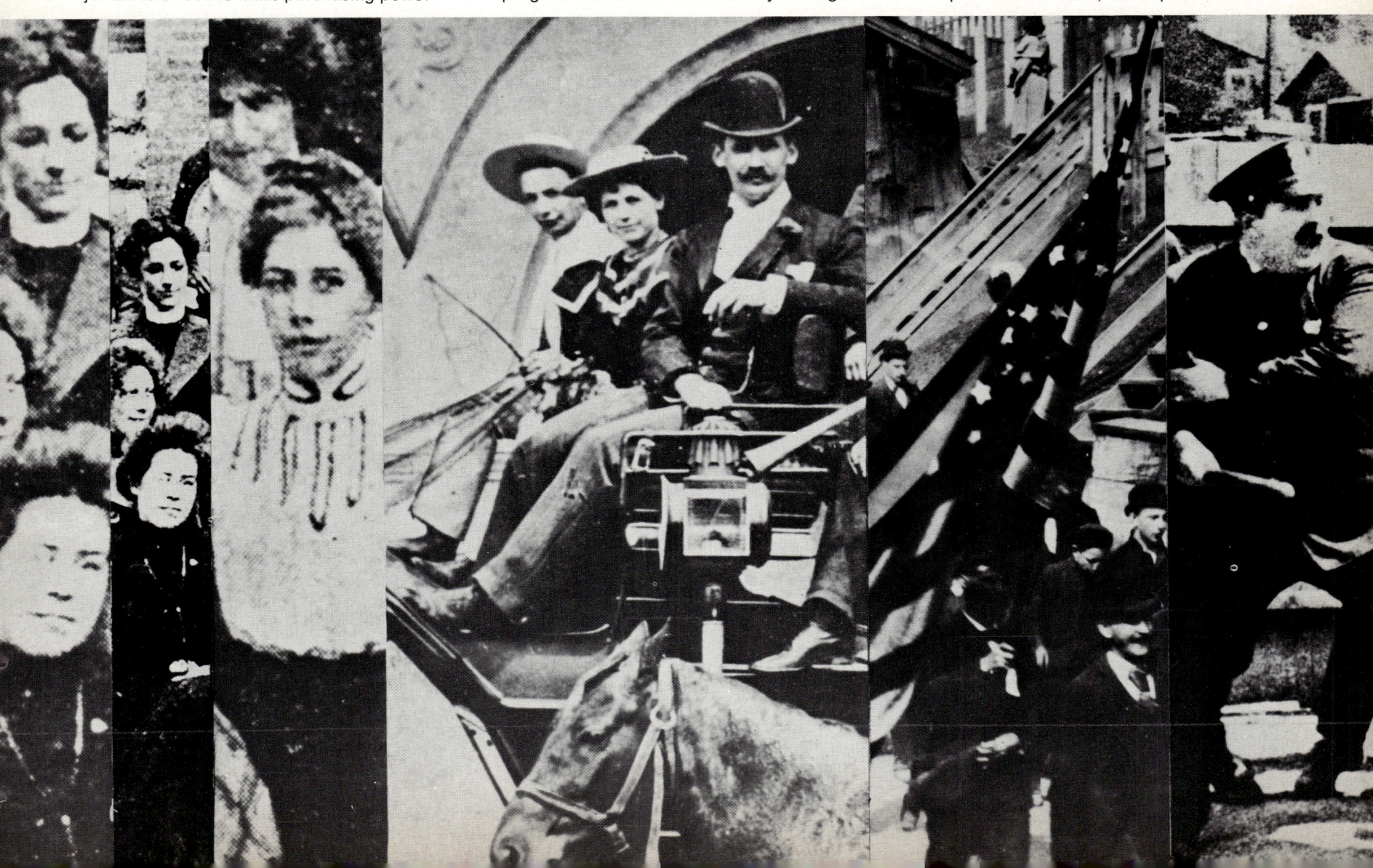

renewing or conserving the natural resources of the country; a body of agricultural activities never yet... served as it should be through the instrumentality of science taken directly to the farm, or afforded the facilities of credit best suited to its practical needs.

The new President meant these words exactly, and as he believed that a modern state could only discharge its immense and increasing responsibilities with strong Executive leadership, he placed himself as President at the vital center of the fight to translate his Inaugural Address into concrete measures for the Congress to enact.

* * * *

Among his predecessors in the history of Democratic Presidents, Jefferson had made the President a party leader. Jackson had made the President both a party leader and a tribune of the people. Cleveland, in his great defensive battles, had made the President's veto power—which is equal to two thirds the combined strength of the Congress—an instrument of public education, and the guardian of Constitutional morality. Now Woodrow Wilson took the permissive clauses of the Constitution and openly made the President the nation's First Legislator.

His success in pushing his reform program through the Congress during the first half of his first term, was beyond precedent. In measure after measure, from the Federal Reserve Act to federal labor legislation, from the creation of a federal farm credit system to the first graduated federal income tax law, from the strengthening of federal antimonopoly weapons to the federal trade acts, the power of the central government was now used to brace the foundations of individual liberty. The by-product was to make the President clearly and plainly the manager-in-chief of economic growth and social justice.

Slowly, reluctantly, but inexorably, the outbreak of the First World War in Europe, thrust Wilson and the Presidency itself into yet a new role. Among post-Civil War Presidents, Grover Cleveland was the first who dealt with a major dispute lying in the field of foreign affairs. The occasion, which grew out of the Venezuela Claims Case, brought a threat of war with Great Britain that had a happy issue—for in the sequel to the confrontation, the United States and Great Britain were brought to a new awareness of how much they had in common. Next came the war between the U. S. and Spain in the time of President McKinley that made the United States something it had never been before — a continental democracy with overseas possessions. After that came the intermittent personal involvement of President Theodore Roosevelt in the affairs of Latin America and in the crises of Europe and the Far East in the opening years of the 20th century.

These developments, however, were dwarfed by the impact of Europe on America and of America on Europe during the First World War. In consequence, Wilson was compelled to make of the Presidency a place of world leadership, and the instrument through which America proclaimed the vision of a world institution that could help keep the peace. From the language of Wilson's Fourteen Points, to the language of the Covenant of the League of Nations, the whole of this was undertaken in the name of the rights of man.

* * * *

The defeat of Wilson's efforts was followed by a turning away by the United States from its duties to the rest of the world—and to itself—by a retreat into isolation, by a concentration of the nation's energies on the good life without thought of what the building of a good society demanded. In Europe, meanwhile, Wilson's defeat was followed by turmoil in one country after another, by the collapse of democratic governments, by acute social and economic strains, and by the rise of the dictators.

The two tendencies, one in the United States, and the other in Europe, converged in the first years of the 1930's in a worldwide collapse of the existing political, social, and economic order.

Here at home, no private individual or groups of private individuals—however well-intentioned—could cope with the facts of the collapse. Nor were the resources of state and local governments in any way equal to the work of reconstruction the hour demanded. Only the powers of the federal government were equal to the undertaking. But that raised special problems. Was it possible to apply the powers of the federal government to the purposes of a <u>controlled</u> revolution? Was it possible to <u>use those</u> powers in ways where the federal government would not be a coercive instrument absorbing all rights to itself—where, instead, it would seek to revolutionize American life in order to create a healthier environment for individual freedom? Was it possible to use those powers in order to revive and expand the wealth-producing activities of a privately owned economic plant, and yet to make that plant serve the general welfare?

The Republican party was paralyzed by these questions—all of which wore the air of the notations ancient cartographers crowded into the margins of their maps once they had drawn the outlines of the world they knew. "Beyond this point," so they used to write, "lies nothing but sandy wastes, full of wild beasts, frozen bogs and Scythian ice." The Democratic party was differently disposed. Embracing all elements and interests in the nation, it wheeled behind the leadership of President Franklin D. Roosevelt, to explore with high excitement the uncharted world ahead, and to bring it under cultivation.

Were errors made along the way? Yes. Were paths taken that might better have been avoided? Yes. Were tools used that fell short of the ends being sought? Yes. But the yes to these and similar questions, sounds in every pioneering project. None, however, sounds as loudly as the net internal achievement of the Roosevelt years. The faith of the people was restored in the power of their governmental institutions effectively to promote the cause of social justice. The frame of American society was strengthened by narrowing the gap between the rich and the poor. New instruments were created to safeguard and promote equality of opportunity among all people alike—and the grounds were laid for bringing the bypassed Negro into the main current of American life. The private enterprise system remained private, but it was braced against its own cyclical maladjustments by the invention and adoption of compensatory governmental props. Thus, despite all the intense and sometimes bitter internal quarrels that marked this work, it was as a united people that America faced the test of the war it was drawn into with the Japanese attack on Pearl Harbor, and it was as a united people that America fought that war to a successful conclusion.

* * * *

Beginning with V-J Day, America seemed to be a new Adam on the first day of a second creation. All the known boundary lines of the past had been erased, and over them all hung the new and awesome fact of the nuclear bomb. There was a time when America could view its domestic and foreign affairs as belonging to separate, self-contained worlds. What happened in one place could run its course for good or ill, seemingly without effect on what happened in a second place for good or ill. Now, however, domestic and foreign affairs merged into one Big Affair so that what happened at home created the pre-condition of what we could do abroad, while what happened abroad predetermined what we had to do at home.

There was also a time when America was at liberty to pick its friends or adversaries one at a time. Now, however, the vacuums the Second World War created in the power structure of Europe and Asia, the revolution of rising peoples throughout the Southern Hemisphere, and the hammerings of aggressive Communism against all soft spots of the globe, denied to America the easy options it once had. If Communism was to be contained without resort to a mutually disastrous nuclear war, then America had to take the lead in forming coalitions of nation-states behind whose ramparts each nation would nurture the strength and the will to develop in its own way.

The Democratic party, as so often in its long history, found itself standing at the point of connection between the unprecedented problems to be faced, and the need to invent new solutions to these unprecedented problems. And as was so often true in its long history, it had the wit, the will, and the leaders to come to grips with new realities and to master them. For if there is a single phrase to cover the Presidencies of Harry S. Truman, John F. Kennedy and Lyndon B. Johnson, it is that they have each in their own way reapplied the idea of the rights of man to the benefit of all men within the United States, and to the benefit of humanity everywhere.

* * * *

No President has God's power to make crabs walk straight, or to build mountains without valleys, and rivers without banks. No President can decree and have it happen that we will all henceforth live in the suburbs of Utopia. Every President works within the framework of a constitutional system of limited government. Every President to some degree at least, is a captive of the unsolved problems inherited from the past, and of the brittle options he faces in the present. But if this means that no President is wholly at liberty to decide what his and the national fate will be, every President is at liberty to decide how he and the nation shall meet their fate whatever it will be. It has been the historic mission of the Democratic party to train men for the office of the Presidency who, in the manner of doing the work that falls to them, instruct the nation as a whole in the meaning of personal and civic virtues. It is this that makes the vision of the rights of man proclaimed in Thomas Jefferson's time and the vision of the great society proclaimed in Lyndon B. Johnson's time, a single vision.

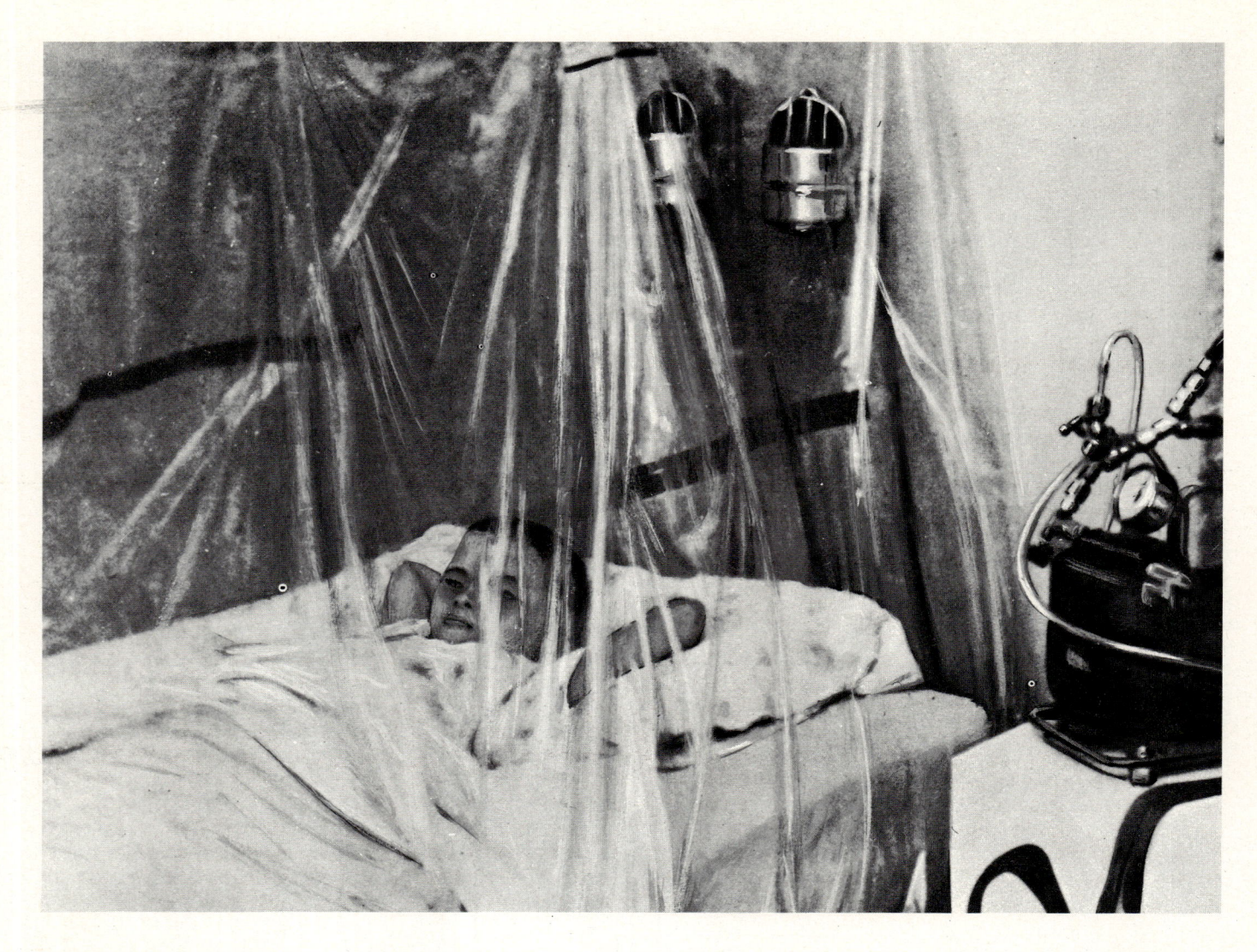

Cystic Fibrosis, an inherited chemical disorder, represents the most serious lung problem among American children. The use of a mist tent (shown above) at night helps keep the air passages clear, important in the treatment of Cystic Fibrosis.
NOTE: In use, mist tent should contain dense fog.

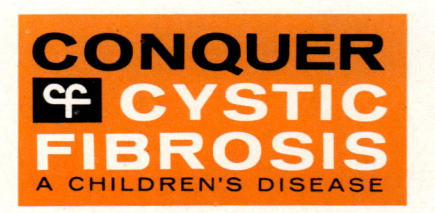

CONQUER cf CYSTIC FIBROSIS
A CHILDREN'S DISEASE

NATIONAL CYSTIC FIBROSIS RESEARCH FOUNDATION
521 Fifth Avenue, New York, New York 10017

This advertisement represents the contribution of the undersigned companies to the public informational activities of the National Cystic Fibrosis Research Foundation.

Bend-Portland Truck Service, Portland, Oregon.
California Cartage Company, Los Angeles, California.
Ellis Trucking Company, Indianapolis, Indiana.
Johnston's Fuel Liners, Newcastle, Wyoming.
Los Angeles Seattle Motor Express, Oakland, California.
Pacific Intermountain Express, Oakland, California.
Texas Oklahoma Express, Dallas, Texas.

She has a rare gift...

It's courage.

Janice's legs are crippled. But there's nothing wrong with the rest of her. She laughs easily. Loves kid games. And she's determined to run, jump rope, dance and play like any other girl her age.

But right now, learning to walk is no picnic. Each step comes hard. Thanks to *you*, she'll beat her problem.

Your Easter Seal contribution last year helped buy expensive equipment to guide Janice's steps, strengthen her legs, and ease her pain. Your contribution helped the therapist and other skilled personnel at your local Easter Seal chapter.

That's why your Easter Seal contribution is so much appreciated. It gives hope and help—instead of pity. All the pity in the world won't do as much good as a single contribution. Your contribution. When your Easter Seals arrive, take the first step for a crippled child. Give to Easter Seals. As you did *last* year.

The first step is yours— your gift to Easter Seals

Send to: Crippled Children, Postmaster (Your City and State)

255,000 CRIPPLED CHILDREN AND ADULTS WERE TREATED LAST YEAR AT EASTER SEAL CENTERS

National Society for Crippled Children and Adults • 2023 West Ogden Avenue, Chicago 12, Illinois

---

This advertisement represents the contribution of the undersigned companies to the public informational activities of the National Society for Crippled Children and Adults.

Consolidated Freightways, Menlo Park, California
D. J. Cronin, Inc., East Providence, Rhode Island
Dixie Highway Express, Meridian, Mississippi.
Floyd & Beasley Transfer Company, Sycamore, Alabama.

Mercury Motor Express, Tampa, Florida.
Osborne & Company, Birmingham, Alabama.
R. C. Motor Lines, Jacksonville, Florida.
Ryder Truck Lines, Jacksonville, Florida.

Count the engines on this corporate-size jetliner. This is the Lockheed JetStar: Four pure-jet Pratt & Whitney powerplants deliver peace of mind as well as power. And the engines speak softly because they are mounted on the aft fuselage — where the noise is behind you. You cruise at 500-550 mph, up to 43,000 feet high — far above the weather. Fly to a nearby city — or to another hemisphere. Take off or land at more than 1,000 airports in the U. S. and Canada — hundreds more in other lands. Lockheed-Georgia Company, Marietta, Georgia: A Division of Lockheed Aircraft Corp.

LOCKHEED
JETSTAR
FLAGSHIP FOR YOUR CORPORATE FLEET

A blast in the Berkeley pit. New concentrator in upper left.

In Montana, Anaconda is moving ahead in these four important ways

1. Expanded copper operations: A revolutionary, new copper concentrator is now operating in Butte, next to the deep-vein and open-pit copper mining operations. This saves shipping a million tons of ore a month to the old concentrator at Anaconda, Montana, 25 miles away. In addition to lower milling costs, it is saving about $3,500,000 a year in rail freight charges.

2. Anaconda Forest Products Division: Before the days of large-scale, open-pit mining in Butte, the production of mine timbers was a big operation at Anaconda's Lumber Department at Bonner, Montana. Now, from 700,000 acres of Company-owned forest lands, this relatively new Division of Anaconda, through vastly expanded operations of logging, milling, fabricating, and nationwide sales, is able to produce annually more than 120,000,000 board feet of commercial lumber and laminated wood products.

3. A metallurgist's dream: Aluminum from U.S. clays. Aluminum comes from alumina. Alumina comes from bauxite, and bauxite comes from far away places . . . like Jamaica. How much simpler if alumina could be economically produced from the abundant high-alumina-bearing clays right in this country. It's been tried, but heretofore never successfully. Now it seems Anaconda metallurgists have the answer. Pilot plant work has proved feasibility. Metal derived from clay has been processed through to fabricated products.

4. New aluminum plants in the works: Engineers are designing a plant to supply clay-derived alumina for Anaconda's total requirement. A new potline is being added to the Columbia Falls, Mont., reduction plant to increase production from 135,000,000 to 200,000,000 pounds yearly.

Anaconda is on the move—in modernization that reduces costs, and in research that points the way to new and diversified products and markets. The Anaconda Company, 25 Broadway, New York, New York 10004.

ANACONDA®

PROFESSOR LUDWIG VON DRAKE'S I.Q.

EYE ACCIDENTS HARM MORE THAN 150,000 AMERICAN YOUNGSTERS EACH YEAR! **BOYS** ARE INVOLVED IN THREE OUT OF FOUR MISHAPS!

SOME CHILDHOOD EYE DEFECTS, IF NOT CORRECTED BY THE AGE OF 6, CAN CAUSE PERMANENT LOSS OF VISION IN THE AFFECTED EYE.

EVERY CHILD'S EYES SHOULD BE EXAMINED BEFORE HE ENTERS SCHOOL!

IF YOU NEED GLASSES --- YOU NEED **SAFETY GLASSES**! THEY HAVE STRONG LENSES THAT ARE SHATTER RESISTANT AND WILL PROTECT YOUR EYES IN CASE OF ACCIDENT.

FOR A **FREE PAMPHLET** ON EYE HEALTH, WRITE TO THE NATIONAL SOCIETY FOR THE PREVENTION OF BLINDNESS, DEPT. MS, BOX 426 NEW YORK 19, NEW YORK.

© 1963 Walt Disney Productions

This advertisement represents the contribution of the undersigned companies to the public informational activities of the National Society for the Prevention of Blindness, Inc.

Bruce Motor Freight, Des Moines, Iowa.
Century Motor Freight, St. Paul, Minnesota.
Cyrus Truck Line, Iola, Kansas.
Illinois California Express, Denver, Colorado.
Red Ball Motor Freight, Dallas, Texas.
Strickland Transportation Company, Dallas, Texas.

If you have a choice, take a fan-jet.

ASTROJET IS A SERVICE MARK OF AMERICAN AIRLINES, INC.

There's extra power in every engine any time you want it.

One time you want it is on your take-off.

On most jets, the surge of power you expected just doesn't feel like a surge at all.

In fact, it usually takes the ordinary jet over a mile to get off the ground.

Would you like to slip into something a little more comfortable?

Take an Astrojet.

All of our Astrojets have fan-jet engines—with enough power to cut one-third of a mile off your take-off alone.

And you get this power on every jet we fly. American Airlines has the largest fan-jet fleet in the world.

American Airlines and its fan-jet engine.

TOTAL CAPABILITY...Single Source Responsibility

To Parsons, versatility means specializing in diversified fields. The breadth and depth of the Company's experience enables it to carry out the most highly specialized project with mature judgment and certainty of performance — *offering all the advantages of total capability...single source responsibility.*

THE RALPH M. PARSONS COMPANY

LONDON
PARIS
WASHINGTON

ENGINEERS · CONSTRUCTORS

LOS ANGELES / NEW YORK

OFFICES IN OTHER PRINCIPAL CITIES THROUGHOUT THE WORLD

WORLD WIDE SERVICES: APPRAISALS AND ECONOMIC STUDIES · ARCHITECT-ENGINEERING · CONSTRUCTION · ELECTRONIC SYSTEMS AND COMPONENTS · MINING AND METALLURGICAL ENGINEERING · PERSONNEL TRAINING · PETROLEUM-CHEMICAL ENGINEERING PETROLEUM PRODUCTION SYSTEMS · PLANT OPERATION · POWER PLANT ENGINEERING · WATER DEVELOPMENT AND SYSTEMS

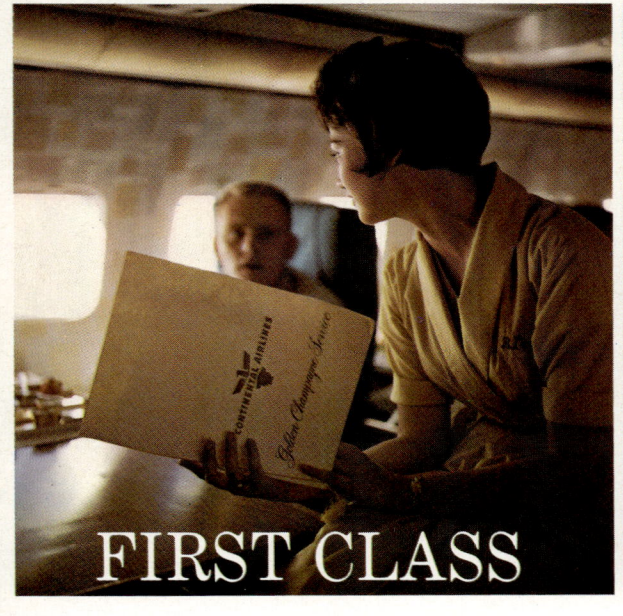

AN IMPORTANT "FIRST" FROM CONTINENTAL AIRLINES
3 CLASSES ON EVERY JET

FIRST CLASS
Luxury, Room, Gourmet Meals
The ultimate in service and privacy. High, wide seats—a table between. Stretch-out leg room. Hors d'oeuvres, cocktails and meals gain from exceptional preparation—all complimentary.

CLUB COACH
Seats are as Wide as First Class
At last, coach passengers can enjoy real roominess. Only 2 seats abreast on one side of the aisle. Hearty meals are complimentary, cocktails moderately priced at appropriate hours.

ECONOMY
Jet Comfort & Speed, Save 15%
All the dependability and convenience of pure jet flight at fares 15% below jet coach. Pioneered by Continental, Economy jet service now brings the lowest fares between Houston and Los Angeles.

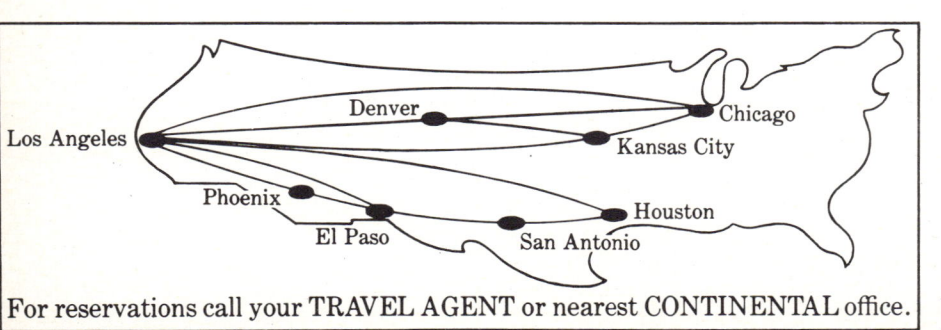

For reservations call your TRAVEL AGENT or nearest CONTINENTAL office.

LOWEST JET FARES BY FAR		NO LOWER JET FARES	
LOS ANGELES—HOUSTON	$72.80	CHICAGO—LOS ANGELES	$85.00
LOS ANGELES—EL PASO	38.65	CHICAGO—DENVER	44.00
LOS ANGELES—SAN ANTONIO	66.95	LOS ANGELES—DENVER	46.00
HOUSTON—PHOENIX	55.65	LOS ANGELES—KANSAS CITY	69.00

all fares plus tax

GOLDEN JETS FLY BETWEEN THE PACIFIC COAST, GREAT LAKES & GULF

CONTINENTAL AIRLINES
...IT'S PEOPLE THAT MAKE THE DIFFERENCE

"Today, the eyes of all people are truly upon us—and our government, in every branch, at every level, national, state, and local must be as a city upon a hill—constructed and inhabited by men aware of their grave trust and their great responsibilities."

John F. Kennedy
Delivered before the Massachusetts Legislature
January 9, 1961

endicott Johnson
all ways a step ahead

ENDICOTT, NEW YORK

MERCURY ARCHIVES

AD 2-20

Travelers to the first national Democratic convention in 1832 came by horse-drawn carriage to nominate Andrew Jackson. Ever since carriages went out of style in the early years of this century, the ways and means of motion have been the concern of Thompson Ramo Wooldridge. TRW products and engineering help keep this country on the move in a multitude of ways. TRW engine valves helped Lindbergh fly the Atlantic. TRW pistons helped the first three racers cross the finish line at Indianapolis. TRW steering linkages help your wife drive to the market. TRW electronic components help ensure the success of virtually every U.S. missile, satellite and manned space flight. And TRW-built spacecraft collect interplanetary data to help man reach for other worlds. TRW is a corporation of selected diversity in the automotive, aerospace and electronics fields, with offices and facilities in Cleveland, Los Angeles and major cities of the world.

TRW
THOMPSON RAMO WOOLDRIDGE INC.

New Jersey welcomes

STATE OF NEW JERSEY
OFFICE OF THE GOVERNOR
TRENTON

RICHARD J. HUGHES
GOVERNOR

It is our New Jersey pleasure to welcome the Democratic national delegates to this outstanding convention resort.

As a Democrat, I am proud that it was my party that first recognized the unique advantages of Atlantic City with its splendid convention facilities and recreational opportunities. Indeed, all New Jerseyans are proud - in our Tercentenary year - to have the eyes of the nation and the world upon our State.

he 1964 Democratic National Convention

We in the Garden State feel certain that those who gather here will find a happy combination of seaside comfort and convenience in doing the work of the Democratic Party and thereby of America. It is our hope that, in the future, the Republican Party too will recognize the wisdom of conducting its political deliberations here in the relaxing atmosphere of Atlantic City.

So, as New Jersey enjoys its first national political convention, I hope that you will enjoy your stay with us and that you will visit our State again and again.

Richard J. Hughes

RICHARD J. HUGHES
GOVERNOR OF NEW JERSEY

August, 1964

EW JERSEY TERCENTENARY · 1664-1964 · PEOPLE · PURPOSE · PROGRESS

John
Fitzgerald
Kennedy

JOHN FITZGERALD KENNEDY

by Arthur Schlesinger, Jr. Former Special Assistant to President Kennedy... Author, Historian... Winner of the 1945 Pulitzer Prize for History... Contributor to magazines, newspapers.

John F. Kennedy would have been 47 years old this year. He looked a good deal younger than that. His face remained youthful, if a little heavier in feature than it had been before the Presidency; and his movements, in spite of the occasional troubles with his back, were lithe and easy. No Democrat will ever forget him at convention time—that tall, slim figure, moving gracefully through the crowd, shaking hands with warm smiles and quick jokes, ascending the platform, waiting for the hall to grow quiet, beginning with a moment of dry wit, then moving into his speech, stabbing the air with his hand for emphasis, so intent that at times he would talk over his own applause, stirring the audience with his summons to the present, inspiring it with his vision of the future. No Democrat will forget him—and no American; for his memory is vivid and immortal. President Kennedy's administration, brief and brilliant, has marked out the directions in which this country must move for years to come. History will record forever the superb leadership he gave America in the fight for progress and justice at home and for peace in the world.

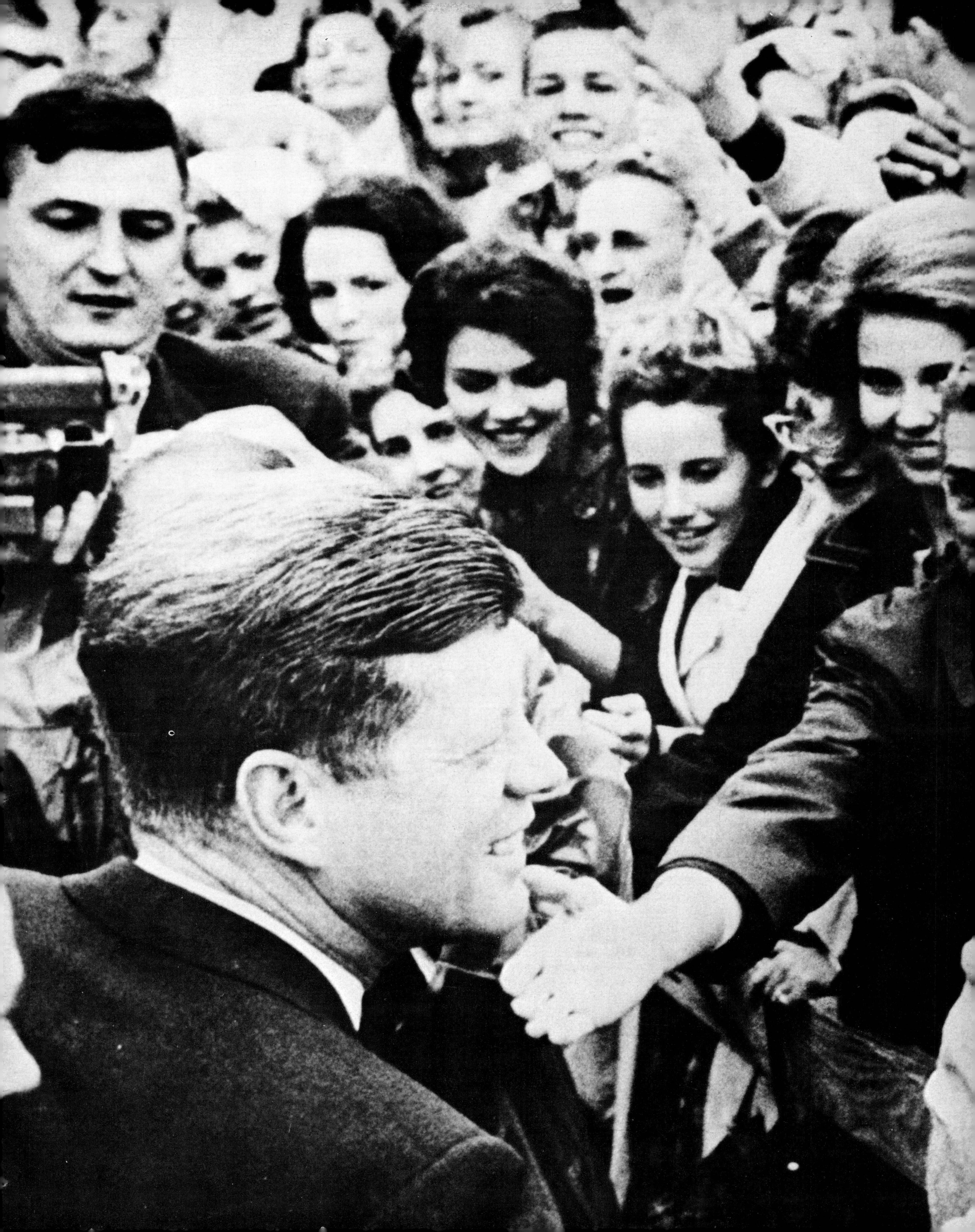

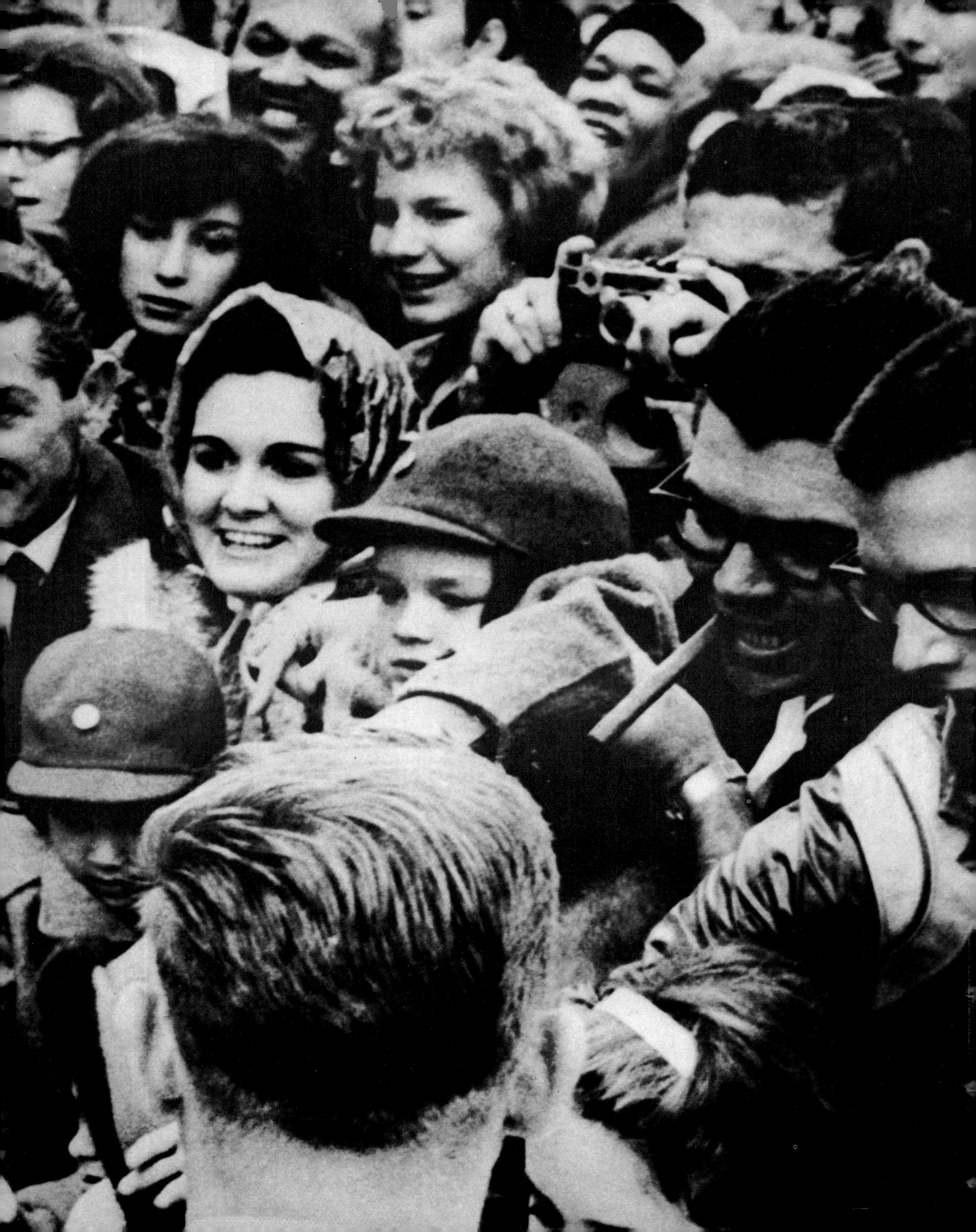

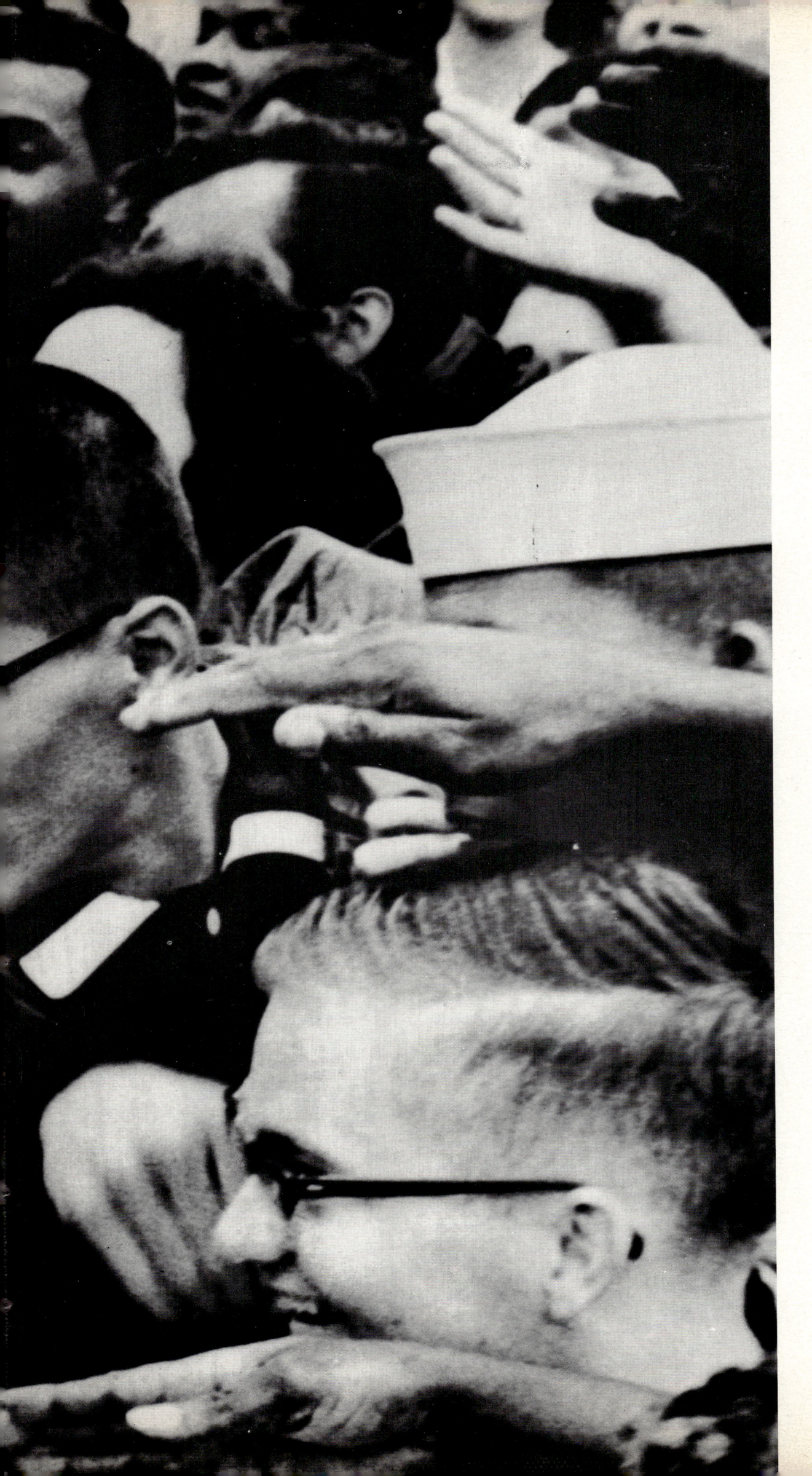

He was born in Brookline, Massachusetts, on May 29, 1917, the second of what would eventually be a family of nine children. His father, Joseph P. Kennedy, was an able young businessman, an Irish Catholic and a Harvard graduate. His mother, Rose Fitzgerald, was the daughter of John F. Fitzgerald—Honey Fitz—a popular Democratic political leader in Massachusetts, congressman and mayor of Boston. The Kennedys were a spirited family, uniting energetic competitive instincts with deep common devotion. Young John Kennedy grew up with his brothers and sisters through the twenties in Massachusetts, in New York and in Florida. He was twelve years old when the Wall Street crash ushered in a new chapter in American history.

As factories closed down, national income fell and unemployment increased, Joseph Kennedy was among the first in the American business community to see the need for positive national action to stop the economic decline. He became one of a small group raising money to back Governor Franklin D. Roosevelt of New York for the Democratic nomination. When Roosevelt became President and launched the New Deal, Joseph Kennedy responded to his call. He served as the first chairman of the Securities and Exchange Commission and later as Ambassador to Great Britain. His son John as a student, first at Choate and then at Harvard, was a strong supporter of the New Deal.

John Kennedy graduated from Harvard in 1940. Later that year his Harvard honors essay, a study of British rearmament policies, was published under the title *Why England Slept*—an unusual distinction for an undergraduate. Before Pearl Harbor, he enlisted in the Navy; and by 1943 he was a lieutenant, junior grade, in command of a PT boat in the Pacific. Everyone knows the story of PT 109 and Lieutenant Kennedy's heroism when a Japanese destroyer sliced his craft in half off the Solomon Islands. He brought the members of his crew three miles to shore, towing one in by his teeth; then swam some distance further to send a message calling for assistance; then sustained the spirits of his men during long hours of anxiety and despair until help came.

After the rescue he returned to the United States, suffering from malaria and an injury to his back on that night in the Solomons. Sickness was not new to him, despite his physical vitality. His brother Robert has told us, "At least one-half of the days that he spent on this earth were days of intense physical pain." But his will to be active was unbeatable, and he was soon restored to health. With the war over, he planned at first to continue a career as a writer. With this in mind, he covered the founding of the United Nations at San Francisco as a reporter. Then his thoughts turned to politics. In 1946 he ran for the United States Congress in the 11th District in Massachusetts. He was elected and served for the next half-dozen years in the House of Representatives. He won steadily increasing respect as an intelligent and effective legislator; and in 1952 he decided to try and move on to the Senate. Though Eisenhower carried the State, Kennedy defeated the incumbent Republican Senator, Henry Cabot Lodge, Jr. Six years later he was re-elected to the Senate by nearly a million votes — the greatest margin in Massachusetts history.

His congressional career was marked by special concern with questions of labor and social welfare at home as well as with questions of foreign policy. But, despite his obvious ability and solid record, some looked with skepticism on the announcement of his candidacy for the Presidency in 1960. This was partly because of his youth and partly because of his religion. But Kennedy, operating with cool efficiency, swept the important primaries and took the nomination on the first ballot in Los Angeles. Then, with equal coolness and efficiency, he destroyed his Republican opponent, Richard M. Nixon, in a series of debates and went on to awaken the nation with a dramatic and trenchant campaign. His theme was the urgency of getting America moving again. "It is time," he would say, "to pick ourselves up and move, to set before . . . the American people the unfinished business of our society . . . to build an image around the world of a strong and vital and progressive society and convince a watching world, as we sit on a most conspicuous stage, that we represent the way of the future."

When he became President of the United States on January 20, 1961, he was something new—not only the first Catholic to be elected President, not only the youngest man to be elected President, but the first American President to be born in the 20th century; this seemed indeed "the way of the future"! The fact that he was succeeding the oldest man ever to serve as President only emphasized the change. As he said in his inaugural address, "Let the word go forth from this time and place, to friend and foe alike, that the torch has passed to a new generation of Americans—born in this century, tempered by war, disciplined by a hard and bitter peace." And John Kennedy spoke for this new generation, not in America alone, but across the world.

Among the men of vast power on this planet, John F. Kennedy in 1961 was unique in having a perspective toward the problems of the world rooted in the experience of our own epoch. The developing nations of the world, it is true, had long since turned to the younger generation of political leadership—the generation of Adoula and Nasser and Sekou Toure and Castro and Nkrumah. This was natural enough: the task of national liberation is often seized by the young and daring. But most of the settled parts of the world had resisted the claims of the generation born in the 20th century. This was just as true of the older states of Asia, like China, India and Japan, as of the states of Europe. And it was just as true of Communist as of Democratic states. When John Kennedy became President, his predecessor, Dwight Eisenhower, was 70, Harold Macmillan was 66, Khrushchev 66, Adenauer 84, de Gaulle 70, Franco 68, Mao Tse-tung 68, Nehru 71, Ikeda of Japan 61. All were old enough to be his father; one, at least, was old enough to be his grandfather. With Kennedy's election the generation which was born during the First World War, grew up during the New Deal, fought in the Second World War and began its public career in the atomic age arrived at last in the seats of power and responsibility.

This fact gave President Kennedy his extraordinary relationship with young people everywhere—not only in the United States but around the planet. No one knew how extraordinary that relationship was until the outpouring of sorrow at his death. And it was not, of course, just the chronological fact of his own youth which won him this loyalty and love. (The world has its young fogies as well as its old.) It was even more the perception and precision with which he expressed youth's vision of the 20th century.

Kennedy once described himself as an "idealist without illusions." His was the sensibility of a man who saw the human struggle, not as a moralist, but as an historian, even as an ironist—but for whom irony never severed the nerve of action.

The experience of his age helped consolidate the stance of detachment: his time was a panorama of disillusion, in which the mature man had but few realities left to rely on—family, friendship, physical courage, intellectual discipline, curiosity, compassion, wit, power. The world outside thus confirmed him in distancing himself from displays of emotion. He was 'cool' in a time where the young valued coolness above all else. Yet there could be no greater mistake than to take Kennedy's coolness for indifference—an error some of his fellow countrymen made before 1960, but few after.

Only the unwary could suppose that his apparent detachment was because he felt too little. It was because he felt too much and had to compose himself for a world which was filled with disorder and anguish. In a press conference a few months before his murder, speaking about the demobilization of the reserves after the Berlin crisis, he said, "There is always an inequity in life. Some men are killed in a war and some men are wounded, and some men never leave the country. . . . Life is unfair." He said this, not with bitterness, but with the knowledge of one who had lived through a bitter age—a knowledge which stamped him as a son of that age.

And he did not say it with acquiescence or defeatism. Hopeless as the world might be, it was a world made by man, and it could therefore be changed by man and even perhaps saved by man. He agreed with Abraham Lincoln who, deeply convinced of the frailty of human striving, nevertheless called for "firmness in the right, as God gives us to see the right." He approached the Presidency, not as an end in itself, but as a means of helping the nation to realize its goals. He was always receptive to new experience, and new experience steadily deepened his sense of what America must do to fulfill its promise. Thus the primary campaign in the barren hills of West Virginia in the spring of 1960 gave his feelings about poverty new concreteness and urgency. He regarded the persistence of want in the affluent society as a national shame and scandal, and he never could understand the complacent rich who, so long as they had all they needed for themselves, were content to starve schools, medical services and social services for their less fortunate fellow citizens. He believed that the time had come for a national assault on poverty. His successor has ably and loyally carried forward his purpose.

And nothing concerned him more in his Presidency than the struggle to assure Negro Americans their equal rights as American citizens. "We are confronted primarily with a moral issue," he said. "It is as old as the Scriptures and is as clear as the American Constitution.... This nation, for all its hopes and all its boasts, will not be fully free until all its citizens are free." So too John Kennedy refused to accept a world living under the threat of nuclear suicide as a permanent reality and, in spite of resistance and discouragement, persevered until he obtained a treaty banning nuclear tests in detectable environments.

Few men have been at such ease in the White House, and few have so effectively understood and used the instrumentalities of power. He gave the executive branch of the government a new inner excitement. He had a dash and style and charm the country had not known since Roosevelt, a disciplined analytical intelligence it had not known since Wilson and an intellectual and cultural range it had not known since Jefferson. He had unlimited curiosity, an exceptionally retentive memory and an endless capacity for responsibility. He was always accessible—to people, to ideas, to experience. Most of all, he had the ability to meet the hard decision head-on, coolly, calmly, decisively. His masterful combination of nerve and restraint during the Cuban missile crisis ended the greatest threat to the peace since the Second World War, knocked the weapon of nuclear blackmail from the Soviet hand and made possible the subsequent progress toward the stabilization of world affairs.

His public vision—the concern for civil rights, for economic growth, for social progress, for peace—impressed people everywhere; but in the end it was the particular union of public and private qualities that moved the world so—that made people mourn him with such an agony of grief after that terrible day in Dallas. Youth, grace, courage, wit, intelligence, realism, idealism—in all these things, he expressed America at its best. He took life seriously, but never himself. He cared passionately, but his passion was understatement. There was not a moment when he was not casual, informal, quizzical; but he remained a man profoundly in earnest. He embodied the skepticism of his generation —the disdain for pomposity, the mistrust of rhetoric, the abhorrence of histrionics, the impatience with the postures and pieties of the past. At the same time, he embodied his generation's hope—for fulfillment in experience, for the subordination of selfish impulses to public purposes, for patriotism and valor and honor. He renewed the oldest traditions, the highest ideals and the best hopes of the republic and gave them new vitality in a troubled age. His death tragically impoverishes the nation and the world. But his life leaves every American new confidence in our ideals and new faith in our future.

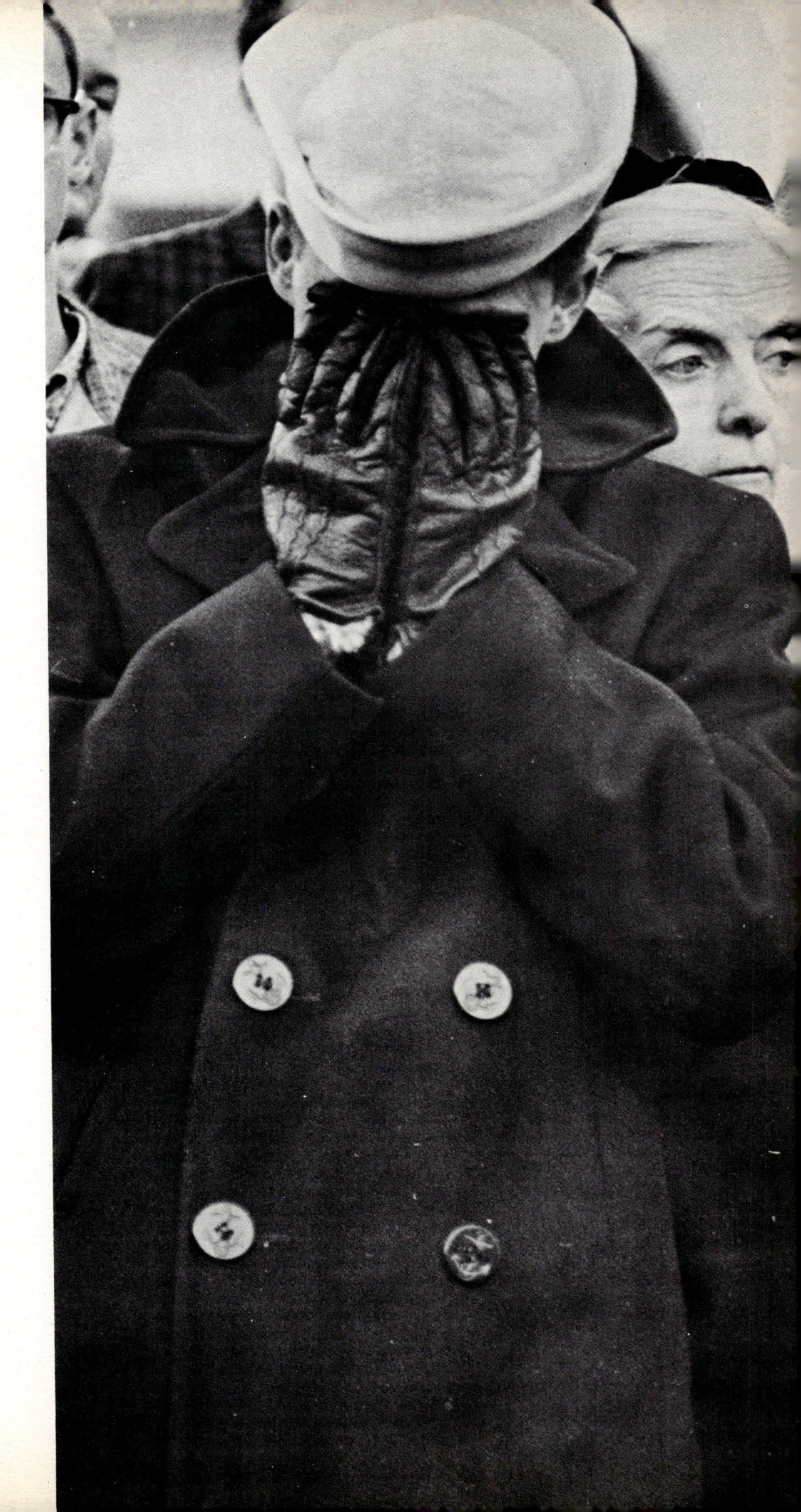

The Kennedy Record

by John Bartlow Martin. Former Ambassador to Dominican Republic... Contributing writer to Harper's, Saturday Evening Post, Reader's Digest, McCall's, Cosmopolitan, Redbook, Look... Author of ten books... Winner of four Benjamin Franklin Magazine Awards.

What did President John F. Kennedy accomplish?

So beloved was he, so brilliant his style, and so overwhelming the world's sense of loss last November, that the man may obscure his own solid achievements. Yet in his 1036 days in the White House, John F. Kennedy accomplished more than many presidents in a full four years or eight.

His programs were his own. Some which he designed he and the Congress completed during his own brief term. Others have since been carried forward to completion by the Congress and his great successor, President Lyndon B. Johnson. Together, these programs reshaped the nation and the world.

John Kennedy once said, "I believe the American people elect a President to act ... New crises, new demands, new pressures, new opportunities must all be met before success can be finally realized." And during his 1960 campaign he time and again declared, "It is time to get this country moving again."

In what direction? How did he translate campaign oratory into programs and action? What did he do?

It was at home, in the United States, that his work began. He himself said, "For unless we are moving here at home we cannot move the cause of freedom around the world." For he knew that strength abroad can be based only on strength at home.

Building on the foundation laid by Franklin Roosevelt and Harry Truman, President Kennedy threw himself into the battle at home on two fronts—the painful struggle for civil rights, the difficult labor for economic growth.

Confronted with a stagnant economy he moved rapidly. Congress extended the minimum wage law to cover an additional 3.6 million workers and raised the minimum wage. It passed the Area Redevelopment Act of 1961, which created new industries and new jobs in 1,000 urban and rural areas in the backwaters of the nation. And today, together with other measures, this program is flowering under President Johnson's leadership as a full-scale war on poverty. President Kennedy's administration eased credit to small businessmen and farmers, tackled the problems of automation, stepped up the fight to protect the consumer from unsafe and ineffective drugs, monopoly and stock market abuses; redesigned the farm program, held the price line in steel, and pressed vigorously to expand exports. Finally, President Kennedy proposed, and under President Johnson's leadership the Congress enacted, the biggest tax cut in American history—a tax cut that will reduce the tax bill of the average taxpayer by almost 20%.

All these were basic economic policies. And their result is already plain to see: a booming economy.

In the eighth month of the Johnson administration, we were in our 42nd month of economic expansion—the strongest and healthiest peacetime expansion in American history.

In the summer of 1963, for the first time in history, 70 million Americans had jobs.

The national unemployment rate has been reduced from 6.9% in February of 1961 to 5.4% in March, 1964.

Personal income has risen more than 70 billion dollars since 1961.

Corporate profits, after taxes, have increased to $27 billion dollars in 1963—up $5 billion from 1961.

Our industrial production index is up 23%.

The stock market has reached all-time highs.

Total farm exports increased 70%.

Total net farm income in 1961-63 averaged a billion dollars a year higher than in 1960.

Grain surpluses dropped to manageable levels.

The dangerous gold drain and balance of payments deficit have been reduced.

All this has been accomplished without inflation. The wholesale price index today stands at virtually the same level as five years ago. And the budget has been reduced for the second time in nine years.

While undertaking the underlying programs which brought economic growth, business recovery, higher employment, and general prosperity, President Kennedy never ceased striving also to make America a better place to live. With compassion, he pressed continually to extend social security, to meet the housing needs of our expanding population, to rebuild the rotting centers of our great cities, to develop our natural resources and safeguard our wilderness heritage for future generations against the encroachments of selfish private interests. And he got results. He would have been the first to say he was not satisfied with the results—President Johnson is still carrying on the fight for hospital insurance for the aged—but his achievements were many. The Housing Act of 1961 made possible the construction of 4.3 million public and private units over the three-year period, including homes for low-income families, college students and the elderly. More than 100 major cities have begun urban renewal programs. New water resource and reclamation developments are underway in the West, research is being pushed to unlock the oceans' resources, and miles of unspoiled beaches and five new National Parks have been opened to the public. And, in the cities, the Department of Justice has vigorously prosecuted the war on organized crime.

The independent regulatory agencies, revitalized by Kennedy appointees, applied themselves diligently to safeguard-

---

"I do solemnly swear that I will faithfully execute the office of President of the United States, and will to the best of my ability, preserve, protect and defend the Constitution of the United States."

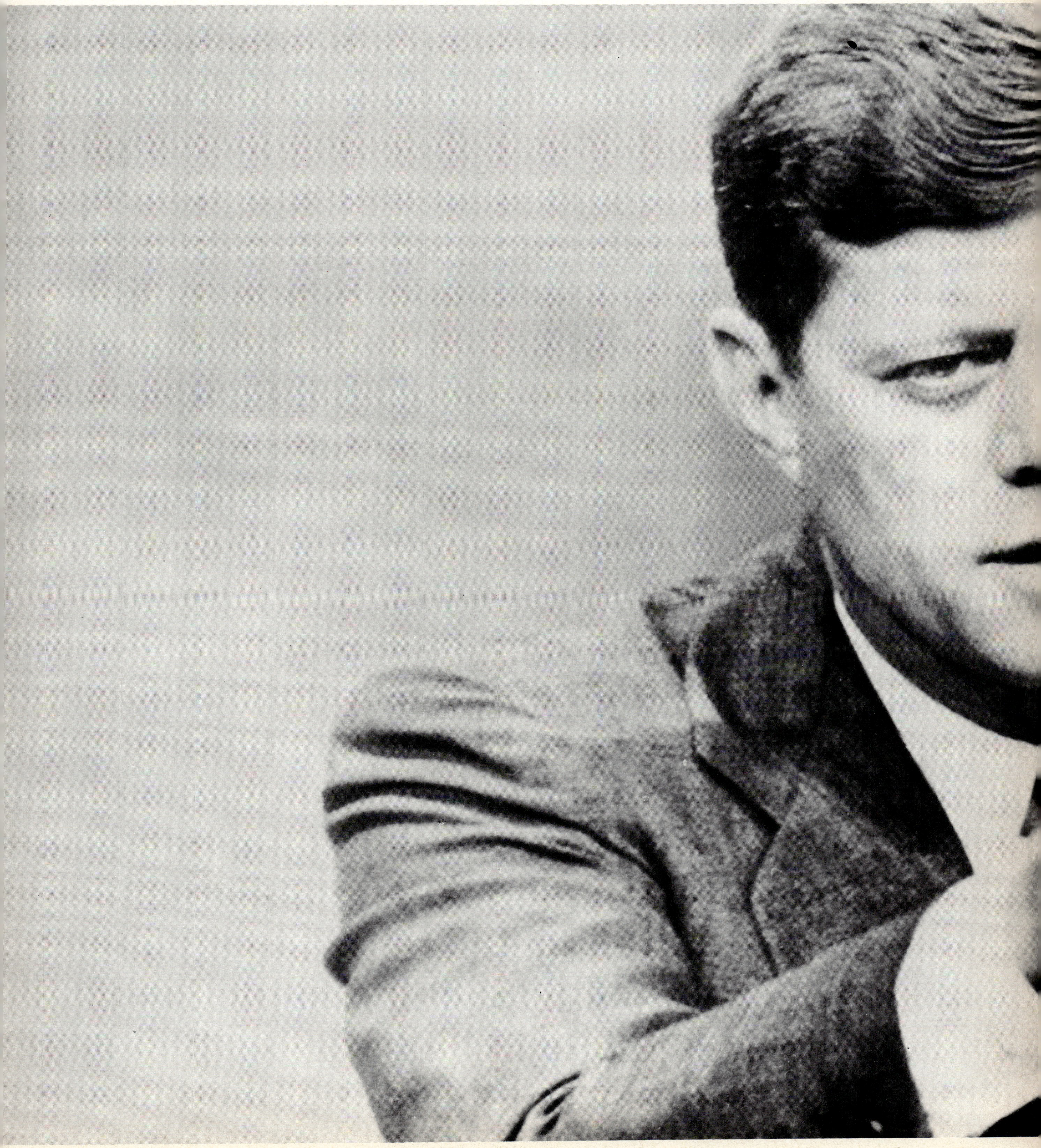

ing "the public interest, convenience, and necessity." The Federal Communications Commission, for example, played a major role in the development of the first Telstar commercial global satellite communications system; obtained rate cuts that make it possible today to telephone any city in the United States for a dollar, and turned the spotlight on the weaknesses of history's greatest communication medium, television.

And President Kennedy's restless mind brought to the forefront of public attention time and again the talent, creativity, and inventiveness which are in the final analysis America's most precious natural resource. The Communist stereotype of a materialistic America—a stereotype which unfortunately had gained substance during the odious years of anti-intellectualism—evaporated during the Kennedy years. For he brought a poet to read a poem at his inauguration; he provided for achievement awards in the arts and sciences; he invited Nobel Prize winners, painters, authors, playwrights, musicians, scientists, and many others to his table; and his White House became not only the repository of the greatest temporal power on earth but a dwelling place for the creative human spirit.

It is, however, almost certain that when the history of President Kennedy's administration is written his greatest achievement at home will be called his fight for civil rights. It is not that he brought to an end the "American dilemma" between our faith that all men are created equal and our practice of treating some men as less than equal. He did not, could not, end this dilemma overnight. But he did what only a great president does: he accepted the burden as his own. In June of 1963 with "fires of frustration and discord" flaming across the nation, he fully committed his own prestige and his nation's when he said, in words that rang around the world and wakened his countrymen's conscience, "Now the time has come for this nation to fulfill its promises... In this year of the Emancipation Centennial, justice requires us to insure the blessings of liberty for all Americans and their posterity—not merely for reasons of economic efficiency, world diplomacy, and domestic tranquility—but above all, because it is right."

No American president after Lincoln had made such a speech. No other president after Lincoln acted so promptly to transform words into reality.

Even earlier, President Kennedy had moved with fairness and resolution to enforce the law of the land; his Justice Department, bravely led by Attorney General Robert F. Kennedy, had worked to ensure Negroes' voting, travel, and educational rights; the President and his Cabinet had appointed many Negroes on their merit to high positions in government; and he had ended job discrimination by Federal contractors and in Federal-financed housing. And the Congress had adopted a Constitutional Amendment prohibiting poll taxes in Federal elections. Now President Kennedy sent to the Congress the strongest and broadest civil rights bill in the history of the United States. And President Johnson, who had long ago pledged his own commitment to the cause of human equality, redeemed that pledge with matchless skill and steadfast courage in the difficult spring of 1964: the civil rights bill has become the law of the land.

2

President Kennedy took office in the most dangerous time in all history. A single false step could destroy not only the United States but civilization itself. By his unique world leadership, both bold and wise, he left the world a different place when he departed.

What did he do in foreign policy?

In his first few months in the White House, President Kennedy found himself confronting the postponed crises of the wasted years — Laos, the Congo, Cuba, Berlin. He plunged into the thick of the fray—achieved a cease-fire in Laos, helped get the Congo out of the jungle and into the UN, virtually isolated Castro and Cuba, heart of an inherited problem, talked bluntly and clearly to Khrushchev at the summit in Vienna, and when Khrushchev delivered his German ultimatum and erected the hated Wall, President Kennedy sent more troops to defend Berlin, asked his trusted Vice-President Johnson to visit Berlin, raising morale, and solemnly told the Communists and the American people in an hour of desperate danger that we wanted peace but would fight if we must. Berlin stood.

Around the world hearts quickened, and statesmen reassessed world politics: America, at last astir, was behaving like a great nation. And her young president had stamped the world with his mark, as cheering millions attested from Bogotá to Berlin, from Puerto Rico to Rome to Dublin. Events rushed on headlong—it is hard to remember that only four years ago Khrushchev was banging his shoe on the desk at the United Nations, that the death of Lumumba meant world crisis, and that not much earlier the first Sputnik had so alarmed us.

Beneath the day-to-day crises that poured into the White House, President Kennedy was devising a strategy for peace. Its rock-bottom foundation was military power. Building on a strong economy at home, he constructed the most powerful defense establishment on earth. Since 1961, under the leadership of Secretary of Defense McNamara, our nuclear weapons in the strategic alert forces have increased 100%, our combat-ready Army divisions 45%, our tactical aircraft procurement 100%, our airlift capability 75%, our strategic bombers on 15-minute alert 50%, our Minuteman production capacity 50%, and, by fiscal 1965, our Polaris submarines by 50%. At the same time, the Defense Department saved money—about $1.4 billion in fiscal 1963 alone. (The Air Force, for example, by simply using what it had, eliminated the need for 102,000 MXY-4A cartridges for starting F-101 and F-102 jets, cutting the cost of each start $24.50—a total saving of $2.5 million.)

Backed by superior force, President Kennedy moved ahead to reshape foreign policy. He ordered a thorough rethinking of our nuclear strategy, a staggering task, going to the heart of our life as a nation.

The previous administration seemed to have assumed that if war came it must be nuclear war—all or nothing. President Kennedy rejected the inevitability of thermonuclear holocaust and such dangerous slogans as "massive retaliation" and "a bigger bang for a buck," built up our conventional forces and counter-insurgency forces, but maintained nuclear superiority and prudently resumed nuclear testing when Khrushchev did. Ably aided by Ambassador Adlai Stevenson, he strengthened the United Nations, but never abandoned his first reliance on our own strength. As he had gathered about him the best Cabinet officers and advisors available, so he sent new and imaginative men abroad to carry out our policies. Around the world, in West Europe, in Asia and Africa and Latin America, inside the troubled Peking-Moscow axis, old alliances shifted rapidly in the 1960's under the pressures of exploding populations and revolutionary movements; and President Kennedy met new perils and opportunities with the intelligent, creative, and courageous leadership that was his hallmark. He maneuvered with great skill to take advantage of the growing Peking-Moscow split. He convinced Khrushchev he meant business. He adopted a new sophisticated policy toward the various Communist nations. With wisdom he sent food to Poland and Yugoslavia. With resolution he stopped Communism at Berlin, in the Congo, in Southeast Asia. With skill and courage, without bombast or humbug, he guided our nation through the dangerous Cuban missile crisis of 1962, when the Communists brought the world to the very precipice of history's first thermonuclear exchange. Today West Berlin is free, none of the 35 new African nations has chosen Communism, India has held her borders against Peking, the United Nations has warded off Soviet attacks on the Secretary General's office, Soviet missiles are out of Cuba, and Cuba is isolated in the hemisphere.

But although his 34 months in the White House were a long series of foreign policy crises, and although he built our defense to unprecedented strength, President Kennedy labored ceaselessly for peace. His imaginative—and successful—race to space strengthened our defense but he also put our satellites to the uses of peace. He established the first Disarmament and Arms Control Agency, and through seemingly endless negotiating sessions it worked tirelessly away. The trade expansion act of 1962, the most thorough overhauling of our tariff policies in a generation, opened new markets to American business, created new jobs at home, and strengthened our ties to our European allies. President Kennedy redesigned our foreign aid programs, shifting from military to development aid, and making sure the money was spent in the United States, not abroad, again helping American labor and business.

And he devised new weapons in the struggle for men's minds in the emerging third world—the Alliance for Progress, Food for Peace, and the Peace Corps. The Alliance for Progress undertook the staggering task of advancing social justice and economic progress in an area of the world that had been ruled by a feudal order for 400 years; and if success has been incomplete, if all the problems were not solved in his 34 months, it is well to remember that the Alliance undertakes nothing less than to lead the Latin American millions out of that 400-year-old darkness and into a brave new world of social justice and economic progress—and to do it by peaceful revolution, not bloody chaos, and under a political freedom unknown in Castro's Cuba. The Food for Peace program, sponsored by the distinguished Senator Hubert Humphrey, not only reduced American surplus farm crops but proved that America is a good neighbor to a hungry world. But of all the new ideas President Kennedy put into action, the Peace Corps almost surely lifted more hearts, stirred more hope, and offered more promise, both here and abroad, than any other. And under the direction of Sargent Shriver, today 7,000 young Americans are working in backward areas of the world, helping the disinherited of the earth to help themselves—and in the process proving once again that the United States is a good friend in time of peace as well as a powerful ally in time of war—and in the process, too, offering to young Americans the chance to serve their country and their own higher aspirations.

Every day of his presidency, President Kennedy concerned himself with peace. He seized every occasion to argue that war was not inevitable for rational men, not even in the nuclear age—to argue that peace was possible. In his inaugural address, he had said, "Let us never negotiate out of fear. But let us never fear to negotiate." Time after time he strengthened the international peace-keeping machinery. Tirelessly he negotiated with our allies and our adversaries. And at length his work bore fruit when the United States, the Soviet Union, and more than 100 other nations signed the limited Nuclear Test Ban Treaty, the first agreement of the human race for mutual self-preservation. Congress ratified it on September 24, 1963, just 58 days before President Kennedy died. He knew it was, as he said, but a small first step on the road to peace that may be a thousand miles long. But he took it proudly for the American nation and the American people he loved. History may consider it his greatest single achievement. It was, in a sense, the capstone of everything he did. For what he did was to re-establish faith in our American ideals of progress and justice, to wipe out the idea that we were a weary old nation outrun by the times, to restore what we stood for in the beginning and are today—a young and progressive nation with much to give the world.

Those were his programs, domestic and foreign, his achievements. They add up to two things. Not only by what he said, or how he behaved, but more importantly by what he did, he gave his country and the world two faiths: faith that human equality is possible, and faith that peace is possible too. This is his monument. This is the torch he passed.

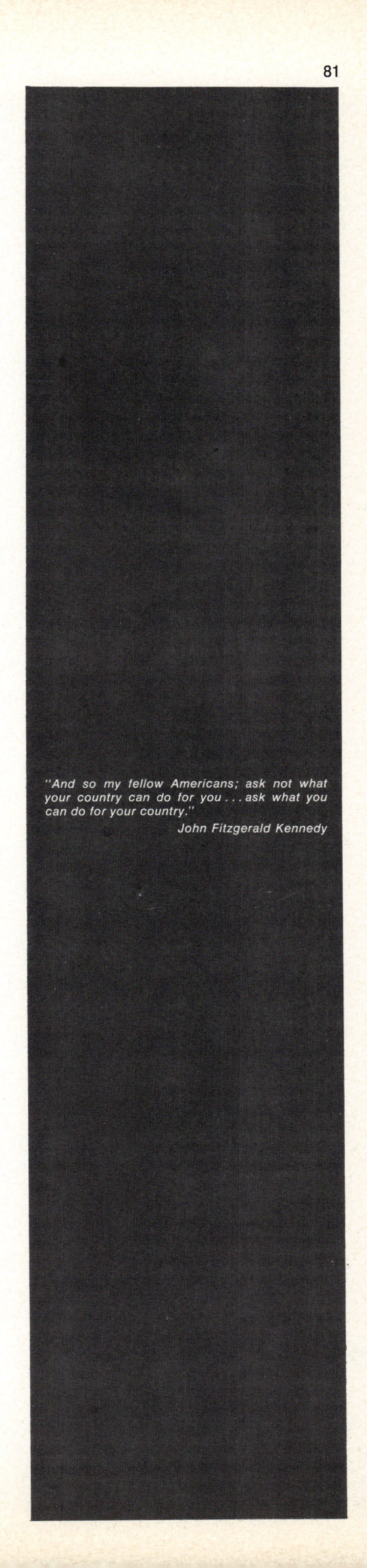

"And so my fellow Americans; ask not what your country can do for you ... ask what you can do for your country."
John Fitzgerald Kennedy

Let's make it a wider world for David too!

One day David will not be a retarded child. He will be one of America's four million mentally retarded adults. *These are not children.** Thanks to the pioneering work of vocational therapists . . . to the pace-setting efforts of the President's Committee on Employment of the Handicapped and its Committee on the Mentally Handicapped . . . and to the retardates who have proved themselves on the job in industry and sheltered workshops, David and the others for whom we labor have hope for a wider world . . . possibly a self-sustaining future . . . a worthwhile existence. *With your professional and personal help, the retarded can be helped.*

Send for FREE COPY of NARC Publications List. It contains many titles of special interest to workers in rehabilitation and vocational training.

* *With apologies to PLAYS FOR LIVING for stealing the title of its new OVR-sponsored play. To show in your area, write PLAYS FOR LIVING, 44 East 23rd Street, New York 10, New York.*

NATIONAL ASSOCIATION FOR RETARDED CHILDREN
386 Park Avenue South, New York 16, N. Y.

This advertisement represents the contribution of the undersigned companies to the public informational activities of the National Association for Retarded Children.

Brady Motorfrate, Des Moines, Iowa.
Cady Moving & Storage Company, Providence, R. I.
East Side Service, Des Moines, Iowa.
Hi-Ball Contractors, Billings, Montana.

Meadows Transfer Company, Bettendorf, Iowa.
Navajo Freight Lines, Denver, Colorado.
Portland Seattle Freight Lines, Seattle, Washington.
Rice Truck Lines, Great Falls, Montana.

Science without technology... is learning without significance. Only when the fragments of many sciences are skillfully woven through technology into need-satisfying goods and services does scientific knowledge assume meaning, purpose, utility. Litton Industries is scientific/technological man, competent in a profusion of disciplines, with a responsive sensitivity to free society's need for advanced military and commercial systems.
Litton Industries, Inc. ⊞ Beverly Hills, California

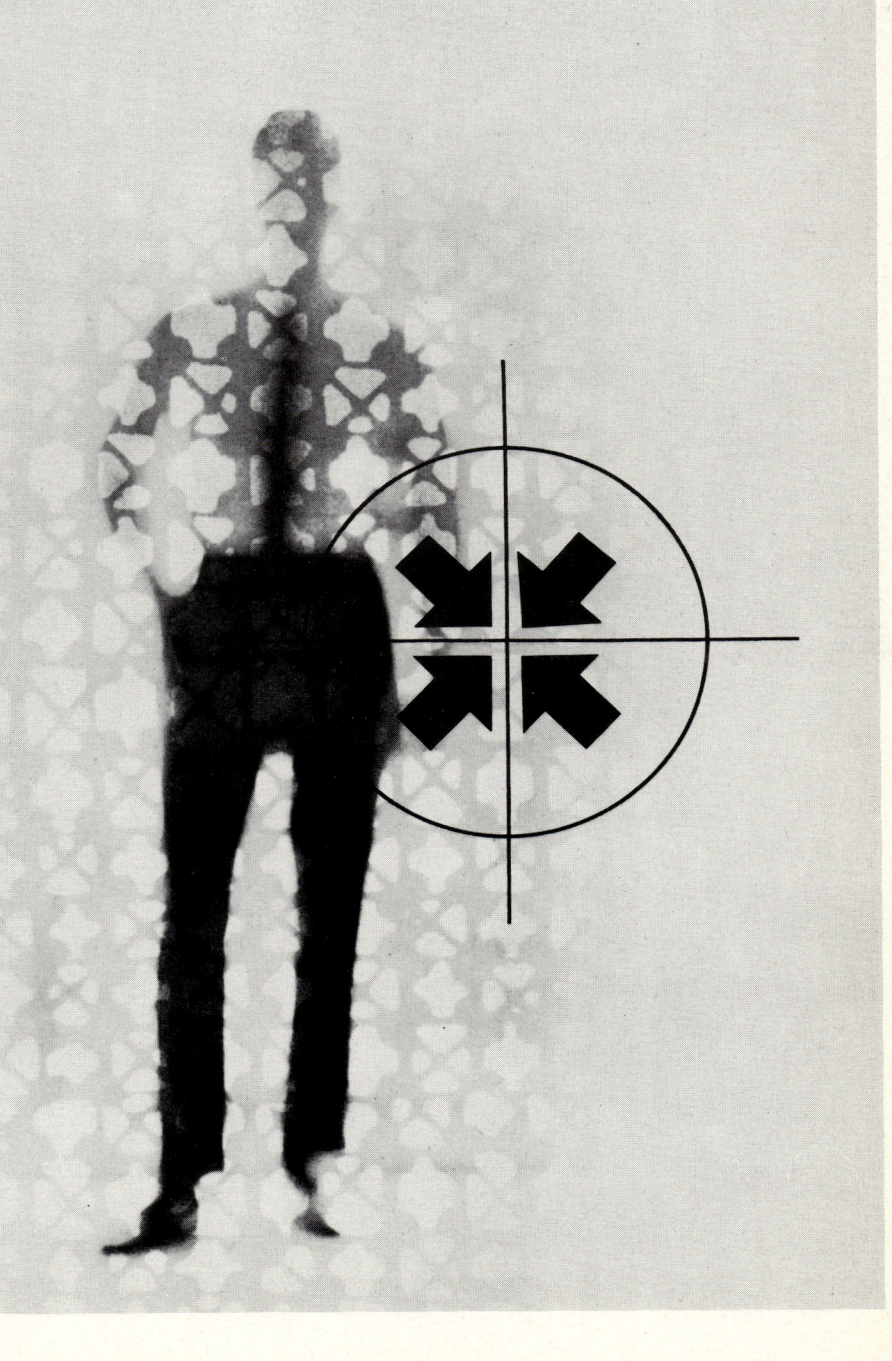

EVERYONE ACROSS THE LAND VOTES FOR CHORE GIRL AND GOLDEN FLEECE

OUR GREAT CANDIDATE...
SUPPORTED BY
A GREAT PLATFORM

the CHORE GIRL® POT CLEANER

NO SPLINTERS

NO RUST

REAL SCOUR POWER

PLIABLE— EASY TO RINSE

SCOURS CLEAN FAST

NON-METALLIC NO SPLINTERS

The GOLDEN FLEECE — Pot Cleaner & Scour Cloth — 3 SCOUR CLOTHS

Metal Textile Company • Roselle, New Jersey • Brandon, Mississippi
A division of General Cable Corporation

After the Convention winds up—unwind with us

(In Bermuda or the Caribbean for as little as $120 round trip)

When all the votes are in, *you're* a candidate for a well-deserved rest.

Let Pan Am take you to beaches, bargains and barrels of fun. Get away from it all on an island with a British, French, Dutch, Danish or Spanish accent.

The weather's marvelous. Warm days, with trade-wind cool nights, this time of the year.

The crowds and the high prices have gone elsewhere.

And you can choose from 15 Pan Am island bargains.

From New York, for example, Bermuda is only $120 round-trip Jet economy. Puerto Rico, $122 Jet Thrift. Nassau, $126 and Jamaica $159 on 17-day Jet tickets. And those are just samples.

For complete information, see the Pan Am representative at the Convention or call Pan Am in Philadelphia at LOcust 9-1300.

Fly from New York, Philadelphia, Baltimore/Washington, Boston or Miami.

You'll have a good feeling every mile of the way, because you'll know you're flying the very best there is: the World's Most Experienced Airline.

A winning ticket, if there ever was one.

YOU'RE BETTER OFF WITH PAN AM—WORLD'S MOST EXPERIENCED AIRLINE
First in Latin America   First on the Pacific
First on the Atlantic   First 'Round the World

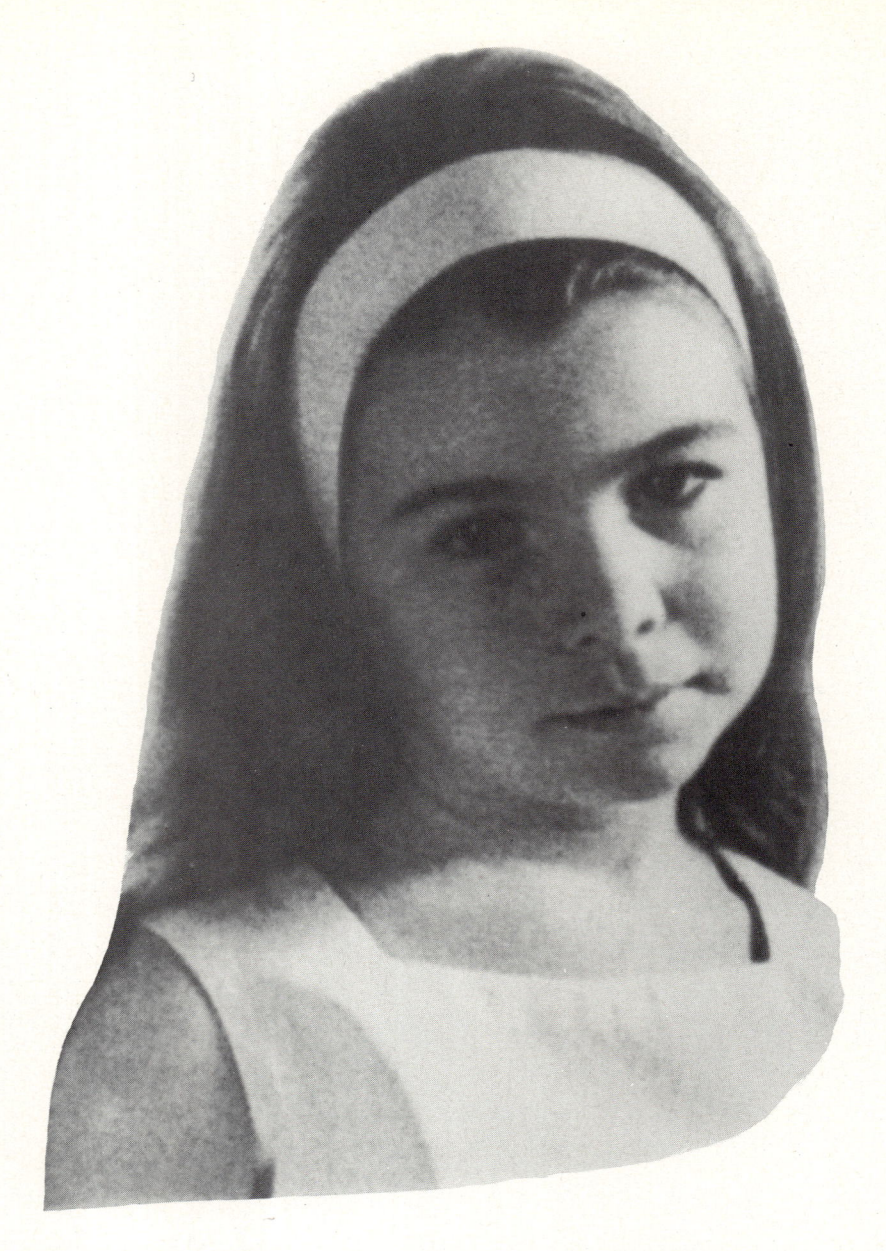

Hope is a warm friend...

A friend who understands... who accepts you as a person when others reject you.

Hope for the child with epilepsy lies in your acceptance. With modern medical treatment most persons with epilepsy can live normal lives. Only misunderstanding and fear stand in their way.

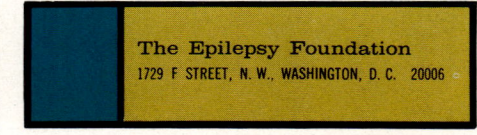

You can be a warm friend... you can be the source of hope for the nation's 2,000,000 sufferers from epilepsy. And it's easy to get the facts.

The Epilepsy Foundation
1729 F STREET, N.W., WASHINGTON, D. C. 20006

Send a postcard to: The Epilepsy Foundation, Dept. T, 1419 H Street, N.W., Washington, D. C. 20005.

(The Epilepsy Foundation is a non-profit, charitable organization. Contributions are tax deductible.)

This advertisement represents the contribution of the undersigned companies to the public informational activities of The Epilepsy Foundation.

Blue Ridge Transfer Company, Galax, Virginia.
Bonney Motor Express, Norfolk, Virginia.
Eastern Express, Terre Haute, Indiana.
Estes Express Lines, Richmond, Virginia.
Felts Transport Corporation, Galax, Virginia.
Houff Transfer, Weyers Cave, Virginia.

The New Dixie Lines, Richmond, Virginia.
Old Dominion Freight Line, High Point, North Carolina.
Overnight Transportation Company, Richmond, Virginia.
Sentle Trucking Corporation, Toledo, Ohio.
Smith's Transfer Corporation, Staunton, Virginia.
The Transport Corporation, Blackstone, Virginia.

Enjoy good old-time beer flavor!

Pabst Brewing Company, Milwaukee, Peoria Heights, Newark, Los Angeles

listen ... to the finest of sound reproduced by the high-fidelity sound components and sound systems of all types made by Ling-Temco-Vought — world leader in sound and electro-acoustic research and development.

LTV ALTEC DIVISION / ANAHEIM, CALIFORNIA   **LTV** UNIVERSITY DIVISION / OKLAHOMA CITY, OKLAHOMA

Grass grows greener...

Jet cargo loads faster...

Sheets are lovelier...

Missiles stand steadier...

WHY?...because FMC's *Niagara* chemicals promote thick turf on golf courses and parkways by destroying grass-killing pests and diseases; because an FMC loader automatically stows 90,000 lbs. of air cargo in 20 minutes; because gaily colored or pure white sheets and pillow cases in a blend with *Avril*® rayon are lustrous and lasting; and because FMC suspension systems support Minuteman ICBM's in underground launching silos. These are FMC ideas at work . . . ideas that benefit nearly everyone in some way every day.

FMC CORPORATION

```
fmc
CORPORATION
```

EXECUTIVE OFFICES: San Jose, California • MAJOR DIVISIONS: American Viscose • Bolens • Canning Machinery • Florida • FMC International • Hydrodynamics • John Bean Inorganic Chemicals • Niagara Chemical • Ordnance • Organic Chemicals • Packaging Machinery • Packing Equipment • Petroleum Equipment • Petro-Tex Chemical Corp. (Affiliate)
PUTTING IDEAS TO WORK...IN MACHINERY • CHEMICALS • DEFENSE • FIBERS AND FILMS

"LOOK AT ME...
I'm Walking!"

Just a few faltering steps...and yet the biggest thrill of his life. What comes next? Will he run and perhaps play like other youngsters? Although science has not yet found the final answer to cerebral palsy, there is much that can be done for the thousands of children who are now afflicted. What is it worth to you to see even one little boy walk? If he lived next door, would you help?

SUPPORT **UNITED CEREBRAL PALSY**

UNITED CEREBRAL PALSY ASSOCIATIONS • 321 West 44th Street, New York 38, New York

---

This advertisement represents the contribution of the undersigned companies to the public informational activities of United Cerebral Palsy Associations.

R. C. Barstow Trucking Company, Hadley, Massachusetts.
Coastal Tank Lines, York, Pennsylvania.
Hall's Motor Transit Company, Harrisburg, Pennsylvania.
Jones Motor Company, Spring City, Pennsylvania.
Mashkin Freight Lines, East Hartford, Connecticut.
O'Keefe Truck Rental Company, Providence, R. I.
Schwerman Trucking Company, Milwaukee, Wisconsin.

...*A stranger to her loved ones*...

Because of pain—the pain of arthritis, a mysterious crippler that attacks so many of its victims in their prime of life. Arthritis disables three times more women than men in the busy, productive years between 30 and 50 . . . the years a woman is needed by her children, who now are going through their troubled teens . . . the years she is needed by her husband, for the comfort and compassion he must have as his career takes exciting, demanding strides.

Because of the pain and crippling that comes with the swelling of her hands, her knees, her joints—arthritis robs a woman of her physical well-being . . . and sometimes, her serenity, her peace of mind, her place in the family and the community.

Arthritis can strike anyone, anywhere . . . women, men, even children. Today no one knows why. No one knows how to prevent it. But some of the best minds in the country are at work in research laboratories and in hospitals all over the nation, seeking solutions to the riddle of this mysterious, crippling disease. The work of these brilliant, dedicated men is supported by your contributions to the March of Dimes.

The National Foundation—March of Dimes
800 Second Avenue, • New York 17, New York

Franklin D. Roosevelt, Founder

This advertisement represents the contribution of the undersigned companies to the public informational activities of The National Foundation — The March of Dimes.

Akers Motor Lines, Gastonia, North Carolina.
Bell Lines, Charleston, West Virginia.
Central Motor Lines, Charlotte, North Carolina.
Georgia Highway Express, Atlanta, Georgia.
Hemingway Transport, New Bedford, Massachusetts.
The Motor Convoy Company, Hapeville, Georgia.

Lyndon
Baines
Johnson

'A President—
Not a Candidate'

by John Steinbeck. Novelist... Winner of Pulitzer Prize in 1940 for the *Grapes of Wrath,* his most famous work... Winner of the Nobel Prize for Literature in 1962... Former European correspondent, New York Herald Tribune.

We Americans are a fortunate breed—lucky in our large, rich slice of the earth which has survived even our own efforts to strip it bare. History treated us kindly in the days of our infancy. Predator nations had other business while we were learning the lessons of nationhood. We find our history strewn with good fortune.

Our nation was designed by a group of men ahead of their time and, in some ways, ahead of ours. They conceived a system capable of renewing itself to meet changing conditions without injury to itself in whole or in part, an instrument at once flexible and firm. We constantly rediscover the excellence of our architecture. It has been proof not only against foreign attack, but against our own stupidities which are sometimes more dangerous.

In reviewing our blessings, we must pay heed to our leadership. Not all of our Presidents have been great, but when the need has been great, we have found men of greatness. We have not always appreciated them. Usually, we have denounced and belabored them living and only honored them dead. Strangely, it is our mediocre Presidents we honor during their lives.

Now we gather at this Convention to nominate a Democrat whom we expect and intend to be President.

I think we all know the peril of the future. The world is restive and nervous. Change is all about us. New nations and alliances are erupting into being, and many of them, from inexperience and ambition, are capable of ill-considered and dangerous decisions.

Only a fool or a rascal believes that we can go back to old positions and attitudes which were ineffective even in their own time. The United States must change to meet change, accommodate when possible and resist when compromise plays out. Americans must accept and encourage change within, social and economic and spiritual, and these things must be done within the equation of our country which has served us so well.

It is said that we demand second-rate candidates and first-rate Presidents. At this time, we may not permit ourselves the pleasant pastime of Camp-Meeting Politicks. We have elected Presidents who had to spend their first terms learning the job, while running for the second term. We haven't time for that now. We require a President who knows not only his own job, but all the other branches of government. We require a President who knows every facet and foible of America—who also knows the world outside our boundaries.

We have one of the best-prepared, most effective Presidents in our history.

Lyndon B. Johnson's preparation for the Presidency begins in his ancestry—in the pioneer people of the land, who settled it, fought for it, developed it and stayed on it. They were always interested and involved in politics, not as a racket, but as the technique and governance of township, of county, of state and of nation. Young Lyndon's training for the Presidency began with his training as an American. He learned the land by working on it. He learned to judge a horse or a heifer or a man by judging them—and sometimes, being wrong. He learned poverty during the great Depression by being poor, and he has never forgotten the lesson.

There is a picture of a little boy, sitting on a door-stoop, face intent and eyes full of questions. Concentration and curiosity he has never lost. He asks questions and he listens to answers.

On finishing high school, the American restlessness struck Lyndon. He abandoned school, wandered to the Far West, worked at any kind of manual labor he could find—shovel work, stoop crops. After a year, he returned home, drove a tractor, handled road machinery, worked with his hands. He learned the needs, the wants, the fears, the exhaustion of laboring men. And this lesson also has remained deep and persistent in him. If he fights poverty now, it is because he knows the face of poverty.

When he went to college, a drive and a concentration came into focus in young Lyndon. He finished four years of college in a little over three years and then became a teacher. He taught boys of Mexican blood and learned to like and to respect them. Many years later, when an American soldier of Mexican ancestry, killed in action in Korea, was refused hometown burial through some small, mean local prejudice, Lyndon Johnson exploded with rage. He used his influence to have the boy buried at Arlington with full military honors. President Johnson's respect and understanding of Latin Americans is greatly responsible for our rapidly improving relations with the countries to the south of us.

No man ever studied the American government more closely than Lyndon Johnson. Beginning as secretary to Congressman Richard Kleberg, then as Congressman and Senator himself, he has absorbed and used the complex and complicated techniques of the Legislative branch. And again, he learned from the inside. He studied the groupings, the alignments, the individual personalities, the rules written and unwritten by which the Congress operates. He learned to reason, to argue, to give and to accumulate loyalties until, when he came to the leadership of the Senate, he was known as one of the most experienced and effective parliamentarians ever to serve.

Lyndon Johnson loves government and loves what he is doing. When other men took long week-ends, arranged tours which amounted to vacations, he worked in his office doing what he liked to do. The result was and is that he can outwork anyone in government and that without strain or exhaustion.

When John F. Kennedy beat Lyndon B. Johnson for the Presidential nomination and asked him to run as Vice President, LBJ stipulated that he must be used, that he must share in the Executive. President Kennedy kept his agreement. As Vice President, Johnson was sent all over the world. He learned about nations—their needs, their wants, their strengths and weaknesses, the character and personalities of their leaders—both actual and apparent. No Vice President was ever given such a comprehensive and concentrated training in the material out of which foreign policy is made. In addition, he sat in the Security Council. He attended all Cabinet meetings, the weekly White House conference with legislative leaders, and meetings of the Secretary of State and Secretary of Defense with the President on problems of security.

In addition, he served as chairman of the President's Committee on Equal Employment Opportunity, Chairman of the National Aeronautics and Space Council and Chairman of the Peace Corps Advisory Council.

His enormous knowledge of and influence in Congress made him invaluable in the presentation of bills the Executive wanted passed.

Then, came the mad and evil day of murder.

There is a photograph of LBJ taking the oath of office of President of the United States. He is standing in an airplane with Mrs. Kennedy beside him. On his face is shock and sorrow and humility, but no weakness. It almost seems that his whole life had been a preparation.

The nation and the world were staggered by the senseless assassination. It is frightening to think what might have happened if a lesser man in character, in training and in experience had been Vice President.

Again, we were fortunate. A questioning world was immediately made aware of our continuity. The command changed, but the Presidency was firm and permanent. Every branch of the nation—civil and military—continued to function without hesitancy and without error. There were no mass resignations, no change of directions or drive. The objectives and policies of John F. Kennedy continued to march along. A strong hand was on the reins of government. We were safe.

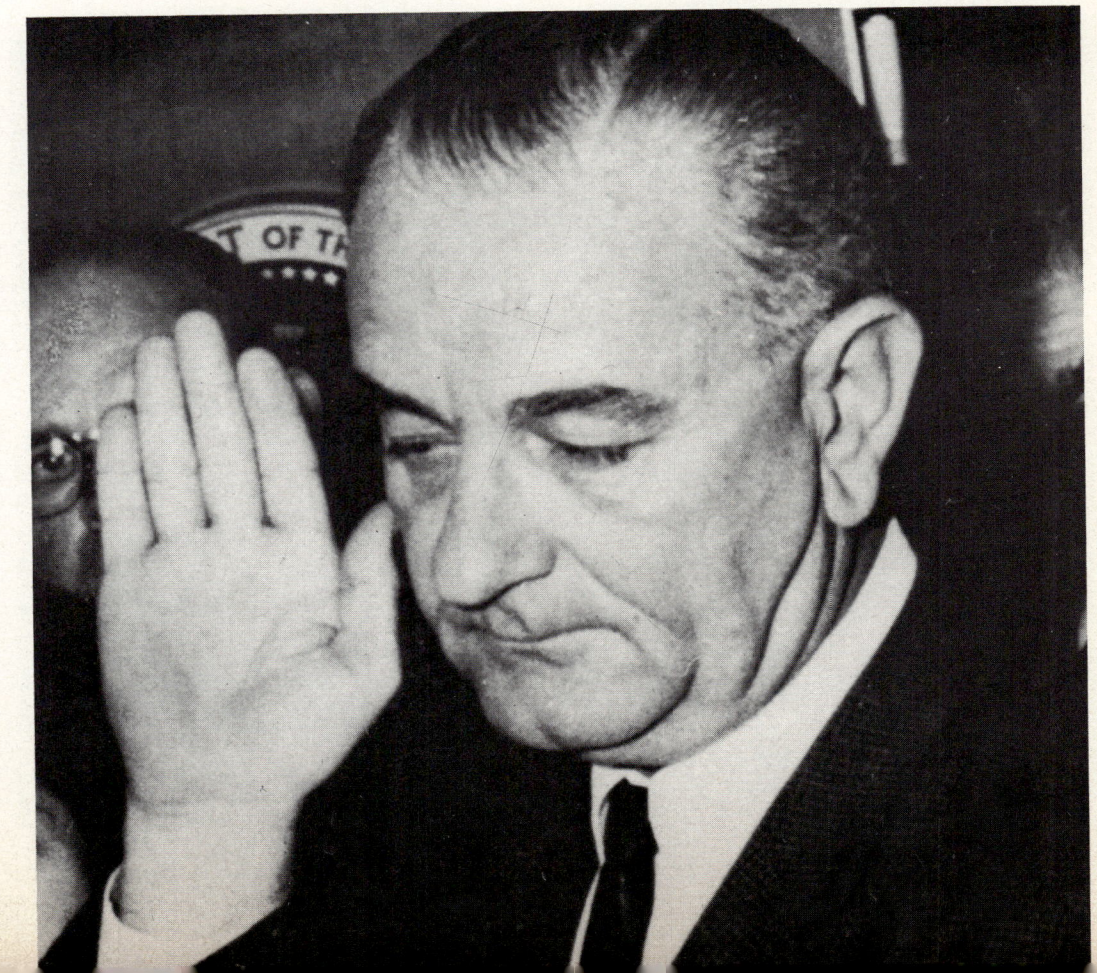

The relationship of Americans to their President is a matter of amazement to foreigners. Of course, we respect the office and admire the man who can fill it but, at the same time, we inherently fear and suspect power. We are proud of the President, and we blame him for things he did not do. We are related to the President in a close, almost a family, sense and we inspect his every move and mood with suspicion. We have made a tough but unwritten code of conduct for him in his private as well as his public life, and the slightest deviation brings forth a torrent of accusation and abuse. The President must be greater than anyone else, but not better than anyone else. We subject him and his family to close and constant scrutiny and denounce them for things we ourselves do every day.

A Presidential slip of the tongue, a slight error in judgment, social, political or ethical, can raise a storm of protest. We give the President more work than a man can do—more responsibility than a man should take—more pressure than a man can bear. We abuse him often and rarely praise him. We wear him out, use him up. And with all this, Americans have love for the President that goes beyond loyalty or party or nationality. He is ours and we exercise the right to destroy him. We insist that the President be cautious in speech, guarded in action, immaculate in his public and in his private life, and in spite of all of these imposed pressures, we are avidly curious about the man hidden behind the formal public image we have created.

What kind of a man is LBJ?

I've asked many questions of people closely associated with him and while there is some small variation in the answers, certain traits of character and nature and of direction stand out.

What does he like?

He likes his work, he believes passionately in the American government, knows as much about it as anyone living and is delighted to be involved in it. This joy in his work protects him from the weariness that comes to men who would rather be doing something else.

He loves his ranch and keeps improving it. The ranch ties him to his youth, his childhood and to his ancestry. It is the same soil, the same rocks, the same trees and brush, the same lazy water. He manages the ranch, judges the stock, rides well and happily. If weary and concerned, a few days on the ranch restore and refresh him.

He loves to hunt, but not necessarily to kill. It pleases him to see the deer romping on his land, to watch the rabbits in the early morning and to hear the quail roar up from the sagebrush. He does not kill for sport—only when he wants a piece of venison or a bird to eat. At the ranch, he falls instantly into the vernacular and the anecdotes of his section. The ranch is his point of departure, his place of contentment and home of return.

How is he to work for?

He is a driver. He sees no reason why others should not work as hard as he does. He demands perfection, and his helpers do their best to give it to him. He excuses a first mistake, considering it a lesson, but he is merciless to the man who fails to learn and makes the same mistake twice.

LBJ has a passion for learning. He listens carefully to all ideas and opinions and, in many cases, uses them after careful consideration. To the man or woman who serves his office well, he gives unlimited loyalty and affection.

Is he generous or stingy?

Impulsively generous. He loves to give presents and they go to high officers and to the girls on his secretarial staff.

What does he hate?

Well, he hates gossip, for one thing. Tell him a piece of malicious gossip and you make him your enemy—even cause him to take the side of the person gossiped about.

He hates cruelty. Abuse or brutality to children or women drive him to rage.

Is he sensitive to criticism of himself?

Not if it is deserved—not if he can learn from it. As an old pro, he understands the give-and-take of political battle. The lunge and parry of candidates do him no hurt. On the other hand, untruth, critical innuendo, secret and malicious attacks that have the quality of gossip—these puzzle him and trouble him, because he is incapable of them himself.

What does he read?

History, sociology, economics and some biography.

What is his favorite pastime? Discussion. It is all a part of his passion for learning. He values any experience by what he learns from it. He learns through discussion with men and women in many fields. He asks questions, listens to answers and remembers. By this pastime, he absorbs facts, ideas and possibilities and also people. His spectacular success as a Senate leader was the result not only of study and experience in the rules and techniques of the Senate, but also of his intimate knowledge and evaluation of the individual Senators. Knowing them as individuals, he was able to approach each man in his own province.

Government is certainly by law, but it is interpreted and administered by men. Very early, LBJ learned that it is necessary to understand both. His understanding of men allows him to make them understand each other and, thence, to approach a common end without friction.

His favorite quotation, Isaiah 1.18, "Come now, and let us reason together," could well be his motto.

What LBJ once learned about Congressmen and Senators, he now applies to heads of foreign states, to leaders of production, of financial groups, to the officers of labor unions. And always, his knowledge of men opens the gates of negotiation where coercion or exercise of power would be bound to fail.

What is his greatest talent as a statesman?

The ability to use his knowledge of men and events in conjunction with his highly developed sense of timing. He is acutely aware that many plans fail because they are too early or too late.

Will he be known as a great President?

If he continues to perform as he has in his first half year, one of the greatest.

It is said that the Presidency of the United States is the most powerful office in the world. What is not said or even generally understood is that the power of the Chief Executive is hard to achieve, bulky to manage and incredibly difficult to exercise. It is not raw, corrosive power nor can it be used willfully. Many new Presidents, attempting to exert executive power, have felt it slip from their fingers, have faced a rebellious Congress, an adamant Civil Service, a respectfully half-obedient military, a suspicious Supreme Court, a derisive press and a sullen electorate.

The power of the President is great, if he can use it. But it is a moral power—a power activated by persuasion, by discussion, by the manipulation and alignment of many small, but aggressive forces—each one weak in itself, but protected by the law from usurpation of its rights or punitive action against it by the Executive. And even if the national government should swing into line behind Presidential exercise of power, there remain the rights, prejudices and customs of states, counties and townships, of management of private production, labor unions, churches, professional organizations of doctors and lawyers, the guilds and leagues and associations. All these can give a President trouble, and if, reacting even to suspicion of overuse or misuse of power, they stand together, a President finds himself hamstrung, strait-jacketed and helpless. It is apparent that the President must have exact and sensitive knowledge not only of his own office, but of all the other branches of government, if his program is to progress at all.

LBJ came to the office as well equipped as any man who has ever taken the oath, but he had to function during a national tragedy. He was committed to carry out the plans and the directions of John F. Kennedy, the force of whose personality did not lessen with his death.

On November 22, 1963, Lyndon B. Johnson became President of a sad and perplexed nation, restive about the future, burdened with civil and foreign problems. In these first few months, he has established a stable and efficient administration, impressed with his leadership. His actions and accomplishments have been astonishing and unprecedented. A review of the record leaves us breathless. And this record is no accident. It is the result of great and increasing skill.

History is moving too fast for America to indulge in the circus of candidacy, baby-patting, blintz-eating, hand-pumping, the tricks, the gambols, gambits and gambles, the stage make-up, the announcements, accusations and revelations. The time for political vaudeville may well be over.

America wants not a candidate—but a President.

And we have a President.

"The Great Society"

President Lyndon Baines Johnson
At The University of Michigan
May 22, 1964

The purpose of protecting the life of our Nation and preserving the liberty of our citizens is to pursue the happiness of our people. Our success in that pursuit is the test of our success as a nation.

For a century we labored to settle and to subdue a continent. For half a century, we called upon unbounded invention and untiring industry to create an order of plenty for all of our people. The challenge of the next half century is whether we have the wisdom to use that wealth to enrich and elevate our national life, and to advance the quality of our American civilization.

Your imagination, your initiative and your indignation will determine whether we build a society where progress is the servant of our needs, or a society where old values and new visions are buried under unbridled growth. For in your time we have the opportunity to move not only toward the rich society and the powerful society, but upward to the Great Society.

The Great Society rests on abundance and liberty for all.

It demands an end to poverty and racial injustice.

But that is just the beginning.

The Great Society is a place where every child can find knowledge to enrich his mind and to enlarge his talents.

It is a place where leisure is a welcome chance to build and reflect, not a feared cause of boredom and restlessness.

It is a place where the city of man serves not only the needs of the body and the demands of commerce, but the desire for beauty and the hunger for community.

It is a place where man can renew contact with nature.

It is a place which honors creation for its own sake and for what it adds to the understanding of the race.

It is a place where men are more concerned with the quality of their goals than the quantity of their goods.

But most of all, the great society is not a safe harbor, a resting place, a final objective, a finished work. It is a challenge constantly renewed, beckoning us toward a destiny where the meaning of our lives matches the marvelous products of our labor.

So I want to talk to you today about three places where we begin to build the Great Society—in our cities, in our countryside, and in our classrooms.

Many of you will live to see the day, perhaps 50 years from now, when there will be 400 million Americans—four-fifths of them in urban areas. In the remainder of this century urban population will double, city land will double, and we will have to build homes, highways and facilities equal to all those built since this country was first settled.

In the next 40 years we must rebuild the entire urban United States.

Aristotle said, "Men come together in cities in order to live, but they remain together in order to live the good life."

It is harder and harder to live the good life in American cities today. The catalogue of ills is long: There is the decay of the centers and the despoiling of the suburbs. There is not enough housing for our people or transportation for our traffic. Open land is vanishing and old landmarks are violated. Worst of all, expansion is eroding the precious and time-honored values of community with neighbors and communion with nature. The loss of these values breeds loneliness and boredom and indifference. Our society will never be great until our cities are great. Today the frontier of imagination and innovation is inside those cities, and not beyond their borders. New experiments are already going on. It will be the task of your generation to make the American city a place where future generations will come, not only to live but to live the good life.

A second place where we begin to build the Great Society is in our countryside. We have always prided ourselves on being not only America the strong and America the free, but America the beautiful. Today that beauty is in danger. The water we drink, the food we eat, the very air that we breathe, are threatened with polution. Our parks are overcrowded. Our seashores overburdened. Green fields and dense forests are disappearing.

A few years ago we were greatly concerned about the Ugly American. Today we must act to prevent an Ugly America.

For once the battle is lost, once our natural splendor is destroyed, it can never be recaptured. And once man can no longer walk with beauty or wonder at nature, his spirit will wither and his sustenance be wasted.

A third place to build the Great Society is in the classrooms of America. There your children's lives will be shaped. Our society will not be great until every young mind is set free to scan the farthest reaches of thought and imagination. We are still far from that goal. Today, eight million adult Americans have not finished five years of school. Nearly 20 million have not finished eight years of school. Nearly 54 million, more than one-quarter of all America, have not even finished high school.

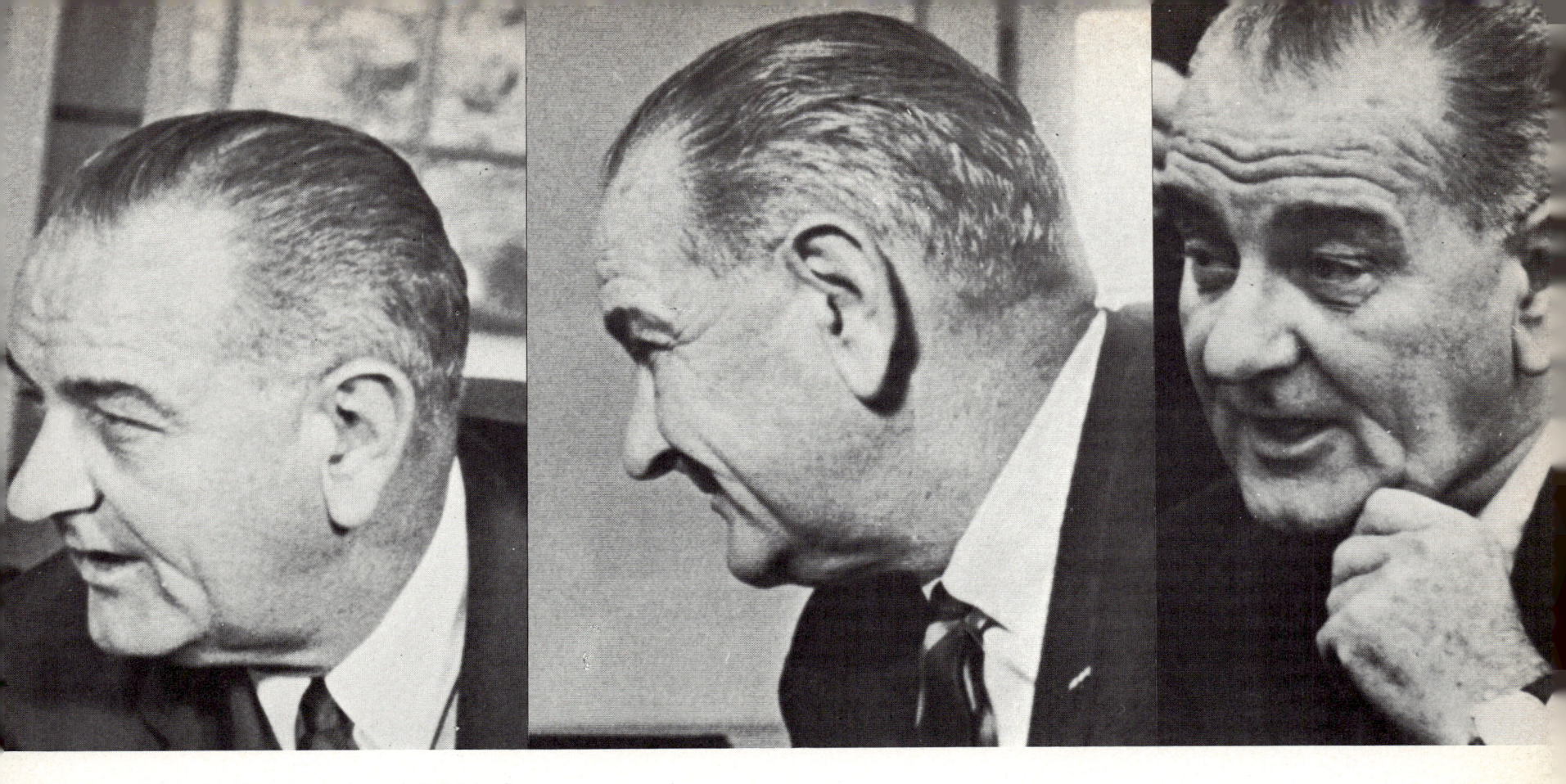

Each year more than 100,000 high school graduates, with proved ability, do not enter college because they cannot afford it. And if we cannot educate today's youth, what will we do in 1970 when elementary school enrollment will be 5 million greater than 1960? High school enrollment will rise by five million. College enrollment will increase by more than three million. In many places, classrooms are overcrowded and curricula are outdated. Most of our qualified teachers are underpaid, and many of our paid teachers are unqualified. We must give every child a place to sit and a teacher to learn from.

But more classrooms and more teachers are not enough. We must seek an educational system which grows in excellence as it grows in size. This means better training for our teachers. It means preparing youth to enjoy their hours of leisure as well as their hours of labor. It means exploring new techniques of teaching to find new ways to stimulate the love of learning and the capacity for creation.

These are three of the central issues of the Great Society. While our government has many programs directed at those issues, I do not pretend that we have the full answer to those problems. But I do promise this: We are going to assemble the best thought and the broadest knowledge from all over the world to find those answers for America. I intend to establish working groups to prepare a series of White House conferences and meetings on the cities, on natural beauty, on the quality of education, and on other emerging challenges. And from these meetings and from this inspiration and from these studies we will begin to set our course toward the Great Society.

The solution to these problems does not rest on a massive program in Washington, nor can it rely solely on the strained resources of local authority. They require us to create new concepts of cooperation, a creative federalism, between the national Capitol and the leaders of local communities.

Woodrow Wilson once wrote: "Every man sent out from his university should be a man of his Nation as well as a man of his time."

Within your lifetime powerful forces, already loosed, will take us toward a way of life beyond the realm of our experience, almost beyond the bounds of our imagination. For better or for worse, your generation has been appointed by history to deal with those problems and to lead America toward a new age. You have the chance never before afforded to any people in any age. You can help build a society where the demands of morality, and the needs of the spirit, can be realized in the life of the Nation.

Will you join in the battle to give every citizen the full equality which God enjoins and the law requires, whatever his belief, or race, or the color of his skin?

Will you join in the battle to give every citizen an escape from the crushing weight of poverty?

Will you join in the battle to make it possible for all nations to live in enduring peace as neighbors and not as mortal enemies?

Will you join in the battle to build the Great Society, to prove that our material progress is only the foundation on which we will build a richer life of mind and spirit?

There are those timid souls who say this battle cannot be won, that we are condemned to a soulless wealth. I do not agree. We have the power to shape the civilization that we want. But we need your will, your labor, your hearts, if we are to build that kind of society.

Those who came to this land sought to build more than just a new country. They sought a free world.

I have come here today to say that you can make their vision our reality. Let us from this moment begin our work so that in the future men will look back and say: It was then, after a long and weary way, that man turned the exploits of his genius to the full enrichment of his life.

he succeeds best who helps others succeed

THIS IS THE SPIRIT OF GROWTH that marks Reynolds Metals Company. A spirit as much in force today as it was yesterday. Growing. Serving. Fulfilling the promise of tomorrow. Developing new and varied uses of aluminum . . . uses that are opening new markets in many lands for this wonderfully versatile metal. Creating new products and services . . . including recent development of new heat treatable alloys for aluminum armor plate and space applications, pipeline joining systems, bridge railing, railroad car equipment, cans and can-making machinery, and Reynolon® plastic films. Research and development that has led to 51 patents this past year alone, including a patent on Reynolds process for rolling sheet by compacting small particles cast from molten aluminum.

New products and services that create new jobs for more people, contributing to the growth and future of our country and Reynolds Metals Company.

Reynolds—where new ideas take shape in aluminum

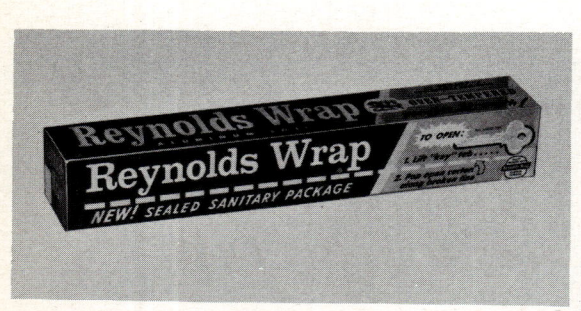

Watch The Richard Boone REYNOLDS ALUMINUM SHOW, NBC-TV, Tuesdays, 9-10 PM EDST

REYNOLDS METALS COMPANY
Employing over 28,800; total payrolls and employee benefits over $210,000,000.
Plants in 19 states: Alabama • Arizona • Arkansas • California • Connecticut • Florida • Georgia • Illinois • Kentucky
Louisiana • Michigan • Minnesota • Missouri • New York • Oregon • Pennsylvania • Texas • Virginia • Washington

REYNOLDS
where new ideas take shape in
ALUMINUM

building a car or a country:

you're in business with USI

Detroit to Dakar, Munich to Manila, the men who mold the future of industry and government are doing business daily with USI. ☐ USI makes and distributes many things for many industries in many countries. USI advanced mechanical and hydraulic automated presses are on the scene from Detroit to Hanover to Tokyo—in every automobile plant throughout the free world turning out complete body parts with precision and rapidity previously undreamed of. In fact, in Japan a whole production line of presses constitute the largest single order for such equipment made in this country for overseas shipment ever... made by USI. ☐ Through its world-wide international divisions, USI distributes or services basic equipment and material needed for the building and development of a country: locomotives in Latin America, tractors in Puerto Rico, air conditioning systems in Africa...the list goes on and on. All over the globe, wherever a country is stretching its roots and feeling its freedom, you will probably find USI. ☐ But USI is more. It is tomorrow's process and today's production. It is elegant nylon stockings and automated teaching machines. In England it is a major manufacturer of oil and hydraulic lift equipment and other heavy machinery; in the Philippines, the largest distributor of basic equipment. No wonder so many people, in so many places, are in business with USI.

U. S. INDUSTRIES, INC., 250 Park Ave., N.Y., N.Y. 10017

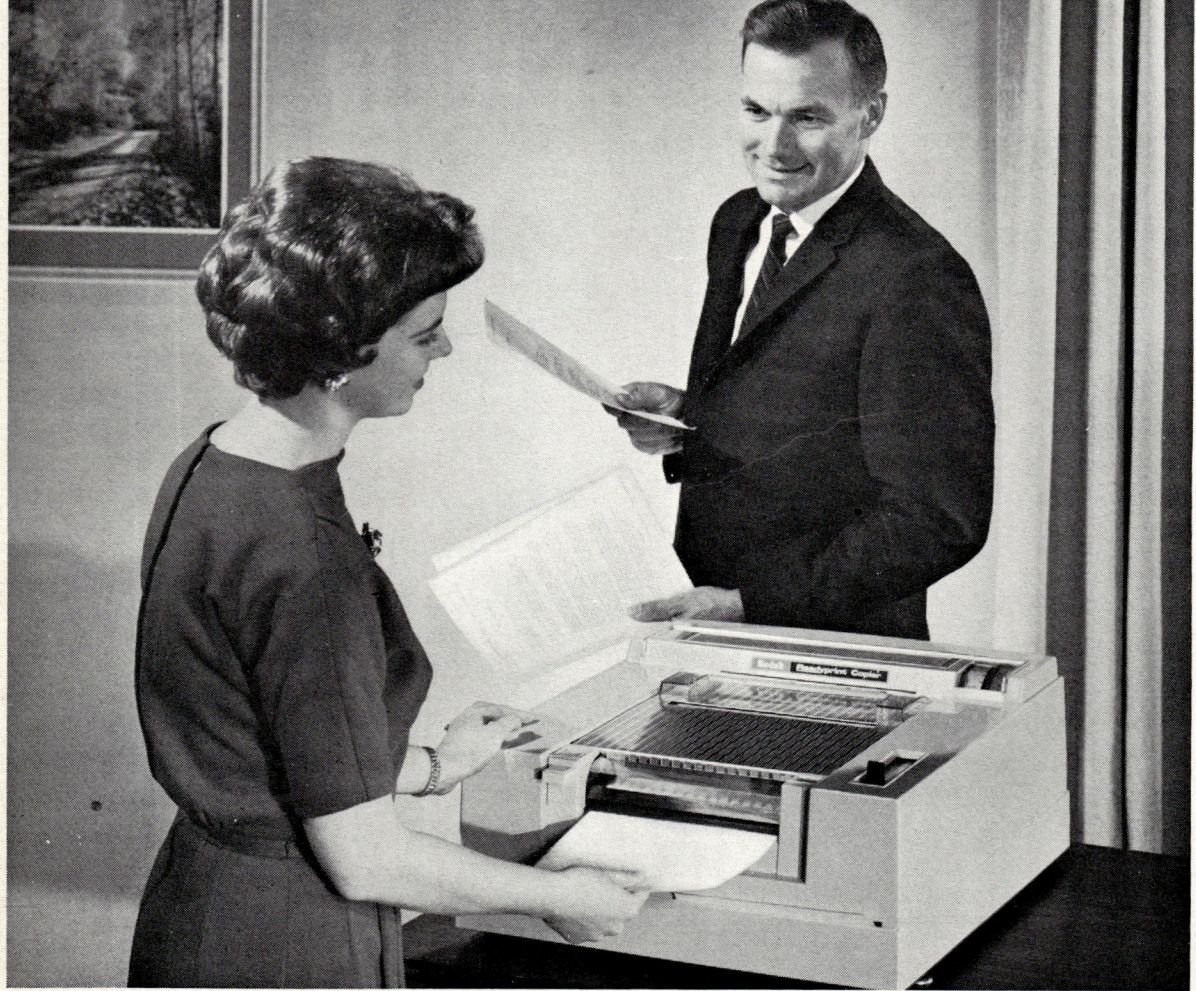

NOW **Kodak**
offers you a choice of TWO great new office copiers

. . . automated, cartridge-loading, specially geared to the needs of today's cost-conscious management!

VERIFAX CAVALCADE Copier

First choice for all-around copying. Makes a top-quality single copy. Turns out at least seven good copies from a 10¢ sheet of matrix. Exposure guide guards against slip-ups. Built-in VERIFAX ACTIMETER Unit ends solution handling.

KODAK READYPRINT Copier

First choice for fast single-copy needs. A completely different process makes this automated copier your first choice when usually only one copy is needed. Just feed the original and negative paper into the copier. Seconds later, with no stripping delay, you have a crisp, photo-exact copy that's good for a lifetime!

See these new copiers at your Kodak Copy Products Dealer's, or send for colorful brochures to Eastman Kodak Co., Rochester, N. Y. 14650.

NEW ADVANCES IN OFFICE COPYING KEEP COMING FROM KODAK

Kodak TRADEMARK

W. Thomas Rice, *President*
Atlantic Coast Line Railroad Company

"Should American Business Have Political Convictions?"

"Without question. For, like individual Americans, American business owes its progress and prosperity to the basic principles on which this country was founded.

"The free enterprise system. The right of self-determination. The right to compete without undue interference. These are the cornerstones that have made this country's business and industrial complex the world's strongest, most efficient, most productive — factors that have given this nation the highest living standards in history.

"For this last reason, if for no other, the American business community must give heed and support to our common political heritage. It must have a political conscience beyond mere partisanship. As with individual Americans, it is the duty of American business to guard against any encroachments into the fabric of freedoms from which we derive our national strength, security and prosperity.

"In this, American business must have political convictions and pursue them with honesty, decency, and courage."

Progressive partner with the auto industry in building America's remarkable mobility

YOUNG SPRING & WIRE COMPANY

DIVISION OF PAUL HARDEMAN, INC.
DETROIT, MICHIGAN

HOW LONG WILL OUR ABUNDANCE LAST?

Within the last hour the world's population has grown by more than 8,400 newborn souls, 292 of them American.

Our abundance will continue to outstrip our needs—if we can continue increasing our productivity. But today American agricultural employment, rural population, and the number of farms are in swift decline. Yet, each acre of those farms yields more; each farmhand controls greater horsepower. Farm machinery ranges from tractors to planes. More than 7,000 aircraft are spraying, fertilizing, and seeding. Result: U. S. crop production at a rate of only two man-days' work per acre—vs. a Far East average of 400.

Helping this production of U. S. abundance, so skillfully managed by the American farmer, Avco supplies many specialized pieces of farm machinery through its New Idea, Ezee Flow, and Barn-O-Matic Farm Equipment divisions. New Idea is offering the Uni-System—a self-propelled power unit with interchangeable machines for picking, husking and grinding corn, and for harvesting. Avco/Lycoming engines power many of the aircraft used in farming today.

Uni-System and other Avco farm machinery will help keep abundance ahead of domestic needs even as our population grows. In the year 2000 we will be feeding ourselves from one-half of the acreage required today. But of deeper significance, recognized by the people of Avco, is the promise such farm machinery holds for the better feeding of other peoples of the world, especially in areas where sufficient food may well mean peace.

If you are interested in joining Avco—an Equal Opportunity Employer—please write. *Avco—leadership in broadcasting; aircraft engines; farm equipment; space and defense research, development and production.*

Avco

Avco Corporation, 750 Third Avenue, New York 17, N.Y.

Is He All Right?

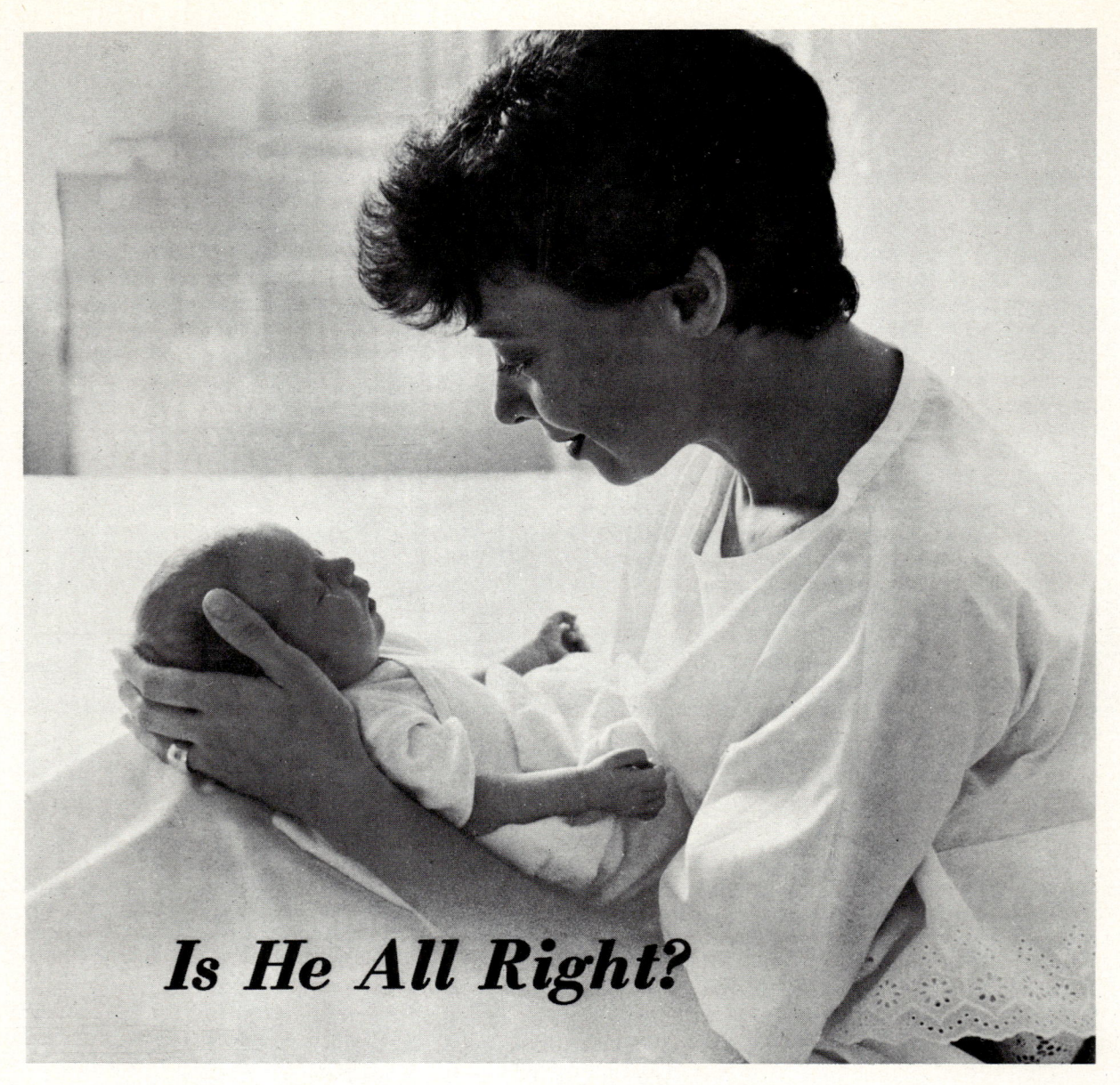

Happily, this time, the answer is yes. But 250,000 times each year across this country, the answer is a heartbreaking, fearful no.

Why does something go wrong when these tiny bodies are being formed? Why is a seriously defective child born to one out of every ten American families?

Can more of these children be helped with present medical knowledge?

What more must we know to prevent this from happening to babies not yet born?

Answers to these questions are being sought in nationwide programs supported by your contributions to The National Foundation-March of Dimes—the largest single source of private support for birth defects research and care in history. These answers will help prevent birth defects, a problem which concerns every family everywhere.

The National Foundation—March of Dimes
800 Second Avenue • New York 17, New York

Franklin D. Roosevelt, Founder

This advertisement represents the contribution of the undersigned companies to the public informational activities of The National Foundation—March of Dimes.

Be-Mac Transport Company, St. Louis, Missouri.
C & D Transportation Company, Newport, Rhode Island.
F. Gilbane, Inc., Pawtucket, Rhode Island.
Interstate Motor Freight System, Grand Rapids, Mich.
Yellow Transit Freight Lines, Kansas City, Missouri.

MARTIN MARIETTA CORPORATION
350 Park Avenue, New York, New York

Appalachian Stone
Headquarters: Mercersburg, Pennsylvania
  Operating Locations: Maryland (five)
  Pennsylvania (fifteen)
  West Virginia

Aetna Portland Cement Company
Headquarters and Plant: Bay City, Michigan

Dewey Portland Cement Company
Headquarters: Tulsa, Oklahoma
  Plants: Dewey, Oklahoma
  Tulsa, Oklahoma

Dewey Portland Cement Company
Headquarters and Plant: Davenport, Iowa
  Terminal: St. Paul, Minnesota

Dragon Cement Company
Headquarters: New Brunswick, New Jersey
  Plants: Thomaston, Maine
  Northampton, Pennsylvania
  Terminals: Boston, Massachusetts
  Elizabethport, New Jersey

Southern Cement Company
Headquarters: Birmingham, Alabama
  Plants: Calera, Alabama
  N. Birmingham, Alabama
  Atlanta, Georgia
  Terminals: Tampa, Florida
  New Orleans, Louisiana
  Meridian, Mississippi

Standard Lime and Cement Company
Headquarters: Baltimore, Maryland
  Plants: Martinsburg, West Virginia
  Pleasant Gap, Pennsylvania
  Woodville, Ohio
  Manistee, Michigan
  McCook, Illinois
  Millville, West Virginia
  Terminals: Baltimore, Maryland
  Washington, D.C.
  Wampum, Pennsylvania

Concrete Materials
Headquarters: Cedar Rapids, Iowa
  Operating Locations: Iowa (ten)
  Kansas (two)

Concrete Products Services
Headquarters: Chicago, Illinois
  Plant: Columbus, Ohio

Manley Sand
Headquarters: Rockton, Illinois
  Operating Locations: Oregon, Illinois
  Michigan City, Indiana
  Sawyer, Michigan
  Festus, Missouri
  Portage, Wisconsin
  Cumberland, Maryland

Superior Stone Company
Headquarters: Raleigh, North Carolina
  Operating Locations: Georgia
  North Carolina (thirty-two)
  South Carolina
  Virginia (three)

The Master Builders Company
Headquarters and Research Laboratory: Cleveland, Ohio
  Plants: Buffalo, New York
  Cleveland, Ohio

Madison Silos
Headquarters and Plant: Madison, Wisconsin
  Other Operating Locations: El Paso, Illinois
  Markle, Indiana
  Detroit Lakes, Minnesota
  Winona, Minnesota
  Falconer, New York
  Marietta, Ohio
  Waupaca, Wisconsin

Southern Dyestuff Company
Headquarters and Plant: Charlotte, North Carolina

Sinclair & Valentine Company (inks)
Headquarters: New York, New York
  Plants: Mobile, Alabama
  Phoenix, Arizona
  Camden, Arkansas
  Oakland, California
  Denver, Colorado
  New Haven, Connecticut
  Norwich, Connecticut
  Hialeah, Florida
  Jacksonville, Florida
  Cantonment, Florida
  Tampa, Florida
  Atlanta, Georgia
  Savannah, Georgia
  Chicago, Illinois
  Monroe, Louisiana
  New Orleans, Louisiana
  Baltimore, Maryland
  Malden, Massachusetts
  Medford, Massachusetts
  Kalamazoo, Michigan
  St. Paul, Minnesota
  North Kansas City, Missouri
  St. Louis, Missouri
  Secaucus, New Jersey
  Albany, New York
  New York, New York
  Charlotte, North Carolina
  Dayton, Ohio
  Rittman, Ohio
  Portland, Oregon
  Philadelphia, Pennsylvania
  Ridgway, Pennsylvania
  Sharpsburg, Pennsylvania
  Memphis, Tennessee
  Nashville, Tennessee
  Dallas, Texas
  Houston, Texas
  Franklin, Virginia
  Richmond, Virginia
  Seattle, Washington

Martin Company
Headquarters: Friendship International Airport, Maryland
  Operating Divisions: Baltimore Division, Nuclear Division & Electronic Systems & Products Division
  Middle River, Maryland
  Canaveral Division
  Cocoa Beach, Florida
  Denver Division
  Denver, Colorado
  Orlando Division
  Orlando, Florida
  The Research Institute for Advanced Studies (RIAS)
  Ruxton, Maryland

Martin Metals Company
Headquarters and Plant: Wheeling, Illinois
Research Laboratory: Portland, Oregon

SERVING ALL AMERICA   MARTIN MARIETTA

M·G·M

suggests an entertainment program for this fall...

OCTOBER

METRO-GOLDWYN-MAYER presents

JANE FONDA · ALAIN DELON · LOLA ALBRIGHT

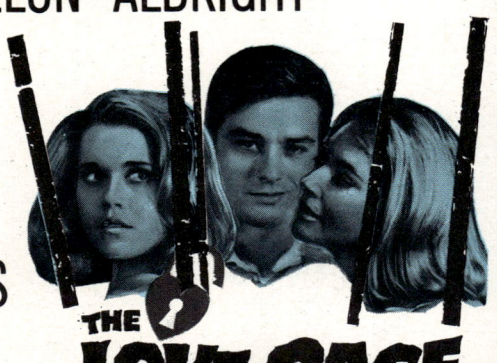

in RENE CLEMENT'S

Based on the novel "Joy House" by DAY KEENE

THE LOVE CAGE

Screen adaptation by RENE CLEMENT · PASCAL JARDIN · CHARLES WILLIAMS · A JACQUES BAR Production

FRANSCOPE

NOVEMBER

METRO-GOLDWYN-MAYER presents A MARTIN RITT PRODUCTION

THE OUTRAGE

starring PAUL NEWMAN

LAURENCE HARVEY · CLAIRE BLOOM · EDWARD G. ROBINSON

Co-starring WILLIAM SHATNER · HOWARD DaSILVA · ALBERT SALMI · Screen Play by MICHAEL KANIN · Produced by RONALD LUBIN · Directed by MARTIN RITT

NOVEMBER

Metro-Goldwyn-Mayer presents A Seven Arts Production

KIM NOVAK · LAURENCE HARVEY

IN W. SOMERSET MAUGHAM'S

OF HUMAN BONDAGE

Co-starring:
ROBERT MORLEY · SIOBHAN McKENNA · ROGER LIVESEY · JACK HEDLEY

Directed by KEN HUGHES · Produced by JAMES WOOLF · Screenplay by BRYAN FORBES

DECEMBER

METRO-GOLDWYN-MAYER presents

JAMES GARNER · JULIE ANDREWS · MELVYN DOUGLAS

in MARTIN RANSOHOFF'S PRODUCTION

THE AMERICANIZATION OF EMILY

Co-starring JAMES COBURN · Directed by ARTHUR HILLER

Screen play by PADDY CHAYEFSKY · Based on the novel by WILLIAM BRADFORD HUIE

A FILMWAYS PICTURE

THE CARLYLE

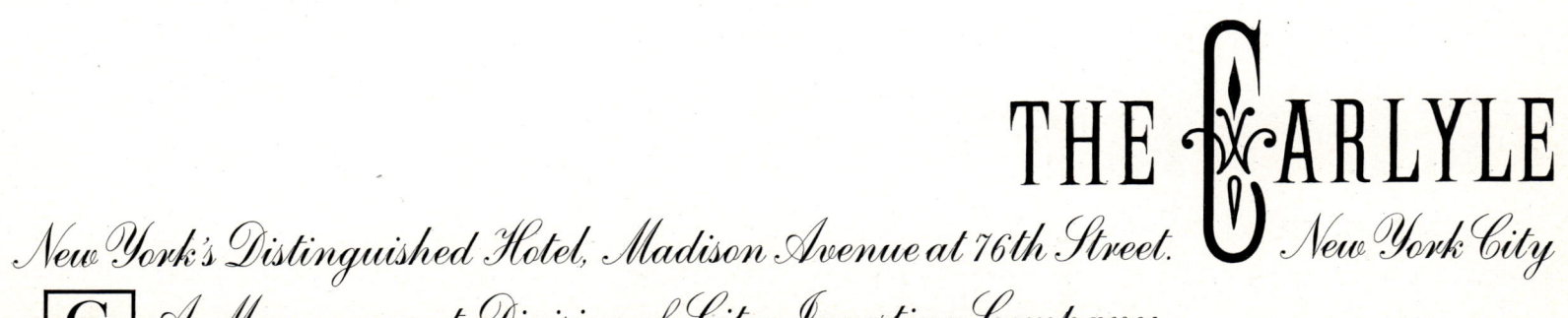

New York's Distinguished Hotel, Madison Avenue at 76th Street. New York City

A Management Division of City Investing Company

**Presidents'
Ladies**

Presidents' Ladies

by Marianne Means. White House correspondent, Hearst Newspapers... Author, *The Woman in the White House*... Contributing writer for magazines.

Her name isn't on the ballot. Sometimes she doesn't campaign much; sometimes she becomes a campaign issue. The Constitution gives her nothing to do, and she will never be paid a cent. Maybe she doesn't even want the honor.

But 32 of 35 American Presidents have brought wives with them to the White House, women of widely varying ages, talents, intelligence, and interests.

Some First Ladies, such as Lady Bird Johnson and Eleanor Roosevelt, have been full partners to the President, active in politics, in the conduct of public affairs, and in efforts to improve the welfare of the country. Some, such as Helen Taft and Florence Harding, were responsible for prodding their reluctant husbands toward the White House. Edith Wilson became "acting President" during her husband's serious illness. Jacqueline Kennedy stimulated a new interest in the arts throughout the country and turned the White House into a museum of American culture.

Only one thing have all First Ladies shared in common: they have fought furiously—and usually futilely—to protect their husbands from the strain of the Presidency.

"The mere fact that she is First Lady, and the highest-ranking woman in the country, is a responsibility," the late President Kennedy once said. Every First Lady has recognized that responsibility, but each has sought to interpret it differently.

President Johnson believes that a First Lady's role is "...to make her husband comfortable and happy and to stimulate and inspire him—and by precept and example attract the admiration of her own sex."

He is enthusiastic about the contributions of Mrs. Johnson to his own Presidency.

"She is helping to bring about more active participation of women in the affairs of the land. She is helping to heal some of the wounds that exist between the North and South and business and labor. She is bringing compassion into the decisions the government must make every day. She also contributes a prudent, practical business judgment to some of the adventures that this government is taking," he says.

President Johnson declares that he discusses most government welfare projects with Mrs. Johnson, such as his anti-poverty program, medical care for the aged, aid to heart and cancer research. She has demonstrated her interest in such programs by making tours to meet the people behind the statistics. She visited pockets of poverty in Pennsylvania and West Virginia to underline the President's program to help those areas. She toured the nation's space center at Huntsville, Ala., to emphasize the President's concern for the U. S. space program. Mrs. Johnson clearly views her role as a full-time job.

A First Lady, however, has no official duties nor authority; the Constitution does not bother to mention her existence at all. While the Founding Fathers were generously creating a Presidency virtually unlimited in scope and power, they gave the President's wife no role to play. She did not even have a title until 1877, when a magazine writer used the expression "first lady" to describe Lucy Hayes.

This was all very well in the late 1700's, when not one in a hundred women could read or write and when female intelligence was rated somewhere around the level of a five-year-old boy. Martha Washington, for example, had never gone to school and spelled so poorly that she was forced to dictate all her letters. (Fortunately, however, her long suit was the social graces, and she managed very nicely in setting the proper social precedents, not too queenly but not too democratic, for future Presidents and their wives to follow.)

The Founding Fathers, with their great vision in other directions, could not foresee that women—wives of plumbers as well as Presidents—would gradually come to play leadership roles in the life of the nation, working side by side with men in every profession. John Adams, who complained that his wife, Abigail, was "saucy" because she proffered him advice, would have been shocked to learn there would be a woman candidate for President in 1964. Even President Johnson, who has done more to bring women into high government jobs than any other President, is slightly astounded at women's progress. He protested wryly that he felt Sen. Margaret Chase Smith had "misunderstood" his desire for more women in federal jobs. "I was referring to an echelon lower than my own job," he grinned.

In the past hundred years, women have passed through a remarkable metamorphosis. First came education, then social acceptance of the single working girl. With the right to vote in 1920, women pushed into the professions at all levels. Today women voters outnumber men, and women are taking an increasing interest in politics. There are two women Senators, twelve Congresswomen, and a number of state legislators and city council members scattered across the country.

As the role of women in general has expanded, so has the role of the highest-ranking woman. The nation now looks to her to set an example in more fields than pie baking and child rearing.

Harry Truman, in his book *Mr. Citizen,* wrote: "I hope someday someone will take time to evaluate the true role of the wife of a President, and to assess the many burdens she has to bear and the contributions she makes." Truman describes his own wife's contributions simply. "She helped me in everything," he says. And he means everything. For Truman insists that he consulted with Bess before every major decision of his life, including whether to drop the atomic bomb on Japan, whether to fight in Korea, whether to initiate the Marshall Plan to rebuild a shattered Europe.

"I discussed all of them with her," Truman declares. Then, as an afterthought, he scowls over his spectacles at his questioner. "Why not?" he asks.

During her nearly eight years in the White House, Bess Truman remained quietly in the background. She never spoke in public. She did nothing to attract attention.

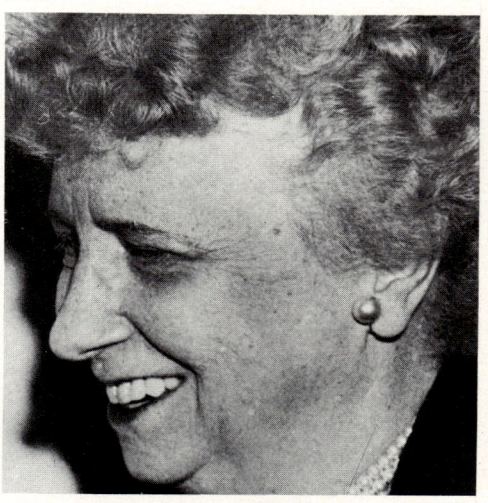

Yet today Truman credits his wife with being "a full partner in all my transactions —politically and otherwise." He frequently followed her advice: "Her judgment was aways good... she looks at things objectively and I can't always," he says. She edited many of his speeches. She campaigned with him and was rarely far from his side. And, as Truman puts it, "...she made sure that the snooty women were well treated."

Until the mid-20th century, however, no President dared pay such tribute to his wife's influence, no matter how much he loved her. Abigail Adams became a campaign issue in 1800 because she was accused of having too much influence over President Adams. Adams, who had few confidants among his male contemporaries, turned to his brilliant wife for counsel on government, politics, philosophy. But once he wrote her grumpily: "I think women better than men, in general, and I know that you can keep a secret as well as any man whatever. But the world don't know this. Therefore, if I were to write my sentiments to you and the letter should be caught and hitched into a newspaper, the world would say I was not to be trusted with a secret."

While Adams was a delegate at the Continental Congress drawing up the Constitution, Mrs. Adams peppered him with letters of advice, imploring him to give votes to women, do away with slavery, and expand educational programs. While in the White House, she liked nothing better than to "pick a political bone" with dignitaries and officials.

Because she was privy to so much that went on in government, one of the political assaults upon Adams which helped defeat his bid for re-election charged that Mrs. Adams had "a degree of public influence over the public conduct of her husband."

During the Civil War Mary Todd Lincoln likewise became an issue to be used against the President. Because of her Southern heritage, she was accused of being a Confederate spy. A joint Senate-House committee was set up to investigate and Abraham Lincoln himself journeyed to Capitol Hill to testify to his wife's loyalty.

And in this century Helen Taft was accused of bossing the President too much. The President called her his "council of war" and she kept his appointment schedule and sat in on all Cabinet meetings. She was not, however, trying to control him—she just wanted to keep him awake. The President had the embarrassing habit of dropping off to sleep in the middle of important conversations so she sat beside him to gently prod him with her fan when he seemed about to doze off.

The First Lady who shattered the concept for all time that a President's wife should remain quiet at home was Eleanor Roosevelt. To her, home was the land, the sea, the air. She was the eyes and ears—and conscience—of a President considered by historians to be one of the greatest. She became so deeply entangled in government affairs Secretary of Interior Harold Ickes complained in his diary: "I wish Mrs. R. would stick to her knitting and keep out of the affairs connected with my department." She travelled around the world, bringing back reports to the crippled President about conditions and opinions in the country, making speeches and appearances on his behalf, and boosting the morale of soldiers overseas during World War I. Her son James (Rep. James Roosevelt of California) called her "a sort of roving one-woman task force for social reform and international good will" and "father's invaluable and trusted right arm."

She championed Negro rights. She championed the unemployed. She stirred the President to action in a variety of causes, particularly the National Youth Administration. Rexford Tugwell, a part of the President's famous Brain Trust, called Mrs. Roosevelt "the keeper of and constant spokesman for her husband's conscience."

She wrote a syndicated column, in which she discussed her favorite projects and controversial issues of the day. She conducted radio broadcasts and held press conferences. The impact of her personality upon the country was impossible to measure, but it was sweeping.

After the death of President Roosevelt, she increased her own prestige and her efforts on behalf of mankind, serving the United Nations. Three American Presidents, United Nations diplomats, foreign heads of state, short-order cooks, secretaries, and miners all called her "the First Lady of the World."

In the grand tradition of Eleanor Roosevelt now has come Lady Bird Johnson. Her influence over the President is unobtrusive but omnipresent. "I want to help," she says simply.

Mrs. Johnson has quickly proved herself to be an active First Lady who refuses to be devoured by ribbon-cutting and posterposing. She brought to the White House twenty-nine years of experience as the wife of a Congressman, Senator and Vice President, and she has put her training to good use. She shares with the President a deep sense of public service.

She has entertained at dinner every Congressman and Senator, most of whom had never before dined at the White House.

She has initiated a series of luncheons for outstanding women in all fields to attract national attention to the contributions women are making in today's world.

She has campaigned by her husband's side throughout his long career and will do so again this fall. She accompanies him on most public appearances, often preceding his speech with a graceful little talk of her own.

"I want to help Lyndon make the people of this country prouder of their country and fuller participants in the life of their government," the First Lady has said.

President Johnson describes his wife as "a soft, kind, modest person with a back of steel." He believes that ". . . she is able to heal the differences between parties, because she has nice things to say about both Democrats and Republicans. She has the peculiar ability to overlook bad qualities and find only the good ones and she genuinely likes people, regardless of their politics."

Mrs. Johnson's business acumen, attested to by the President, enables her to speak with authority on many affairs of government in which few First Ladies have dared interest themselves. She managed her husband's Congressional office when he enlisted in the Navy during World War II. For many years she handled the Johnson family business enterprises all by herself while her husband concentrated upon his political career. (When he became President, the family corporation was put into trust.)

She has exerted her energies on behalf of youth, making special appeals for the Girl Scouts and 4-H groups, and hostessing special programs for young people at the White House.

And her exceptional warmth and vivaciousness have already brought her a popularity accorded only the most outstanding First Ladies.

In the first six months of 1964, Mrs. Johnson traveled 30,000 miles over Appalachia to the West Coast, underlining her husband's program. With the warm personal touch, she visited and spoke to people living in "pockets of poverty" to underline her husband's program for them.

Her visits to housing projects for the aged, to one-room schools in the Kentucky Mountains, and to Radcliffe College in Massachusetts helped draw back the curtain a little wider on the national needs.

"In the space age," she often declares, "passive citizenship is a luxury no one can afford."

Every First Lady makes her distinctive mark. Mrs. Kennedy added glamor and excellence in taste to American life. President Kennedy listed as his wife's greatest contributions as First Lady ". . . her emphasis on creative fields, her concentration on giving historical meaning to the White House furnishings, and her success as an ambassador on the trips she has made with me abroad. And by carrying out her primary responsibility to support her husband and care for her children well, she is doing her real job as a woman."

Presidents through the years have held varying concepts of how their wives should behave in the public eye. President Kennedy believed that ". . . any First Lady will do all right if she is herself." Grover Cleveland, however, advised his wife she would get along as First Lady if she did not try anything new (at issue was Mrs. Cleveland's desire to go horseback riding, which no First Lady had ever done).

President Eisenhower took a limited view of a First Lady's responsibilities, centering on the areas of hostess and wifely duties. "In the White House you need intelligence and charm — to make others glad to be around you," he said.

President Roosevelt, on the other hand, was not even upset when Adolf Hitler ranted in 1934, "Eleanor Roosevelt is America's real ruler." Roosevelt knew better than anyone else that Hitler was exaggerating, and he used to remark every time his wife's uninhibited remarks or energetic projects raised a storm of controversy, "Lady, it's a free country . . . If you get me in hot water, I'll manage to save myself."

It is often written that there is no training for the Presidency, for no man who is not President can know the full extent of the awful burdens of the office. But in campaigning for the job and in the years of public service which must precede a nomination, a candidate does receive some preparation in the art of governing.

For the First Lady, however, there is truly no adequate preparation. Several First Ladies have not even been interested in politics. Few women came to the White House equipped by background to cope with the sudden focus of national attention, the demands of leadership in social and cultural fields, and the duties necessary to ease the President's work load. (Mrs. Johnson is one of those few.)

Only three women in history married Presidents. (Edith Galt married Woodrow Wilson on Dec. 15, 1918; Frances Folsom married Grover Cleveland on June 2, 1886; and Julia Gardiner wedded John Tyler on June 26, 1844.) The others married engineers, lawyers, soldiers and businessmen. Only five had college educations. Abigail Fillmore, Grace Coolidge, Helen Taft, Caroline Harrison, and Eleanor Roosevelt had been school teachers; Florence Harding ran a newspaper. The others had no independent careers. (Mrs. Kennedy worked a few months as an inquiring photographer.)

Nonetheless a great number of First Ladies have left behind solid contributions to the nation and most developed into valuable helpmeets to their husbands. Each has interpreted her role according to her own best talents and temperament.

Mrs. Johnson is a people-person; her influence is felt today most strongly in the realm of human relations and the national welfare.

Lou Hoover was national president of the Girl Scouts and built the organization from a membership of 10,000 to nearly one million. Abigail Fillmore launched the first permanent White House library. Dolly Madison, who is usually thought of only as a fabulous party-giver, persuaded President Madison to rebuild the nation's capitol in Washington on the site where the British burned it during the war of 1812. (He originally favored moving the capitol and rebuilding it in Philadelphia).

Sarah Polk served as her husband's chief assistant and private secretary in the White House. Lucy Hayes was a temperance leader and because she banished even wine from the White House was dubbed "Lemonade Lucy." Caroline Harrison was one of the founders of the Daughters of the American Revolution. Helen Taft, all by herself, persuaded William Howard Taft not to accept Theodore Roosevelt's offer of a Supreme Court Justiceship, so that he would be eligible for the Presidential mantle. (Taft himself desired the bench more than the White House, but he followed his wife's urgings.)

Of all First Ladies, history treats Florence Harding the most unsympathetically. Its judgment is harsh, too, on her husband, Warren Gamaliel Harding, the only President who totally and miserably failed the American people.

The Presidency is the master force for shaping public policy; as Franklin Roosevelt put it, "pre-eminently a place of moral leadership." But Harding's inability to cope with the responsibilities of the White House led to incredible shame and corruption, including the jailing of a Cabinet member (Secretary of the Interior Albert Fall, convicted of fraud in the Teapot Dome scandal).

Harding never displayed much understanding of political issues and principles; he was an amiable puppet who simply did what people told him. And his chief advisor and promoter was his wife. She called herself "the President-maker." The President constantly bowed to her will; as a Christmas present he let her pick which prisoners were to be pardoned. She had a hand in most of the high Federal appointments and there is ample evidence that she knew more about what was going on in his corrupt administration than he did.

When Harding died in August, 1923, Mrs. Harding promptly burned all his official and private papers. The nation will never know if she sought to protect his memory or his duplicity—or her own collaboration.

The First Lady who actually came closest to bearing the responsibilities that the Constitution has given the President alone was Edith Galt Wilson.

Woodrow Wilson still had a year and a half of his second term to serve when he was partially paralyzed by a stroke in 1919.

For six weeks, no one saw the paralyzed President but his wife and doctor, Admiral Cary Grayson. For months after that, only an occasional secretary or official visitor was allowed to speak to the President for brief moments. Yet the government went on as usual.

Edith Wilson insisted upon referring to this period as her "stewardship"—which implies management within delegated authority, but no assumption of independent policy-making authority. Others, however, called her "acting President" and "regent."

The First Lady screened all pending affairs of state, postponed some, handled some herself, and brought the most important up with the ailing President. Then she carried out his instructions. She gave all orders orally, so as not to leave a record that might later raise Constitutional questions about her authority. She appointed two Cabinet members, telling them she was acting on behalf of the President.

She protected her husband so zealously from visitors that he was isolated from public opinion and the Senate's mood. Unaware of the full bitterness in the Senate toward the League of Nations, Wilson refused to compromise its provisions and thereby sealed its doom with his own sickly hand.

And so, it is clear that if the present trend continues First Ladies of the future will play ever more influential roles in the conduct of the Presidency. And why not? After all, a wife is the first to see her husband in the morning and the last to see him at night and she understands the President of the United States better than anybody else in the world.

"We have long neglected the mentally ill... this neglect must end"

John F. Kennedy   Feb. 5, 1963

Let Us Carry On... GIVE for MENTAL HEALTH

The National Association for Mental Health, Inc. • 10 Columbus Circle, New York 19, New York

---

This advertisement represents the contribution of the undersigned companies to the public informational activities of the National Association for Mental Health.

Auclair Transportation, Manchester, N. H.
Dameo Motor Transportation, Somerville, N. J.
Greens Storage Warehouse, Providence, R. I.
Rogers Cartage Company, Chicago, Illinois.
St. Germain Motor Transportation, Woonsocket, R. I.
Schuster's Express, Colchester, Connecticut.
Spector Freight System, Chicago, Illinois.
Transamerican Freight Lines, Detroit, Michigan.
Wooleyhan Transport Company, Wilmington, Delaware.

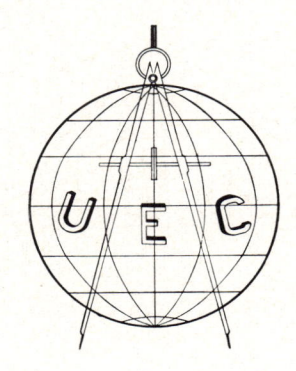

CONSULTING ENGINEERS

UNIVERSAL ENGINEERING

CORPORATION

Research and Development
Field and Laboratory Analyses
Studies and Reports
Engineering and Geological Surveys
Civil and Structural Engineering Design
Construction Supervision
Soils Engineering

DAVID NASSIF - President   WILLIAM A. HENDERSON - Vice President

---

MAIN OFFICE

38 CHAUNCY STREET   BOSTON, MASS. 02111

Area Code 617   542-8216

Independent financing of scholarship aid

A nationwide, cooperative program of assistance to students of exceptional ability and to the colleges they select

This program, as now financed, is the largest independent scholarship program in the history of American education. It provides opportunity for contributing donors to preserve their identities and their own objectives, and to increase greatly the effectiveness of scholarship contributions.

MERIT SCHOLARSHIPS
are administered through the
NATIONAL MERIT SCHOLARSHIP CORPORATION
1580 Sherman Avenue, Evanston, Illinois

This program merits your financial support

This advertisement represents the contribution of the undersigned companies to the public informational activities of the National Merit Scholarship Corporation.

All States Freight, Akron, Ohio.
Dixie Ohio Express Company, Akron, Ohio.
Roadway Express, Akron, Ohio.
Suburban Motor Freight, Columbus, Ohio.

UNIVERSAL CITY STUDIOS
THE ENTERTAINMENT CENTER OF THE WORLD

UNIVERSAL CITY, CALIFORNIA

Give to fight

MS
Multiple Sclerosis

the great crippler of young adults

You can send your contributions in care of your local Postmaster, or to:

NATIONAL MULTIPLE SCLEROSIS SOCIETY
257 Park Avenue South, New York, New York 10010

This advertisement represents the contribution of the undersigned companies to the public informational activities of the National Multiple Sclerosis Society.

Automobile Carriers, Flint, Michigan.
Automobile Transport, Wayne, Michigan.
Bolin Drive-A-Way Company, Cleveland, Ohio.
Cassens Transport Company, Edwardsville, Illinois.
E & L Transport Company, Dearborn, Michigan.
Liquid Transporters, Louisville, Kentucky.
Vehicle Leasing Company, Kenosha, Wisconsin.
Vehicle Leasing Corporation, Kenosha, Wisconsin.

The World's Largest Manufacturer of Surgical Dressings Welcomes the Democratic National Convention to Atlantic City

Our Credo

WE BELIEVE THAT OUR FIRST RESPONSIBILITY IS TO THE DOCTORS, NURSES, HOSPITALS,
MOTHERS, AND ALL OTHERS WHO USE OUR PRODUCTS.
OUR PRODUCTS MUST ALWAYS BE OF THE HIGHEST QUALITY.
WE MUST CONSTANTLY STRIVE TO REDUCE THE COST OF THESE PRODUCTS.
OUR ORDERS MUST BE PROMPTLY AND ACCURATELY FILLED.
OUR DEALERS MUST MAKE A FAIR PROFIT.

OUR SECOND RESPONSIBILITY IS TO THOSE WHO WORK WITH US—
THE MEN AND WOMEN IN OUR PLANTS AND OFFICES.
THEY MUST HAVE A SENSE OF SECURITY IN THEIR JOBS.
WAGES MUST BE FAIR AND ADEQUATE,
MANAGEMENT JUST, HOURS REASONABLE, AND WORKING CONDITIONS CLEAN AND ORDERLY.
EMPLOYEES SHOULD HAVE AN ORGANIZED SYSTEM FOR SUGGESTIONS AND COMPLAINTS.
SUPERVISORS AND DEPARTMENT HEADS MUST BE QUALIFIED AND FAIR MINDED.
THERE MUST BE OPPORTUNITY FOR ADVANCEMENT—FOR THOSE QUALIFIED
AND EACH PERSON MUST BE CONSIDERED AN INDIVIDUAL
STANDING ON HIS OWN DIGNITY AND MERIT.

OUR THIRD RESPONSIBILITY IS TO OUR MANAGEMENT.
OUR EXECUTIVES MUST BE PERSONS OF TALENT, EDUCATION, EXPERIENCE AND ABILITY.
THEY MUST BE PERSONS OF COMMON SENSE AND FULL UNDERSTANDING.

OUR FOURTH RESPONSIBILITY IS TO THE COMMUNITIES IN WHICH WE LIVE.
WE MUST BE A GOOD CITIZEN—SUPPORT GOOD WORKS AND CHARITY,
AND BEAR OUR FAIR SHARE OF TAXES.
WE MUST MAINTAIN IN GOOD ORDER THE PROPERTY WE ARE PRIVILEGED TO USE.
WE MUST PARTICIPATE IN PROMOTION OF CIVIC IMPROVEMENT,
HEALTH, EDUCATION AND GOOD GOVERNMENT,
AND ACQUAINT THE COMMUNITY WITH OUR ACTIVITIES.

OUR FIFTH AND LAST RESPONSIBILITY IS TO OUR STOCKHOLDERS.
BUSINESS MUST MAKE A SOUND PROFIT.
RESERVES MUST BE CREATED, RESEARCH MUST BE CARRIED ON,
ADVENTUROUS PROGRAMS DEVELOPED, AND MISTAKES PAID FOR.
ADVERSE TIMES MUST BE PROVIDED FOR, ADEQUATE TAXES PAID, NEW MACHINES PURCHASED,
NEW PLANTS BUILT, NEW PRODUCTS LAUNCHED, AND NEW SALES PLANS DEVELOPED.
WE MUST EXPERIMENT WITH NEW IDEAS.
WHEN THESE THINGS HAVE BEEN DONE THE STOCKHOLDER SHOULD RECEIVE A FAIR RETURN.
WE ARE DETERMINED WITH THE HELP OF GOD'S GRACE,
TO FULFILL THESE OBLIGATIONS TO THE BEST OF OUR ABILITY.

Johnson & Johnson

AND ITS FAMILY OF COMPANIES
NEW BRUNSWICK, NEW JERSEY SINCE 1886

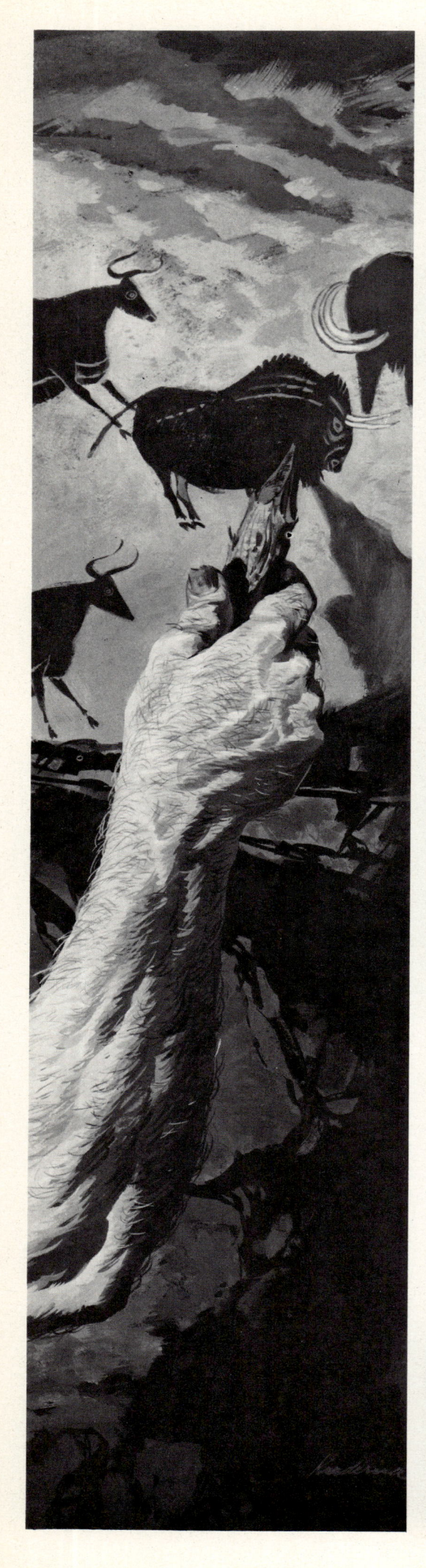

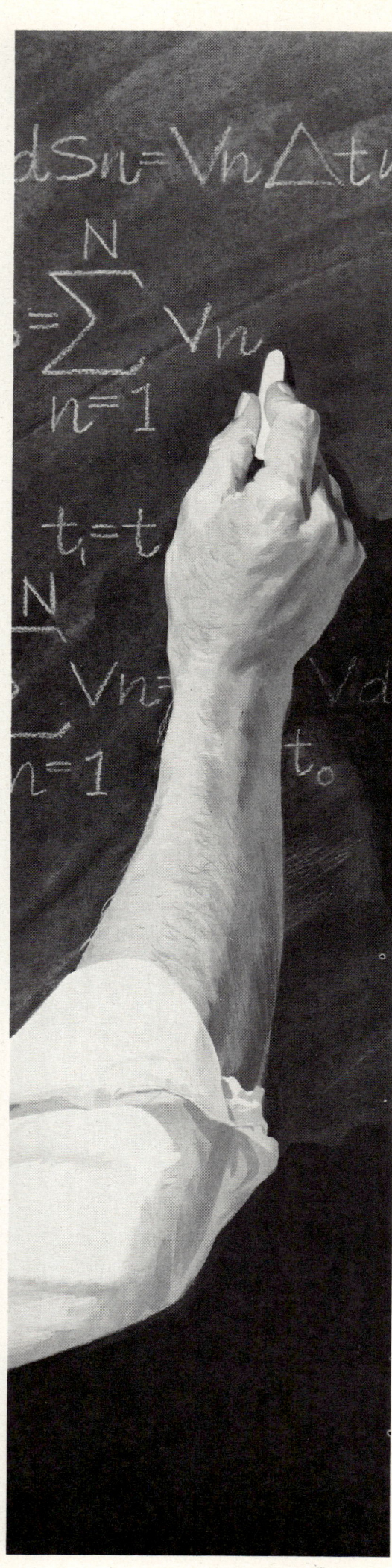

imagination has
no beginning...
no end...

Today's astonishing progress in
electronics is no accident — for the field
has attracted the kind of imaginative
people who have always set the bench
marks for man's progress. Hughes
was built by people like these. They are
prepared to cut away old restraints;
to plunge ahead to new discovery; to
build and prove the "impossible." In just
a decade they have made Hughes
one of America's leading producers
of advanced electronics.

```
------------------
|     HUGHES     |
------------------
```
HUGHES AIRCRAFT COMPANY

Hughes Aircraft Company,
Culver City, El Segundo, Fullerton,
Newport Beach, Malibu, Oceanside,
Los Angeles, California; Tucson, Arizona

ATLANTIC CITY CONVENTION HALL will be the site of another dramatic scene like this Democratic National Convention meeting. Three York centrifugal chillers, with a combined capacity of 3,300 tons, provide cooling capacity for the entire building. Mechanical Contractor, Araco Co., Phila.; Mechanical and Electrical Engineers, Meyer, Strong and Jones, New York.

Delegates in Atlantic City Convention Hall cooled by YORK!

A solid vote for solid comfort! Every delegate to this 1964 Democratic National Convention will enjoy ideal comfort—thanks to the advanced air conditioning system that was installed just a few weeks before the Convention.

Three York compressors provide the chilled water that cools the entire Convention Hall, including the committee rooms. This modern system dehumidifies as it cools... assures a better climate for delegates, twenty-four hours a day!

When you plan air conditioning for any kind of building, have your architect or consulting engineer talk to York, pace-setters in creating better climates for over 75 years. Or write York Corporation, Subsidiary of Borg-Warner Corporation, York, Pennsylvania.

YORK®

THE QUALITY NAME IN AIR CONDITIONING AND REFRIGERATION

Building
the Great
Society

"The success of a party means little unless it is being used by the nation for a great purpose."
—President Woodrow Wilson

Every period in our history has offered challenges to greatness. But there have been times when the challenges went unmet, when political success became the end in itself—not a means to a higher end. Inevitably such periods of national self-indulgence have led our nation to turn to Democratic leadership for creative and imaginative programs to move America ahead again.

Among the great challenges which summoned the Democratic Party to leadership in the 1960's, two—Space and the Atom—are unique to our age. A third—Education—is as old as the republic. And upon our response to these challenges depends our success as a free people, a progressive republic and a Great Society.

Here is a report on the party's leadership in Education, Space and the Atom in a Great Society.

Education for the Great Society

From our founding years, America has turned to education to chart our course at moments of climactic change—in building a republic after a revolution; in civilizing frontiers as we moved westward across a continent; in restoring a nation after a civil war; in reshaping an economy turning from agriculture to industry.

Through these years education has animated us, given us direction, provided us with faith that what is good today can be made better tomorrow. One aspect of our faith has been the goal of universal education, equal educational opportunity for all our people. Like most great goals, it has long remained an objective not easily attained. But now, in recent years, we are making powerful efforts to reach it.

In January 1963, President Kennedy reaffirmed his commitment to American education, bringing its cause dynamically and dramatically before the 88th Congress in his third message on education. He called for the most comprehensive and far-reaching educational legislation ever proposed by an American President. Addressing the Congress and the people, he said:

"Education is the keystone in the arch of freedom and progress. Nothing has contributed more to the enlargement of this Nation's strength and opportunities than our traditional system of free, universal elementary and secondary education, coupled with widespread availability of college education...

"The problem here proposed... provides for economic growth, manpower development, and progress toward our educational and humanitarian objectives. It encourages the increase of the knowledge, skills, attitudes, and critical intelligence necessary for the preservation of our society. It will help keep America strong and safe and free."

The 88th Congress passed more significant legislative measures for education than any Congress in history. President Kennedy was dead, but his leadership had given American education new impetus in meeting its responsibilities of today, new promise toward fulfilling its responsibilities of tomorrow.

President Johnson, who guided these measures through Congress and signed them into law, called them "new landmarks in educational progress" and pledged his energies to carry forward the "unfinished business" of education that still remained. The new legislation, now in effect, enables American education to meet certain immediate, specific needs:

—Under the Higher Education Facilities Act, substantial and urgently needed funds are authorized to help our colleges and universities build classrooms, libraries and laboratories, preparing these institutions for the surging enrollments in the years just ahead.

Today more than 4 million students are enrolled in our colleges and universities. By next September, more than 5 million will be enrolled. By 1970, there will be 7 million or more—almost twice the number at the start of this decade.

—Under the Vocational Education Act,

Federal funds together with matching State and local funds will bring vocational training, long neglected, into harmony with the economic realities of our time.

Millions of young Americans today lack the necessary advanced skills for modern employment. As our technology grows in complexity, old jobs will become extinct and new jobs will be created. The new legislation will make our vocational schools responsive to these changes as they occur.

—Under the Mental Retardation Facilities Act, grants are authorized for research and the training of teachers of some 5 million handicapped children, including those who are impaired in hearing, sight, speech and the emotionally disturbed.

Today only one-fourth of these handicapped children are given special educational opportunities. Three-fourths are struggling to keep up in regular school grades, or are not in school at all. They need specially trained teachers, who are now in short supply. The new legislation will increase the ranks of these teachers, bringing to the physically and mentally handicapped a maximum potential for leading useful, productive lives.

—Under the Library Services and Construction Act, funds are provided to develop and improve library services in urban as well as rural areas, to build libraries for approximately 18.5 million Americans previously denied them, to bring seriously needed improvement to libraries for 100 million others.

Today's library is not only a place of study and research. It is also a busy market place of ideas, a reservoir of information, and a source of continuing cultural and social enlightenment. The new investment in good public library service is a direct and highly productive contribution to the intellectual life of the Nation.

—Under various other Acts are provisions to help build 25 to 30 new community colleges every year, to help build graduate schools and facilities in at least 10 to 20 major academic centers, to expand student loans enabling some 70,000 to 90,000 additional students to attend college every year, to increase funds for educational research into new and better means of teaching.

The new legislation, as President Johnson said, "...is concrete evidence of a renewed and continuing national commitment to education." But it "...will still not do the whole job of extending educational opportunities to all who want and can benefit by them, nor in meeting our growing national needs."

The challenge to American education has been partially met in this sixth decade of the 20th century. The unfinished business of education continues to challenge us. It has become high priority business of the Administration. Specifically, it calls for "early, positive action" to make up for past neglect and to move forward in new directions and with new purpose.

—It calls urgently for measures to help our elementary and secondary schools meet acute shortages of classrooms and qualified teachers in a day of rapidly growing enrollments. These schools are the foundation upon which education ultimately depends.

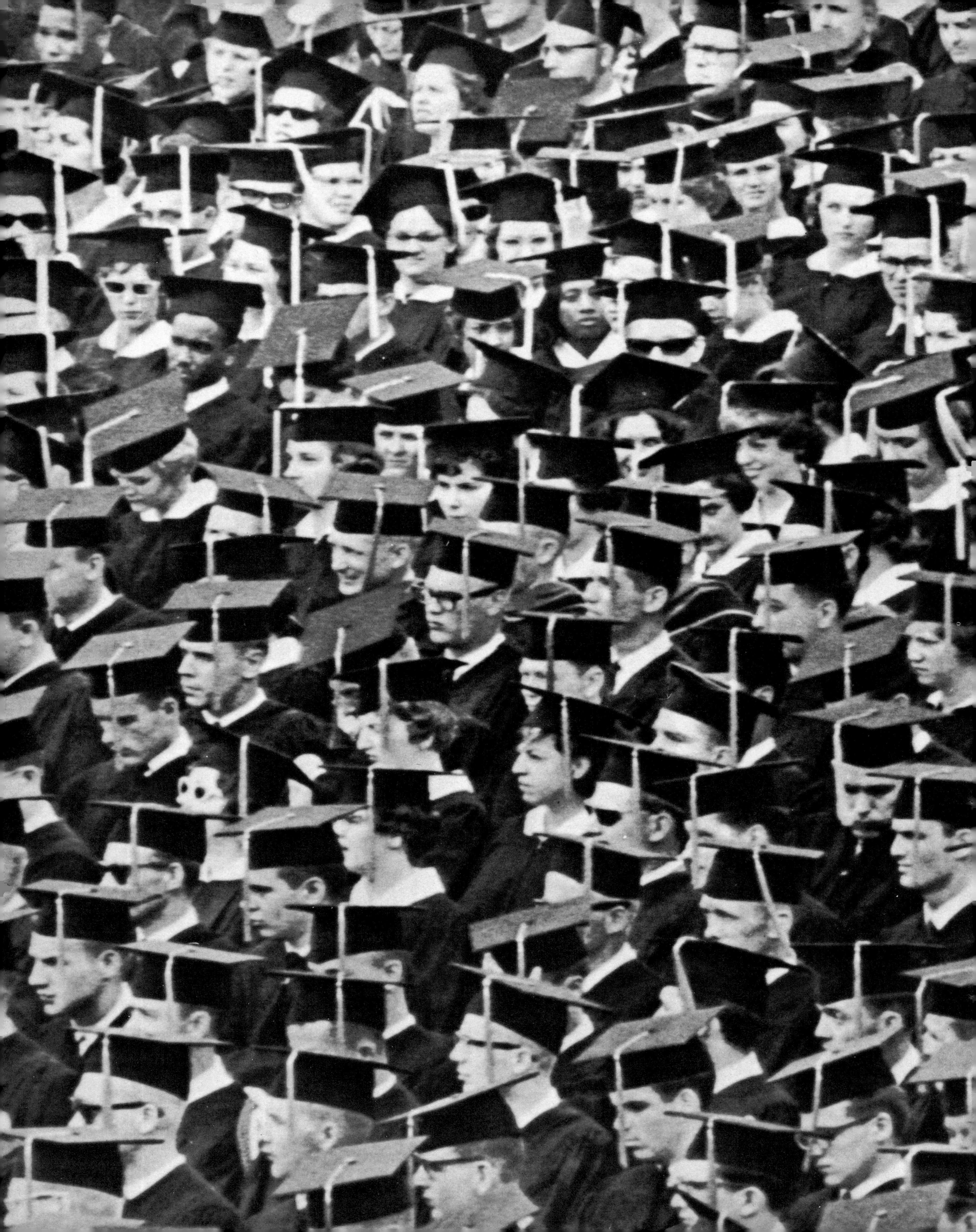

—It calls for increased graduate fellowships to prepare more men and women to teach in our expanding universities. While our college enrollments will almost double in the decade between 1960 and 1970, the proportion of new professors with doctoral degrees is in steady decline. To increase quantity while quality drops means higher education in name alone—but mediocre education in fact.

—It calls for increased work-study programs and student loans to enable capable but needy youth to attend college. Today, between 25 and 40 percent of our most able students do not continue their education beyond high school, chiefly because they cannot afford to do so. To permit levels of income to determine levels of learning means the denial of equal opportunity and the loss of our most precious resource, our skilled and educated youth.

—It calls for bold new efforts to expand educational opportunity in the slums of our cities and in our depressed rural areas. Measures to accomplish this purpose are embraced in the Economic Opportunities Act—the President's anti-poverty program. Through educational grants to impoverished areas, this program aims to improve teaching in low-income areas, establish learning and study centers, combat adult illiteracy, create co-ordinated counseling services, enrich cultural backgrounds and assist the children of poverty toward as high a level of education as they are capable of attaining.

In a day when unemployment rises wherever educational attainment is low, when incomes rise wherever educational attainment is high, there is no doubt that poverty and lack of education are closely linked. There is no doubt that of all the challenges to education, the challenge of poverty is the greatest. And there is no doubt that America, in becoming a Great Society as well as a powerful one, can and will meet that challenge.

As President Johnson has said:

"We must seek an educational system which grows in excellence as it grows in size."

FROM RYAN'S SPECTRUM OF CAPABILITIES:

HIGH-PERFORMANCE V/STOL AIRCRAFT

Which V/STOL concept is best? That depends upon the mission to be flown.

Whatever the mission requirement, Ryan will continue to make significant contributions to successful V/STOL technology.

Three current Ryan V/STOL projects, each of a different technical approach, are illustrated here.

On these, and on such pioneering projects as the X-13 Vertijet, the VZ-3RY Vertiplane and the YO-51 Dragonfly, Ryan has expended nearly four million engineering/developmental manhours. Notable gains in V/STOL technology have resulted from Ryan's original work on direct thrust systems, variable nozzles, jet reaction controls, unique V/STOL simulation, auto-stabilization and deflected slipstream aerodynamics.

But V/STOL is only a single band in Ryan's broad spectrum of capabilities.

Ryan Firebees have tested more U.S. surface-to-air and air-to-air weaponry than any other jet target missile. Ryan Doppler equipment contributes to the navigation of fixed-wing aircraft, helicopters and space vehicles.

Lightweight Ryan structures support the solar cell panels on Mariner, Ranger and Transit V spacecraft.

In many fields of aeronautics, electronics and astronautics, strength for tomorrow is being forged today — at Ryan!

RYAN AERONAUTICAL COMPANY • SAN DIEGO • CALIF.

NEWEST RYAN V/STOL is Army XV-5A, lift-fan research aircraft built under contract to General Electric. Designed to take off vertically on no more power or fuel than is needed for high speed cruise, the XV-5A is now in flight test.

FLEX WING STOL "FLEEP," popular name of the easy-to-fly XV-8A, is under study by Army's Transportation Research Command as an aerial "truck," capable of operation in rugged areas.

TILT-WING V/STOL TRANSPORT XC-142A is being built by Ryan (jointly with Vought and Hiller) for Army, Navy, Air Force. It will be capable of lifting troops, equipment into unprepared areas under all weather conditions.

RYAN

The role of the
motion picture camera
is to roam the hills and valleys
of the free world...
revealing and not concealing,
reporting and not distorting,
enriching and not enslaving,
indulging democracy
and not demagoguery...
yesterday, today, and tomorrow.

Joseph E. Levine, President
Embassy Pictures Corp.

'Rest Assured'...on New York Central

Sleepercoach

Private Room $7 plus low coach fare!

"Take the Central to the Fair"

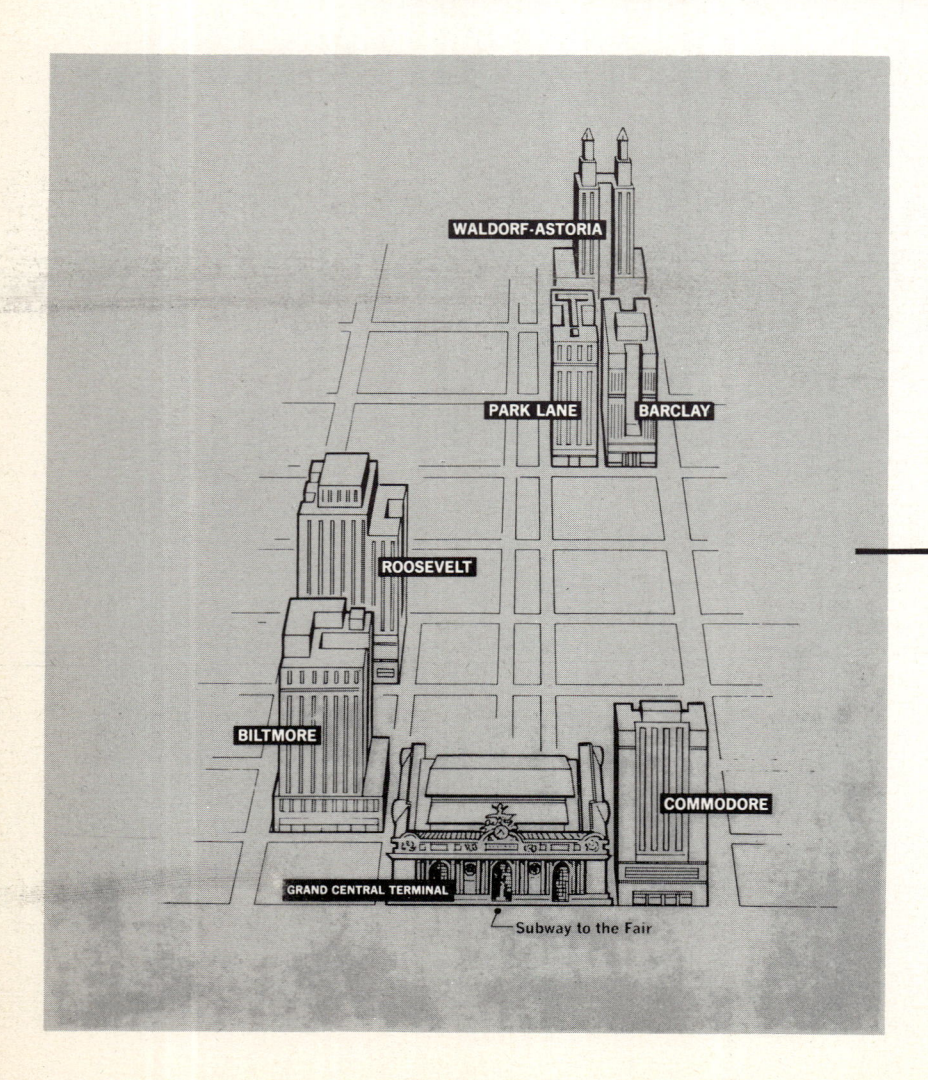

Stay at one of our World-famous Hotels when you visit the New York World's Fair

BARCLAY Lexington & 48th St., NYC
BILTMORE Madison Avenue & 43rd St., NYC
COMMODORE Lexington Avenue & 42nd St., NYC
PARK LANE Park Avenue & 48th St., NYC
ROOSEVELT Madison Avenue & 45th St., NYC
WALDORF-ASTORIA Park Avenue & 50th St., NYC

The Fair is only 17 Minutes away from Grand Central Terminal

From Grand Central Terminal in New York City, you can get to the Fair quickly by direct express subway service via the Queens-Flushing Line. Running time 17 minutes—fare 15 cents each way.

Wind he's got plenty of . . .

Do you?

You should.

It's so important to keep on breathing.

After all, you're a candidate too. For health. For a reasonably long life.

If you're short of breath . . . if you cough too much . . . you may find it tough to win. Don't take chances with these symptoms of respiratory disease.

Take good care of your wind; you'll need it as long as you live. This is the recommendation of your local Christmas Seal organization and the National Tuberculosis Association.

Short of breath?
Cough too much?
Don't take chances.
See your doctor.

NATIONAL TUBERCULOSIS ASSOCIATION, 1790 Broadway, New York, New York 10019

This advertisement represents the contribution of the undersigned companies to the public informational activities of the National Tuberculosis Association.

Associated Truck Lines, Grand Rapids, Michigan.
Belger Cartage Service, Kansas City, Missouri.
Hugh Breeding, Inc., Tulsa, Oklahoma.
Campbell "66" Express, Springfield, Missouri.
Lyons Transportation Company, Erie, Pennsylvania.
Norwalk Truck Lines, Norwalk, Ohio.
Norwalk Truck Lines of Delaware, Lancaster, Pennsylvania.

Help me fight Arthritis

*"**My nickname used to be 'Champ'** . . . I used to be the pitcher of our softball team. I used to play basketball and ski. And I was quite a swimmer—up until I got arthritis. I've had arthritis since I was 14 and it's become part of me. Sometimes I try to forget about it, but the minute you put me in a hospital and I'm here month after month—so many long discouraging nights that I sit and stare out the window—this is when I wonder, 'What's the use?' I'd like to get back into some work I could achieve in. Maybe it would be some work where I could help others who need help. And maybe, someday, I could think of marriage. But now I sit in the hospital and wonder, 'Why is this such a long stretch?' I hope I don't have to come back."

*from an interview with a Boston teacher, an arthritis victim

Give TO THE ARTHRITIS FOUNDATION

ARTHRITIS AND RHEUMATISM FOUNDATION, 10 Columbus Circle, New York 19, New York

"CARE TODAY . . . AND A CURE TOMORROW"

This advertisement represents the contribution of the undersigned companies to the public informational activities of the Arthritis and Rheumatism Foundation.

Denver Chicago Trucking Company, Denver, Colorado.

Hillside Transit Company, Milwaukee, Wisconsin.

Ringsby Freight Lines, Denver, Colorado.

B. J. Kirk Transportation Company, Pawtucket, R. I.

Rhode Island Sand & Gravel Company, Hillsgrove, R. I.

CREATIVE ENGINEERING
at your service

Continental Motors' outstanding record of power plant research, development, and production is now 62 years deep. It includes major advances in propulsion of all sorts —specialized power for use on land, at sea, in air. Continental capability, fully implemented by equipment and engineering knowhow, includes complete testing facilities— environmental, altitude, components—using the most modern equipment to be found today. Inquiries as to specific capabilities are invited.

CONTINENTAL MOTORS HAS OPEN CAPACITY FOR SHORT-RUN PRODUCTION ASSIGNMENTS. ADDRESS LYNDON DIVISION, 8647 LYNDON AVE., DETROIT 48238

CONTINENTAL MOTORS CORPORATION
DETROIT · MUSKEGON

"A Position of Pre-eminence"

Highlights of Major Accomplishments in the National Space Program

In mid-1964, the United States had moved to the halfway point in the broadened, accelerated National Space Program which the Kennedy-Johnson Administration advocated that the nation carry out during this decade.

The program has created resources of great space competence on which the nation can now draw for purposes of security and to spur progress in a wide range of scientific and technical fields. These resources include:
- A world-wide tracking and data acquisition network
- The series of successful weather satellites
- Echo, Telstar, Relay, and Syncom communications satellites
- Space boosters of tremendous thrust and high reliability for many different types of mission
- Manned and unmanned spacecraft of advanced design for exploring near space, deep space, the moon, and the planets
- Orbiting observatories that will study the earth, the sun, and the stars
- Extensive ground facilities for fabricating, testing, launching, and controlling the new rockets and spacecraft—facilities that will be basic national assets for many years to come
- Research and development centers staffed with skilled and experienced personnel to study what the United States requires and can accomplish in space and to guide the efforts of industry in producing the rockets, spacecraft, and other equipment needed to achieve space pre-eminence
- Strengthened space research capabilities in our universities
- Creation of a versatile and efficient industrial base capable of meeting any national need in space

The National Aeronautics and Space Administration (NASA) performs the civilian part of the program and also contributes research and development aid to many defense projects. The Department of Defense, in turn, shares appropriate knowledge from its military projects with NASA.

Detailed reporting of the long list of American achievements in space to date would require a shelf of thick volumes. Here, in brief, are typical examples:

Mercury to Gemini to Apollo

The Project Mercury series, the nation's first stepping stones to manned space flight, was completed when Astronaut Leroy Gordon Cooper completed 22 orbits around the earth and brought his Faith 7 spacecraft to a faultless ocean landing in the North Pacific near Midway Island and within sight of the "recovery" aircraft carrier Kearsarge. With astronauts aboard, there were two relatively short Mercury space flights over the Caribbean Sea and four orbital flights that repeatedly criss-crossed much of the globe. The flights confirmed that, given spacecraft, space suits, and other equipment that could seal in some of the conditions of earth environment, men can live, and perform piloting and other duties while traveling nearly 18,000 miles per hour through regions where there is neither air nor weight.

Following Mercury is Project Gemini, in which relays of two astronauts each will train in space toward the decade's major United States manned space flight goal—the Project Apollo exploring expedition to the moon—and for other missions valuable to science and technology for both civilian and defense requirements.

A full-scale model of the Gemini spacecraft was successfully tested in orbit on April 8, 1964. This paved the way for the first manned Gemini flight, expected late this year, with two astronauts aboard. Gemini flights will increase competence in manned flight in space and help perfect techniques of rendezvous and docking—joining and fastening together objects in space. These techniques must be mastered for the more difficult space flight tasks essential to achieving over-all space competence for the United States.

Landing American explorers on the moon was urged as a national goal by the late President Kennedy because the undertaking will carry forward at a rapid rate all elements of space flight technology the nation must develop to achieve pre-eminence in space. Now, some three years after the Congress endorsed President Kennedy's proposal, good progress has been made on nearly every facet of this vast undertaking. The major contracts have been signed with industrial firms (some 93 cents of every dollar NASA spends goes to industry) and work is well under way or nearing completion on the ground facilities necessary for Apollo. Development of the gigantic Saturn V launching vehicle, which will generate seven and a half million pounds of thrust as it takes off to carry the Mercury astronauts to the moon, is being directed by the Marshall Space Flight Center, Huntsville, Alabama.

The astronauts for the historic journey have been selected. They are undergoing extensive training for the mission.

Various "modules" or sections of the Apollo spacecraft in which the lunar voyage will be made are being fabricated and tested.

Scientists, engineers, architects, draftsmen, technologists, artisans, clerks, laborers, educators, management personnel—an estimated 300,000 of them by the end of the decade in nearly every State of the Union—are being assigned their tasks. In NASA centers, contractors' facilities and university laboratories, more than half that total are already at work on individual tasks to fit them into the grand design of the American expedition—round-trip

480,000 miles—to our nearest neighbor in space. Scientists expect U. S. exploration of the moon to unlock many of the mysteries of the universe and to pay other expected and undoubtedly unforeseen dividends of immense value to national progress and stability and to the well-being of mankind as a whole.

Twenty-three astronauts were selected and given rigorous courses of training for the more demanding space flight projects beyond the Mercury program — the two-man Gemini and three-man Apollo manned space flights. With six of the original seven astronauts still in the program, the National Aeronautics and Space Administration possessed an unmatched competence in skilled and highly trained space pilots. The astronauts in the program have amassed more than 82,000 hours of flight time, most of it in late model jet aircraft. It is estimated that more than 2,000 hours of space flight time will be accumulated in Gemini and Apollo flights before the manned exploration of the moon is undertaken late in this decade.

Launch vehicles, the basic rocket power needed to hurl spacecraft into earth orbits or to immense distances from this planet, are the keys and the pacing items to space pre-eminence. The United States has been lagging behind the Soviet Union, and is now surpassing that country, at least for the time being.

The Saturn I, successfully tested in January 1964, is more powerful than any other booster known to exist in the world. It has the power to orbit a weight equivalent to seven Mercury spacecraft — weighing about 3,000 pounds each—at the same time, or twice the weight of the Soviet Vostok spacecraft. An improved Saturn, scheduled for flights in 1966, will be able to orbit a payload equaling 10 Mercury capsules in weight. When the Saturn V goes into service later in this decade, the United States will be able to launch into Earth orbit payloads as heavy as 80 Mercury capsules or to send the 90,000-pound Apollo spacecraft to an orbit around the moon. (From this orbit, the small LEM, or landing craft, will carry two astronauts to the surface of the moon for scientific work, and back again to the main Apollo craft which will return them to Earth.)

The world's first successful test flight of a liquid hydrogen-fueled rocket, the Centaur, was the last space vehicle launching from Cape Canaveral, on the eve of Thanksgiving, 1963. The next day, President Johnson announced that America's principal spaceport would henceforth be known as Cape Kennedy, in honor of the late President. Centaur demonstrated the practicality of using the volatile liquid hydrogen for high-energy thrust power in space.

The road into deep space for men and robot spacecraft quite literally demands pouring miles of concrete on earth. In the past three years, work has proceeded rapidly in building the ground installations the nation must have to master space. These spaceports and spaceyards are helping to breathe new vigor into the national economy while preparing the Nation for a wide range of future missions in space. At Cape Kennedy, Florida; at Michoud, Louisiana, near New Orleans; in Hancock County, Mississippi; and at the new Manned Spaceflight Center, near Houston, Texas, the National Aeronautics and Space Administration is creating long-range service facilities that will be useful far beyond the present decade.

In the direct practical use of space technology, NASA has made outstanding progress with its experimental communications, weather, and navigation satellites.

Global Teleradio Linkage Via Satellite

To date, NASA has launched three different kinds of experimental communications satellites. The Echo balloon satellite contains no receiving or transmitting equipment but reflects signals from one station to another. The active repeater stations, Relay and Telstar, at medium heights, have given the world its first live transoceanic television broadcasts. The world's first synchronous satellite, Syncom, appears to be suspended in one part of the sky some 22,300 miles above the earth. Syncom has demonstrated the feasibility of using three or four "stationary" satellites to tie all countries together in a global telecommunications network.

Congress had endorsed the policy of private ownership of communications satellites — by the Communications Satellite Corporation.

The National Aeronautics and Space Administration will continue communications satellite experiments until the best system, or combination of systems, can be ascertained and offered to the Communications Satellite Corporation.

Satellites Scan Weather Patterns

NASA's experimental Tiros weather satellites—eight launched by May 1964—have produced more than 350,000 useable photographs of cloud masses, giving the U. S. Weather Bureau a potent new tool in weather forecasting. Tiros has been put into day-to-day service despite its "experimental" status. The satellite has televised back to earth, on many occasions, the first warning signals of hurricanes and typhoons building up in their spawning grounds, far more quickly than could other means of weather observation. The time saved by the early Tiros warnings has spared thousands of lives by making it possible to evacuate localities in the path of hurricanes and typhoons.

The latest Tiros contains a new Automatic Picture Transmission system whereby an inexpensive ground station (costing approximately $30,000) located anywhere on earth, can request a picture of local weather from Tiros as the satellite passes over the area, and receive the photo in a matter of minutes. Several nations have purchased APT equipment, and other nations have expressed interest in this new weather prediction aid.

The U. S. Weather Bureau estimates that if it could make reliable weather forecasts just five days in advance, the United States could realize a saving of some $6.7 billion a year—nearly $1.5 billion more than the present annual cost of the space program—in such areas as agriculture, water resources management, surface transportation, retail marketing and the lumber industry. World-wide savings would be many times greater.

Indirect Dividends

Beyond the prime goals of the space program, valuable side benefits have come and will continue to accrue to the economy because the exploration of space demands entire new technologies and people trained and experienced in them.

In working with new materials, new sources of power and propulsion, new techniques and new processes, the men and women in the factories, the universities and the government laboratories have produced many innovations that are finding use in industry. NASA has initiated a program of codifying these space-oriented innovations, and disseminating information about them to industry in general so that they may be applied to production of non-space items.

Space Exploration Enriches Science

The Nation has amassed an unprecedented wealth of scientific knowledge in space over the last few years. Scientific satellites and deep space probes have revealed important new information about the nature of the universe — information which will have a lasting effect on mankind, and which can be used for the betterment of human conditions throughout the world. Until recent times, space was thought of as a "void."

Today, through space exploration, it has been discovered that space is teeming with vast interacting forces and energies —solar winds, magnetic fields, radiation belts and other phenomena the nature of which is still only barely understood. It has been learned, too, that these forces and energies in space have a direct influence on the earth's atmosphere and the weather systems in it. As more is learned about the phenomena of outer space and their effect on earthly weather, the stronger becomes the possibility that one day man may be able to control the weather. Should that day come, the deserts could be reclaimed, great new farmlands could be opened, and abundant harvests could end the specter of hunger.

As an example of scientific work, the 1962 - 1963 flight of NASA's Mariner II Venus probe to the vicinity of that cloud-wrapped planet was one of the most notable achievements in the history of science. The flight was remarkable for a number of reasons. A complicated mid-course guidance maneuver was carried out by remote control when Mariner was 1.2 million miles from earth, enabling the spacecraft to pass within 21,000 miles of Venus. From Mariner's instruments, scientists learned that Venus has a smog-like atmosphere some 20 times heavier than Earth's, that at ground level the temperature is about 800 degrees Fahrenheit— hot enough to boil lead — and that the planet probably rotates only once in its year, if at all. These and other Mariner findings taught science more about Venus than has been learned in the 400 years since the invention of the telescope.

On June 29, 1961, the United States achieved a "first" with the successful orbiting of the Defense Department's Transit 4A satellite, containing a nuclear power source for the on-board electronic equipment. The device functioned extremely well, and the satellite continued to transmit for almost two years.

U. S. Leads in Successful Launches

All in all, the United States has sent into space more than 200 satellites and probes —civilian and military—on a wide range of scientific and technological missions. In 1963 alone, this country successfully sent aloft more spacecraft than the Soviet Union had orbited in the six years since Sputnik I.

In the early years of the U. S. Space effort, three or four out of every five launch attempts failed. During the past three years, the ratio has reversed. In 1963, for example, the NASA launch record was 85 percent perfect.

International Programs

In the international cooperative program of NASA, sounding rocket and satellite programs, exchanges of scientific data and other cooperative ventures are now carried out with 67 other countries, in which there are no exchanges of funds. Each participating nation pays the costs of its own space activities. Further, international cooperation has enabled the United States to extend its network of tracking and data acquisition stations across the face of the globe.

James McDivitt, now in training as a Gemini astronaut, spoke to 53 representatives of free world nations at the Washington International Center on May 14, 1964. Said McDivitt: "Flying in a Gemini space capsule will be the biggest thrill of my life. And when I am circling the earth, especially when I am over your individual nation, I hope that each of you will look up and say: 'There goes a friend.'"

That is typical of the spirit that motivates the National Space Program.

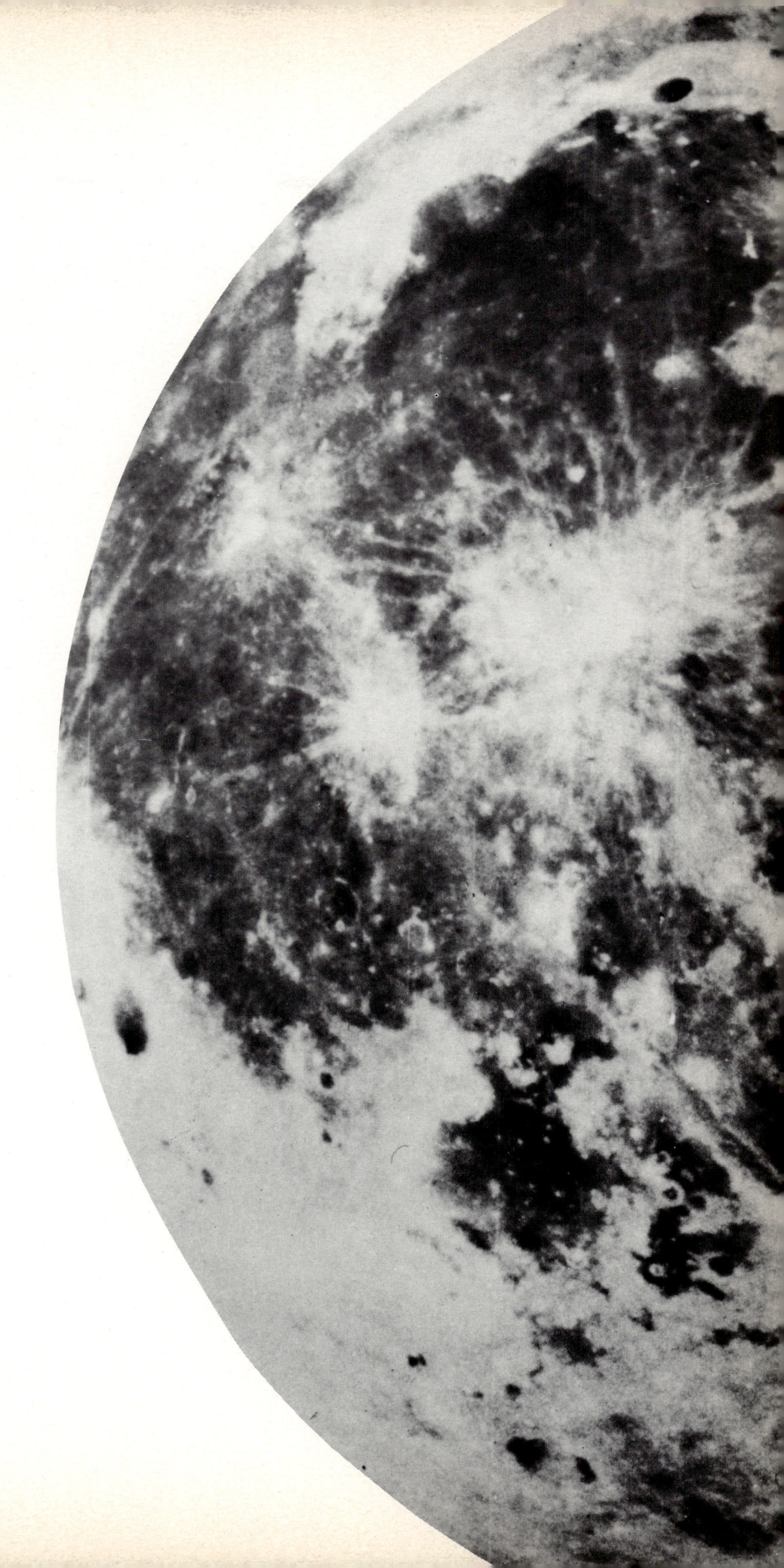

The Peaceful Role of Atomic Energy

While scientists and engineers watched from a safe distance, a thermonuclear device equal in power to one hundred thousand tons of TNT was exploded 635 feet beneath the barren Nevada desert.

Within seconds, twelve million tons of rock, sand and alluvial soil were hurled skyward in a mighty eruption that momentarily hid the desert from view.

When the dust had settled, a yawning crater 320 feet deep and 1,280 feet wide gaped in the desert floor.

The experiment, which took place at the Atomic Energy Commission's Nevada Test Site on July 6, 1962, and resulted in the largest single-shot excavation ever made by man, was the first nuclear earth-moving experiment in the AEC's "Plowshare Program"—named from the Biblical reference in Isaiah 2:4 that "...they shall beat their swords into plowshares, and their spears into pruninghooks..."

As such, it dramatically pointed the way to an expanding role for nuclear energy into an ever-increasing number of important civilian uses.

From the fateful day when the first atomic bombs were dropped on Japan to end World War II, much of the public impression of atomic energy has been drawn from memories of the devastating power of the atom as a weapon.

Now, however, though national defense rightly remains a major concern of the nation's atomic program, new and ever more vital uses are being found for this man-made source of energy.

The Nevada experiment was based on belief that the enormous energy locked up in a compact quantity of nuclear material could do more than spread destruction.

It was based on the firm conviction that this same energy could be used for peaceful purposes—in this instance, for the excavation in a few seconds of a vast quantity of earth.

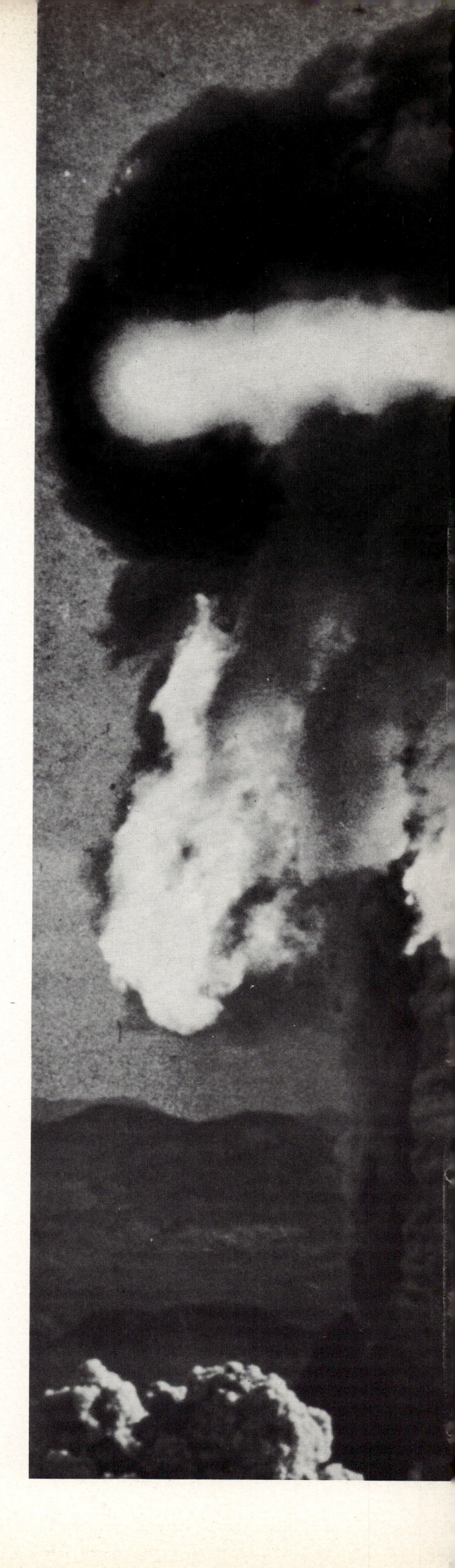

From the results of this and other experiments, the use of nuclear explosives for building a new, sea-level canal across the American Isthmus can be considered.

It is expected that such a canal can be excavated far more quickly and cheaply by nuclear means than by the use of conventional means.

Other facilities for which Plowshare excavation methods may be technically feasible include such major projects as harbors, reservoirs, and highway building.

Recently, for example, the Atcheson, Topeka and Santa Fe Railway Company and the California Division of Highways cooperated with the AEC in making a feasibility study of the possible use of nuclear explosives to blast a cut 10,000 feet long, ranging from 100 to 350 feet deep, and 325 feet wide at the bottom, through the Bristol Mountains in California.

The cut would result in the removal of about 68 million cubic yards of rocks—ten times the quantity of earth removed by the Nevada explosion. The cut would easily accommodate double tracks for the railway and eventually eight lanes for the highway.

The study indicated that the project is technically feasible and recommended that a preliminary site investigation be performed to verify assumptions made in the study.

But the ability of relatively small amounts of nuclear material to generate explosions of great magnitude is just one of the unique aspects of atomic energy that is enabling it to play its expanding role in a growing list of civilian uses today.

Two other aspects are equally important in this regard.

One is the compactness and long-lasting characteristics of nuclear material when used as a fuel.

For example, the potential energy contained in one pound of uranium—a cube measuring an inch on each side—is equal to that contained in 1,500 tons of coal!

One of the principal costs in the production of electricity is the cost of transporting conventional fuels, such as coal and oil, from mine or well to a central power generating station.

Thus, because of its compactness, transportation cost for a nuclear fuel such as uranium is negligible by comparison.

Widespread use of atomic energy to generate electric power would bring cheaper electricity to all consumers, and would tend to equalize electric power costs throughout the country. Many large areas which have been hampered in their industrial growth because of their distance from supplies of conventional fuel would therefore be put in a position to realize their full industrial potentials.

An added benefit would be that our supplies of coal and oil, which are not limitless, could be preserved for uses for which these materials are uniquely suited.

A considerable start along the road of atomic-generated power already has been made.

Some 14 civilian power reactors, operated for the most part by private and public utilities, already are supplying more than a million kilowatts of electrical power capacity in areas scattered throughout the country.

By the end of 1964, the nuclear electrical power capacity of the United States will be doubled—to more than two million kilowatts.

By the end of the decade, American homes, churches, schools, businesses and industries are expected to be using more than five million kilowatts of electrical power capacity based on the atom.

The compact and long-lasting qualities of nuclear fuel also make it useful for propulsion—especially for ships.

Nuclear-propelled merchant vessels can be built to carry more cargo than conventional merchant ships because the space needed for oil storage can be used for freight instead.

Nuclear-propelled ships can carry this cargo faster over longer runs without slackening speed.

This is because the oil needed to drive a conventional ship at high speeds over long trade routes would weigh more and take more space than would be economically feasible.

The United States has built the N. S. Savannah, the world's first nuclear-powered cargo-passenger ship, to demonstrate the feasibility of using energy from the atom for merchant shipping.

The U. S. program for the development and construction of nuclear submarines and surface ships has given this country a deterrent force that has played a vital role in protecting our national interests and in preserving the peace. Through the use of nuclear propulsion for naval vessels, we have attained a pre-eminent position in naval power.

A growing application of nuclear power for propulsion appears to lie ahead in the space age.

With a nuclear rocket, the weight of a spaceship that would be assembled, say, for a trip to Mars could be held to between one million and three million pounds.

That of a completely chemically powered spaceship would be about ten million pounds.

The eight- to nine-million-pound weight differential, entirely accounted for by the weight of the extra chemical fuel that would be needed, could well be the deciding factor in determining whether a trip to Mars were feasible.

Scientists and engineers concluded, in fact, that nuclear-powered rockets are essential to extensive future space exploration.

The AEC and the National Aeronautics and Space Agency are engaged in a joint program looking toward the development of a nuclear rocket. Another program is aimed at the development of compact reactors and radioisotopic power generators to provide energy for instrumentation and to maintain conditions under which astronauts can live in space and in other environments such as the moon's surface.

In more prosaic, but equally important fields, programs also are under way to find more uses for civilian reactors.

For centuries, for instance, one of man's most persistent dreams has been the conversion of salt water to fresh, drinkable water. This already has been accomplished by means of heat from conventional fuels, but at costs that do not yet make the large-scale distillation of salt water economically feasible.

It now appears that giant nuclear desalination plants powered by reactors whose heat also will be used to generate another salable product—electricity—may be an important answer to the problem of salt water conversion.

Reactors already have been used to provide space heat, as well as power, at remote military installations far from sources of conventional fuel supplies.

Such reactors have operated at an army base under the Greenland ice cap, in Alaska and in the far reaches of Anarctica.

It is not inconceivable that useful civilian applications for such reactors may be found one day in the reasonably near future.

The second unique aspect of atomic energy is its accompanying radioactivity.

With a nuclear reactor, for example, it is possible to make many radioactive materials which can be extremely useful in industry, agriculture, medicine and other fields.

Because of its ability to change the molecular structure of many materials, to penetrate solids and to be measured with great accuracy, radiation has come to be of immense value in industry.

In one of the newest experimental uses of radioisotopes, wood is impregnated with a simple liquid plastic and then is subjected to intense radiation from a radioisotope—a radioactive form of some well-known element.

The small molecules of the original plastic are changed into larger molecules in such a way that a solid wood-plastic material is produced. The resulting product is stronger, harder, bends better and is more resistant to warping than ordinary wood. The combination of plastic and wood is expected to have a host of uses in making consumer products.

Radioisotopes can be used to trace complicated manufacturing and industrial processes, can be used in gauges to measure the thickness of materials and, in many applications, are superior to conventional X-ray equipment in industrial radiography work.

Low-dose radiation treatment of certain foods to inhibit the growth of bacteria promises new benefits to industry and consumer alike.

Preliminary results show that tomatoes and several varieties of fish and fruit can be kept under refrigeration from days to weeks longer as a consequence of radiation pasteurization.

Work on developing this process is continuing.

One military program has demonstrated that it is possible to keep certain foods, including bacon, for months without refrigeration by means of high radiation dose sterilization.

In agriculture, one use of radioisotopes has been to demonstrate more efficient and economical ways to use fertilizers. Another has been to develop better diets for farm animals, thus increasing supplies of meat, milk and eggs. Still another has been the control of insects, the study of diseases, and internal virus infections of farm animals. Work on the breeding of new and superior strains of food plants and grains also is under way.

One of the most important uses of radiation in the newly expanding role of atomic energy has been in medicine.

The use of radioisotopes has provided some truly astonishing advances in fundamental medical research and in the diagnosis and treatment of disease.

One such advance in treatment may serve as an example.

It has long been known that removal of the pituitary gland brings dramatic temporary relief to many cancer patients.

But such an operation is both difficult and dangerous.

Now, however, the gland may be destroyed by planting pellets of a radioactive isotope within it.

The procedure is much less dangerous than surgery and the results, in general, have been pronounced most encouraging.

Such great advances as these, made possible by this new, man-developed source of power and radiation, give indication that atomic energy is now at the threshold of an expansion that may affect almost every facet of human life.

United States Lines Company

— SALUTES THE —

United Seamen's Service

"A home away from home for the men of the American Merchant Marine"

United States Lines Co., One Broadway, New York, N. Y. 10004

COMPLIMENTS OF

BROWN & POMERANTZ

CONSULTING ENGINEERS

CHRYSLER BUILDING
NEW YORK, N. Y. 10017
Cable Address - SYBROWN - Telephone - YUkon 6-7155

HE BEAT HEART ATTACK

...he's going back to work

Today three out of four who survive first heart attacks go back to their jobs, resume their roles in their homes and communities. It wasn't always so. Research, speeded by Heart Fund dollars, helped bring about this change through new advances in treatment and rehabilitation.

But those who survive are fortunate. More than 500,000 Americans, young and old, die each year of heart attack.

Research is the way to better control and prevention of heart attack. Give to your Heart Fund to support research aimed at cutting down the toll of this No. 1 U.S. killer.

More will LIVE the more you GIVE HEART FUND

AMERICAN HEART ASSOCIATION, INC., 41 East 23rd Street, New York, New York

---

This advertisement represents the contribution of the undersigned companies to the public informational activities of the American Heart Association, Inc.

Arkansas Best Freight System, Fort Smith, Arkansas.
Arrow Transportation Company, Providence, R. I.
Jack Cole Company, Birmingham, Alabama.
Garrett Freight Lines, Pocatello, Idaho.
Gordons Transports, Memphis, Tennessee.
Huber & Huber Motor Express, Louisville, Kentucky.
Southeastern Freight Lines, Columbia, South Carolina.
Watson Wilson Transportation System, Omaha, Nebraska.

FRANK COWAN PHOTO

Don't ever go away again, daddy!

Her Dad is one of the sensible ones. He went to his doctor as soon as he noticed a cancer danger signal. Thanks to his prompt action, his cancer was discovered when it was still in its early stages, and the prospects for cure are more favorable.

Do you know Cancer's Seven Danger Signals? 1. Unusual bleeding or discharge. 2. A lump or thickening in the breast or elsewhere. 3. A sore that does not heal. 4. Change in bowel or bladder habits. 5. Hoarseness or cough. 6. Indigestion or difficulty in swallowing. 7. Change in a wart or mole. If you notice one of these signals and it lasts more than two weeks, see your doctor. It may not be cancer, but only a doctor can tell.

Play it safe and see your doctor once a year for a health checkup, too. And help research and education save lives by sending your check to "Cancer," c/o Postmaster.

AMERICAN CANCER SOCIETY
219 East 42nd Street, New York, New York 10017

This advertisement represents the contribution of the undersigned companies
to the public informational activities of the American Cancer Society.

Carolina Freight Carriers Corporation, Cherryville, N. C.
Jacobs Transfer Company, Washington, D. C.
McLean Trucking Company, Winston-Salem, N. C.
O'Boyle Tank Lines, Bethesda, Maryland.
Petroleum Heat & Power Company, Providence, R. I.
Pilot Freight Carriers Corporation, Winston-Salem, N.C.
Standard Transportation Company, Pawtucket, Rhode Island.

Now...
About
"Politics"

THINK
THEN
KENTUCKY FOR JOHNSON
DISTRICT of COLUMBIA SUPPORTS
Indiana Hoosier State FOR Johnson
Indiana Hoosier State FOR Johnson
OHIO FOR Johnson

Conventions And Communications
by Sidney Hyman

Much has been said about the way television has changed the national nominating convention, and much of what has been said is true. It is true, for example, that TV tends to act like a policeman on the beat, breaking up convention "rumbles." The delegates know that a protracted floor fight can lead to sharp words—whose use can fly out of control to hurt the party with the viewer-voter. It is also true that TV has affected the reading of the platform, the introduction of "favorite sons," the choice of people to second nominations, the length of speeches, the use of "graphics" to illustrate party positions, and above all, the timing of the main events of the convention program.

But if all this and more like it is true, the implied notion that TV is the first instrument of communication ever to impose its own authority on the form and force of the convention system, is false. It is but the latest in a long line of mechanical inventions that have deeply affected the convention system, back to the birth of the system itself.

Until the 1830's, for example, the use of the Congressional caucus to make party nominations could be justified merely by citing the great physical barriers that impeded the movement of any body of Americans from all the states to one central meeting place. Inland travel, whether by roads or river routes, was as uncomfortable and hazardous as it was expensive and time-consuming. It therefore made sense to entrust the nomination of Presidential and Vice-Presidential candidates to party leaders who were already assembled in Washington as members of the Congress.

This, in fact, was the view expressed in 1823 by the members of the Democratic-Republican party in Lancaster County, Pennsylvania, when members elsewhere urged the displacement of the Congressional caucus by some other nomination method. "The best and most exceptional method" for nominating a President and Vice President, said the Lancaster men in a 'resolution' addressed to the general public, "would be a convention of delegates from all the States of the Union." However, this would be "entirely impracticable from the immense extent of the country, and from the great expense necessarily incident to the attendance from the extreme parts of the Union." Under the circumstances, the "old and tried mode" of nomination—the Congressional caucus—remained the best alternative.

The birth of the Railroad Age in the 1830's made it possible in an increasing degree to assemble party members "from the extreme parts of the Union"—and thus to consolidate the human basis for the convention system that was born at that same time. At the first Democratic Convention, for example—the one held in Baltimore in 1836—the delegates came from twenty-two states and two territories. But the disproportion in the size of the delegations still mirrored the physical limitations on travel in the interior of the country. Thus on the roll call of 626 names, the states closest to the convention city—Virginia, New Jersey, Pennsylvania and Maryland—alone accounted for 422, or two-thirds of the total. After that, however, as railroad tracks were gradually laid in all directions, nominating conventions became more truly national in their human composition, and delegate votes were more equitably apportioned among the various states.

* * * *

While the railroad "nationalized" the nominating convention, the invention of the telegraph changed the tempo and often the outcome of convention proceedings. So much so, that a telegram from a candidate to his floor managers or to other leading personages at the convention, became a recurrent cause for high drama.

The first case in point occurred only five days after Samuel F. B. Morse on May 24, 1844, tapped out his pioneering message for transmission over the telegraph line newly laid between Washington and Baltimore. On May 28, the Democratic Convention met in Baltimore, and its proceedings were reported in Washington by telegraph bulletins hung in the rotunda of the Capitol. The next day—May 29—the delegates voted to make James K. Polk of Tennessee the Presidential nominee. Then, in their choice of a Vice-Presidential nominee, they paired Polk with Senator Silas Wright of New York. Since Wright was a personal friend and political ally of Martin Van Buren, his nomination was meant to be a friendly gesture to Van Buren whose own bid for the Presidential nomination had foundered on the two-thirds rule.

Wright, all the while, had remained in Washington, and he learned of his Vice-Presidential nomination as he scanned the telegraph bulletins in the Capitol's rotunda. He immediately directed the telegrapher on duty to send the following message to the convention: "Washington. Important! Mr. Wright is here, and says, nay to the New York delegates, that he can not accept the nomination." Soon afterward, it occurred to him that the text might be construed as a threat to bolt the ticket. So he had the telegrapher send a second message: "Again, Mr. Wright is here, and will support Mr. Polk cheerfully, but can not accept the nomination for Vice President." When all this was received and read at the convention, the delegates jeered loudly. They refused to believe that the messages were authentic. The next day, however, a courier on horseback reaching Baltimore after a dash from Washington, brought the delegates (who had already voted to adjourn) a message confirming Wright's refusal.

In later years, convention managers at the receiving end of telegrams sometimes found it convenient to ignore the messages sent them by candidates. The text book case involved Abraham Lincoln and the 1860 Republican Convention in Chicago. Lincoln, in Springfield, had received word that his managers were promising everything on earth and in the sky above to win delegates to their side. Whereupon Lincoln wired them: "I authorize no bargains, and will be bound by none." To this, one of his managers fervently said: "Damn Lincoln!" And he went ahead with his own bargaining, trading and promising.

Closer in time to our own, was the fateful effect a telegram had on the 1912 Democratic Convention. When the convention met in Baltimore, the two main contenders for the Presidential nomination were the Speaker of the House Champ Clark and Governor Woodrow Wilson of New Jersey. Neither man had a majority of the delegates, much less the two-thirds that were required to win the nomination. Yet the struggle between the two men was eclipsed at the start of the convention by a telegram William Jennings Bryan sent to all aspirants for the nomination, demanding that a progressive and not a reactionary Democrat be chosen as the convention's temporary chairman. Wilson, in reply, telegraphed back: "You are quite right." But the other aspirants took evasive action or equivocated in their replies. The difference won Bryan to Wilson's side, and the delegates who followed Bryan's lead were to have a decisive effect in producing Wilson's eventual nomination.

* * * *

To an equal degree, the outcome of the same convention hinged on the dramatic use of yet another new instrument of communication—the telephone.

On the ninth ballot, Champ Clark won a majority of the votes, and on the tenth ballot, gained two more, though the Wilson lines, braced by Bryan men, held firm. At the same time, however, past precedent said that when a candidate won a majority of the delegate votes, he almost always went on to win the two-thirds required to nominate. V. F. Combe, Wilson's manager, who knew this historical fact, was panicked by it, and meant to have Wilson withdraw from the race.

The most reliable story of how he tried to do this is told by Louis Brownlow, at that time a reporter for the *Nashville Banner,* and in later life a leader in the creation in the United States of a science of public administration.

McCombe, on the convention floor, had sent Brownlow to a certain room in the Emerson Hotel in Baltimore. He was to get and hold Wilson on the phone until McCombe himself reached the same room. Brownlow placed the telephone call, and in the interval before the connection was made, into the hotel room came McCombe with William Gibbs McAdoo on his heels.

"Mac," said McCombe to McAdoo, "Wilson must withdraw!"

"He must not!" shouted McAdoo.

At this moment, the telephone connection with Wilson was made. "Governor," said Brownlow, "Mr. McCombe wishes to speak to you."

McCombe was a very slight man, not very strong, and now in a palsy of fear. McAdoo was very tall, very strong and very sure of himself. He brushed McCombe aside with a sweep of his forearm and seized the telephone. "Governor," he said, "McCombe is going to beg you to withdraw. I ask you not to. He is the only one of your friends who is afraid." McAdoo then handed the telephone receiver over to McCombe who pleaded with Wilson to recognize the fact of a majority vote for Clark, and to withdraw in order to save the party that would otherwise be split.

There was a brief moment of silence at the other end, and McCombe turned the receiver over to Brownlow. Wilson's voice at last came through. "May I suggest," said he, "that you tell my friends of the press that I shall not withdraw." Nor did he. And the course of American history subsequently moved in directions it might not otherwise have gone.

* * * *

The first time a transatlantic cablegram played a decisive part in a nominating convention was during the 1888 Republican Convention at Chicago. James J. Blaine, a previously defeated Republican Presidential nominee, was on a holiday in England with Andrew Carnegie. But so firm was his hold on the minds of the delegates that they refused to take seriously his earlier letters to Republican leaders, asking that his name should not be put forward as a candidate. At the convention itself, when it became evident that Senator John Sherman of Ohio, the front-runner, had failed to consolidate his strength after five ballots, the convention adjourned for a weekend. Sherman's managers, fearing a stampede to Blaine, tried during the recess to get Sherman to withdraw in favor of William McKinley. McKinley, so they told Sherman by wire, would consolidate the "anti-Blaine" forces and thus save the party from the "Blaine lunatics." Sherman refused to be persuaded. He wired back to Mark Hanna who was quietly working for McKinley: "Let my name stand. I prefer defeat to retreat . . . I like McKinley, but such a movement would be unjust to others . . . a broach of implicit faith."

The Blaine men, for their part, sensed the imminent defeat of Sherman, so they bombarded their hero with cables, urging him to reverse his stand and come out openly as an avowed candidate. Blaine cabled back from London: "Earnestly request my friends to respect my Paris letter" (in which he had refused to stand for nomination). He also advised the delegates to refrain from casting any votes for his name. Even this did not put an end to the exhortations of his friends at the convention. They cabled Andrew Carnegie, Blaine's host in England, asking for his help. Carnegie begged, but Blaine stood firm. All that remained for Carnegie to do was to send the Blaine men a cable in secret code, advising the convention in Blaine's name to pick Benjamin Harrison for President. This was done on the eighth ballot.

* * * *

Beginning in 1924, when the death struggle between Al Smith and William Gibbs McAdoo in the Democratic Convention extended for a record 103 ballots, the convention walls no longer set the boundaries of the convention. Nor were the candidates and the delegates the only ones who engaged in exchanges of messages. Thousands of pairs of headphones on thousands of homemade crystal radio sets made the nation itself both a gallery and a source of influence on the convention proceedings. Candidates and delegates alike now began to "hear from people" at every turn.

Beginning with this time, too, the whole style of American oratory was forced to accommodate itself to the discipline of the radio microphone. Spread-eagle bombast and bluster became "old-fashioned." The shouting that was required if a speaker expected his voice to carry the length of a hall or for any distance in the open air, no longer would do. A conversational style of oratory was demanded by radio that brought the speaker into "the front parlor of the American home," and this style was all the more strongly reinforced by the demands of TV.

* * * *

The invention of the airplane, like all the other inventions, profoundly affected the work of the nominating conventions. While the conventions were still in session, it became possible for candidates remote from the scene to send and receive emissaries who had something important to say face-to-face that could not as well be said by any other means of communication—and that could affect the results of the convention. And again, the advent of the airplane made it possible for Franklin D. Roosevelt to end the old custom governing the acceptance of a Presidential nomination. Beforehand, a newly chosen candidate waited for days until a formal delegation chosen by the convention called at his home to inform him of his nomination, and to hear his "acceptance speech." In the case of his own 1932 Presidential nomination by the Democratic Convention, F.D.R. flew out to the convention site in Chicago, and there delivered his "acceptance speech" in the presence of all the delegates. So it has been ever since with all newly chosen nominees.

In The Beginning Is The Word
by Sidney Hyman

Human speech is a record of human experience, and as experience changes, new words come to birth while old ones pass away or live on through altered meanings. So it has been with the words that crop up when Americans "talk politics." Some continue the original meaning they had in Greek, Latin, Old English, French and Dutch. Some underwent a sea change in their journey to America. Some are native born, with a lineage that goes back to Colonial days—or only to yesterday. Anyway, here is a list of words we use when we "talk politics," where they came from, and how they acquired the meaning they now have.

Ballot is derived from the Italian ballotta, the diminutive of balla—meaning "little ball." The Italian ballotta referred to round objects or little balls used in casting votes.

Band wagon was the high-structured and ornately decorated wagon that carried the musicians who led a circus parade. P. T. Barnum, the American showman, is credited with having invented the phrase in 1855, but it did not come into common political use until the first years of the 20th century when the New York Post on September 4, 1906, referred to "... many of those Democrats who rushed into the Bryan band wagon." The political practice the phrase describes was, however, an invention of the Whig Party during the 1840 log cabin and hard cider campaign. The Whigs used a circus band wagon to lead their parades in that campaign, while office seekers and others who wished to identify themselves prominently with the Whig candidates, climbed on the band wagon and rode with the musicians.

Bolt. An Old English term meaning "arrow" or "shaft," migrated into the world of horse-racing, and from there into the world of politics. A horse that ran away or suddenly got out of control was said to bolt, perhaps because the speed of its movement suggested an arrow or a shaft of lightning. An early recorded use of the term in a political sense appears in an entry John Quincy Adams made in his diary on April 9, 1808. Adams, then a Senator, commented on two Senate members who deliberately absented themselves from the chamber because they did not want to vote for either side of a disputed issue. "This," said he, "is sometimes called bolting, and sometimes flying the course."

Boss is derived from the Dutch baas, which originally meant "uncle," but came to mean "head of a household," "chief," "overseer" or "master." As early as the 1670's, the word had entered common American speech via the New York Dutch, and in its Americanized spelling boss referred to an employer or superintendent of labor crews. With the construction of canals and railroads, the term was carried from New York into adjoining states and finally all over the country. In its political sense, boss came into common use after the Civil War.

Campaign is taken from the Latin campus, meaning "field." For a while after the Constitution was adopted in 1789, Americans used the English term canvass to describe their election contest. But in the early 1800's, as voting rights were won by increasing numbers of Americans, American politicians came to compare election contests to a military operation and called it an electioneering campaign. Still later, this was simplified to campaign, while other military terms—strategy, battle, camp, high command, and war chest— came to be used in connection with the word campaign.

Candidate comes from the Latin candidus, meaning "shining" or "white." A person in ancient Rome who sought high elective office customarily appeared among the citizens in public places dressed solely in a white toga to symbolize purity of purpose, while the absence of any undergarments symbolized humility— and also made it easy to show battle scars to voters. The Romans thus came to call such a person candidatus, which became candidate in English. Candidateship and then candidature were used by the British to describe the act of standing or running for office. Americans for a while used the latter form, but gradually substituted the more easily spoken candidacy.

Caucus is an American invention, but language scholars sharply disagree about how it came to birth. Some say it is derived from the Algonquin Indian caucauasu signifying "elder," "counselor" or "one who advises, urges, encourages, pushed on." Some connect it with another Indian kaw-kaw-was, meaning "talk." Some trace the word to a pre-Revolutionary War political organization that met at "West-Corcus" in Boston, and came to be known as the Caucus Club. Others say it was derived from the word caulker—meaning one who drives oakum or old rope into the seams of vessels; and on this theory, the Caucus Club itself was merely a corruption of Caulker's Club, an organization whose members were identified in one way or another with Boston's shipping interests.

Dark horse was originally English racing slang. It has been suggested that the term originated in a trick practiced by jockeys who dyed the hair of well-known fast horses in order to enter them in races under other names. The horses were generally dyed black, and the jockeys and their friends would then bet heavily on them and make a clean-up. In a retrospective view, American political historians refer to James Knox Polk, the 1844 Democratic candidate for President as the first dark horse to emerge from a nominating convention. But the first explicit use of the term in its political sense is believed to have been applied to Rutherford B. Hayes, the 1876 Republican nominee for the Presidency.

Demagogue is derived from Greek demos, "people," and agogos, "leading." In ancient Greece a demagogue was originally an orator or leader who took the part of the people against other interests in the state. As such, the term had a respectable echo. But as time wore on and it was observed how often the demagogues led the people astray, the term gradually came to signify a misleader rather than a true leader of the people. It was in that sense that it entered the English language around 1650. In Great Britain the practices of demagogues are called demagogism or demagogy, while the Americanized term for those same practices is demagoguery.

Dyed in the wool originated in the days of vegetable dyes and homespun clothes. The coloring lasted better when the raw wool was dyed before instead of after weaving. In its political sense, dyed in the wool signifying "ingrained," "thorough" or "complete," dates from the Jackson era. Thus John Quincy Adams, in a reference to a Jefferson birthday dinner in Washington, wrote in his diary for May 22, 1830: "Eight members of the Pennsylvania delegation, Jefferson Republicans dyed in the wool, agreed to go."

Favorite son is a term most people properly associate with the Presidential nominating convention. But in its political usage, it is as old as the Federal Government. On May 1, 1789, for example, the New York *Daily Gazette* hailed the first President as, "Washington, the favorite son of liberty." By the 1820's, the term suggested a political leader whose strength lay more in his native state than in the nation at large. The rise of the convention system for making Presidential nominations merely sealed that new meaning.

Fire eater entered the English language around 1670 and referred to a magician who pretended to swallow fire. It entered the vocabulary of American politics after the 1845 admission of Texas into the Union, and was used by Northerners to describe Southern extremists who openly advocated secession from the Union.

Forgotten man is an old English phrase which was used by Lord Byron and even by earlier writers. But in 1883 it was first popularized in the United States by William Graham Sumner, professor of political and moral science at Yale University. The meaning Sumner gave to it was the opposite of the one it acquired in more modern times. To him, the forgotten man was the hard-working, solid citizen and taxpayer who was exploited by the "wrangling grabbers, loafers and jobbers."

Later, in 1897, Walter Hines Page, who was to be American Ambassador to England during the Wilson Administration, used the forgotten man as the title of an address he gave at North Carolina Teachers' College at Raleigh, and that drew widespread attention in the South. In Page's view, the forgotten man meant the "average man." But then, Governor Franklin D. Roosevelt in his pre-Convention campaign for the 1932 Democratic Presidential nomination, gave the forgotten man the meaning of the "underprivileged man" or the "underdog." Thus in an Albany radio speech on April 7, 1932, Governor Roosevelt said: "These unhappy times call for the building of plans that rest upon the forgotten, the unorganized by indispensable units of economic power, for plans like those of 1917 that build from the bottom up, and not from the top down, that put their faith once more in the forgotten man."

Franchise, meaning "the right to vote" is derived from the Old French franc, "free," since only freemen had the right to vote.

Hat in the ring came directly from sporting slang in the American West where it was customary for a man to volunteer to enter a boxing or wrestling match by throwing his hat into the ring. This practice in turn was a survival of the old "gage of battle" where a person willing to fight in support of his claims cast his glove or cap on the ground, and his opponent designate was left with the choice of picking it up or not. Hat in the ring in the sense of a political willingness to be a candidate for office was popularized in February 1912 by ex-President Theodore Roosevelt when he was asked during a stop in Cleveland, Ohio, if he meant to run for the Presidency that year. "My hat's in the ring," replied Roosevelt. "The fight is on and I'm stripped to the buff."

Henchman is believed to be derived from Anglo-Saxon hengst, "stallion," and "man." In this sense, a henchman was someone who looked after the horses, an important function among the Anglo-Saxons. Though the term died out in England during the seventeenth century, it survived in Scotland to mean an attendant to a Highland chief. Here, especially, the word conveyed an honorable mode of action. In the United States, however, henchmen was used as early as 1839 to convey the sense of political lackeys who automatically do anything asked of them by their leaders, however, questionable.

Hustings is derived from Anglo-Saxon hus, "house," and thing, "assembly." Originally it was a royal household council, but the term was later applied to a court of justice. Thus the supreme Court of London, held in Guildhall before the Mayor, Recorder, Sheriffs and Alderman, was called the Hustings Court, while the platform at the upper end of the hall where the magistrates sat was called the husting. The term became associated with political campaigning and electioneering because Parliamentary candidates, prior to a reform in 1872, were nominated and addressed the voters from the hustings in the Guildhall. In the Americanized version, the term first applied to any place where political speeches were made and then to campaigning and electioneering in general.

Mending fences acquired its political meaning from a speech made by John Sherman when he was serving in the Hayes Cabinet as Secretary of the Treasury. Sherman, a native of Mansfield, Ohio, had a farm nearby which he had rented to a tenant. In 1879, his return to Mansfield led a number of reporters to ask if his purpose was to seek the governorship of Ohio. Sherman publicly insisted that he was back merely to inspect his run-down farm. "I found when I arrived in my old home," said he to a Mansfield crowd that serenaded him at evening time, "that the papers said I came West to seek the nomination for governor. I came purely on private business—to repair my fences and look after my neglected property." The reporters seized upon the references to fences and construed them as having a political significance. Mending fences afterward became a byword to describe every politician who is engaged in strengthening his political position.

Keynote was borrowed from the vocabulary of music where the keynote is the note or tune on which a system of notes is based. It entered the American political vocabulary toward the close of the 19th century.

Kiss of death which appears in many places from the Babylonian Talmud to Chaucer's *Canterbury Tales* was a kiss given to one just before dying and symbolized a final leave-taking. The phrase in its political meaning was popularized in 1926 when Governor Alfred E. Smith of New York applied it to William Randolph Hearst's support of Ogden L. Mills, the Republican candidate for Governor. Governor Smith may have had in mind the Judas kiss—kissing before killing.

Lame duck was originally part of English stock market slang where a broker or stock jobber who would not or could not make good his losses, was said to "waddle out of the alley like a lame duck." In this sense, the term was imported into America. The transition to politics was natural, but the earliest known use of the term in a political sense did not occur until 1863 when the *Congressional Globe* referred to "...a receptacle of 'lame duck' or broken-down politicians."

Off the record and **On the record** had their origins in courtroom proceedings. When the proceedings were suspended for an informal conference between a judge and the contending lawyers, the recorder was told by the judge: "This is off the record." When the official proceedings were resumed, the judge told the recorder: "This is on the record." Only what was "on the record" could be considered in judicial review.

The two terms entered the vocabulary of American politics beginning in 1873 when the official proceedings of the Congress were first published daily in the *Congressional Record*. Members then referred to formal and informal statements as being respectively "on the record" and "off the record." However, the term did not enter into common political usage until after the first World War when it gained wide currency because of an informal talk President Woodrow Wilson had given at the White House on February 28, 1919, with members of the Democratic National Committee.

Ovation is of Latin origin and referred to the second of two grades of ceremonial honors the Roman Senate conferred upon victorious commanders. The highest grade was the triumphus, where a general wore a laurel crown and toga embroidered with gold stars and carried a scepter in one hand and a laurel branch in the other. Riding a circular chariot drawn by four horses, he was preceded by the Roman Senate, magistrates and musicians, and was followed by his fettered captives, the spoils of victory, and his entire army in marching formation. When the procession passing through Rome reached the Capitoline Hill, sacrifices were offered and the hero was entertained at a public feast. The lesser of the two grades of honor was known as ovationem, from ovare, "to rejoice" or "to exult." A general who was thus honored entered the city on foot or horseback and was crowned with myrtle instead of laurel. The political sense of the word ovation still tends to be restricted in meaning to popular applause or a mass tribute to a public person.

Peanut politics had its origin in the fact that until the early part of the nineteenth century, peanuts were regarded in America as unfit food for the upper classes and were eaten only by poor whites and slaves in the South. Hence peanut came to mean anything small, trifling or of little value. The earliest known instance where the word picked up the further word "politics" is dated 1887.

Platform is derived from Old French plateforme, which literally meant a plane or a flat form, and which figuratively came to mean a ground plan to build by, or a written outline, a sketch or a scheme for action. The earliest known use of platform in an American political sense, occurs in one of the resolutions adopted by the 1844 Democratic National Convention. It read: "The Whigs, whether on the Lexington platform or some other noncommital platform, will be and must be at once known as the party that opposed their country in her just and generous war." By 1848, a single declaration in a political platform was already being called a plank.

Roorback, meaning a lie about a political candidate launched just before the votes are due to be cast, is derived from a story published in 1844 to injure James K. Polk, the Democratic candidate for President. On the eve of the election, the Ithaca (New York) *Chronicle* printed what purported to be an extract from *A Tour Through the Western and Southern States* by a Baron Roorback. The extract, as widely reprinted in other Whig newspapers, described a slave camp where forty-three slaves "...had been purchased by the Honorable J. K. Polk, the present Speaker of the House of Representatives, the mark of the branding iron, and the initials of his name, on their shoulders, distinguishing them from the rest." The extract was later proved to be a forgery. There never was any such writer as Baron Roorback. But ever since roorback has meant a last-minute canard published on the eve of an election.

Smoke-filled room in its political sense was popularized by Kirke L. Simpson of the Associated Press in connection with the nomination of Warren G. Harding by the 1920 Republican National Convention in Chicago. Before the convention opened, Harry M. Daugherty, Harding's campaign manager, reportedly predicted that once the convention was deadlocked, "... some twelve or fifteen men, worn out and bleary-eyed for lack of sleep, will sit down, about two o'clock in the morning, around a table in a smoke-filled room in some hotel and decide the nomination. When that time comes, Harding will be selected." At five o'clock on the morning of June 12, 1920, Simpson filed a story beginning: "Harding of Ohio was chosen by a group of men in a smoke-filled room early today as Republican candidate for President." Later the same day the convention nominated Harding by an overwhelming majority and smoke-filled room took its place in the American political vocabulary.

The political practice represented by the term, however, went back to colonial days. Thus in February, 1763, John Adams wrote in his diary: "This day learned that the Caucus Club meets, at certain times, in the garret of Tom Dawes, the Adjutant of the Boston Regiment. He has a large house, and he has a movable partition in his garret which he takes down, and the whole club meets in one room. There they smoke tobacco till you cannot see from one end of the garret to the other. There they drink flip, I suppose, and there they choose a moderator, who puts questions to the vote regularly; and selectmen assessors, collectors, wardens, pre-wards, and representatives are regularly chosen before they are chosen by the town."

Stalking horse is derived from a horse used by hunters in stalking game. Since wild animals and birds generally take horses for granted, Old English hunters concealed themselves behind a trained horse or even a dummy horse to get within shooting range without alarming their quarry. It was in its meaning as a decoy or pretext put forward to conceal real intentions, that the phrase first passed over into American political usage. Thus Thomas Jefferson in explaining why he changed his mind about the merits of agriculture to the exclusion of manufacturing, complained in 1816 about those who used his "... former opinion only as a stalking horse, to cover their disloyal propensities to keep us in external vassalage to a foreign and unfriendly people." After that, the term in political usage increasingly came to mean a candidate who runs to split the opposition without expecting to win himself.

Steam roller, meaning high-handed methods to overcome political opposition, dates from 1908 when the Republican National Committee met in Chicago a week before the Republican nominating convention to decide on contested delegates and to make up the temporary roll. President Theodore Roosevelt was then trying to dictate the nomination of his handpicked understudy, William Howard Taft. But there was strong opposition from a number of quarters, and many delegate seats were contested. However, the Roosevelt-Taft members of the national committee, acting with mechanical precision, decided the contests in favor of their own faction, thus giving the Roosevelt-Taft delegate control of the convention.

Oswald F. Schuette, a political writer for the Chicago *Inter-Ocean,* who was covering the Republican National Committee meeting, emerged from the meeting place after one of the sessions to see a steam roller standing in a vacant lot where it was being used in an advertising stunt. It bore a sign reading: THE STEAM ROLLER VAUDEVILLE AT THE AUDITORIUM THEATRE. Schuette was at once struck by the idea of comparing the methods of the Roosevelt-Taft committeemen with the object in the vacant lot. The next day in his report in the *Inter-Ocean* he said that the Roosevelt-Taft men had flattened out the opposition like a steam roller. Other newspapers promptly seized on the simile, and it caught the popular fancy as well.

Stump in connection with politics is of American origin where the first recorded use of the term is dated 1816. Along the western frontier, candidates for office sometimes resorted to the stump of a tree as a rostrum from which to address the backwoods voters. The practice spawned a whole family of terms—stump speech, stump speaker, take the stump, stump the State or nation.

Straw vote, as an unofficial poll taken before an election to get the drift of public opinion, apparently originated in America —though the references to "straws in the wind" go back to Biblical times. In 1774 Joseph Galloway, member of the First Continental Congress, wrote that the Massachusetts delegates were "warm in their Behaviour and Conversation very modest, yet not so much as to throw out Hints which, like Straws and Feathers, tell us from which Point of the Compass the Wind Comes." As a political practice, the first use of a straw vote to forecast the result of an election, is attributed to Charles "Calico Charlie" Foster, who was elected Governor of Ohio in 1879.

Sufferage in the sense of the right to vote, is related to the Latin suffragium. As such, the Roman practice which gave rise to the political meaning of the term was similar to the one described in connection with the word ballot as derived from the Italian word ballota. That is to say, it signified something broken off, such as a piece of shell or potsherd used in voting. In this way it came to mean a voting tablet and the right to vote.

Ticket is a corrupted form of French etiquette. The root of the latter word signified "to stick," and hence the term came to mean a label, bill, card, sign or notice stuck on a post or wall. In the time of Louis XIII, persons received at court were given cards of directions and regulations and those who wanted to do the proper thing were careful to follow the directions on the etiquettes. "That's the ticket," meaning "that's the right thing," is a survival of this practice. Ticket in its political sense, however, is of American origin. Here, as early as 1711, a slate of candidates nominated for office by a fraction was called a ticket. The term in its political sense, came into widespread use the first years of the 19th century. Straight ticket, scratched ticket, split ticket, mixed ticket and general ticket all date from the same time.

Unit rule is one of the oldest—and most disputed—devices in American politics. Thus when the South Carolina legislature appointed John Rutledge, Christopher Gadsden and Thomas Lynch to attend the 1765 Stamp Act Congress held in New York, it was agreed that they should act as a unit and be bound by a majority. Again, one of the first acts of the First Continental Congress in 1774 was to decide that the delegation from each Colony should have only one vote. There was enough opposition to this decision so that it was deliberately noted in the Journal of the Congress that this was a temporary decision and was not to be taken as a precedent. However, the method was retained and even the Declaration of Independence was adopted under the unit rule. And again, after much discussion, the Continental Congress which adopted the Articles of Confederation in 1777, adopted the provision that "in determining questions in the United States in Congress assembled, each state shall have one vote." The method continued in force until the Constitution went into effect in 1789. After that, under the Constitution, the unit rule was prescribed only in cases when the House of Representatives chooses a President.

Vote is derived from Latin votum, "vow," "prayer," "wish" or "desire." Votive, votary and vow are from the same source. Vote in the sense of casting a ballot was used in English in the sixteenth century, and in that sense, was transplanted in meaning to American soil.

A History Lesson About Dark Horses

by Sidney Hyman

It is no accident that American more so than British politics, has looked to the race track as a source of its imagry. In America a man runs for office. In Britain he stands for it. With us, moreover, since we have no tight party discipline and few safe elective offices, political fortune appears more of a gambling affair—though with a strong moral streak as we bet on right and wrong.

Naturally, therefore, we apply to our politics various figures of speech from the place where running and betting meet openly in their most dramatic focus. Thus in Presidential politics, we talk of "grooming a candidate for a race," the "stable" he came from, and whether he is a "favorite" or "front runner." We talk of a candidate's "rounding the bend" or "entering the home stretch;" of his being a "runner-up," an "also ran"; or of his "winning by a nose" in a "photo finish" — followed, of course, by "the payoff."

Of all such talk, the phrase "dark horse" candidate when sounded at a convention has the most romantic overtones. The picture it conjures up is the picture of a convention deadlocked in the ballotting between two leading candidates. Neither one will give way to the other. Personal animus or fundamental disagreement over the issues stand in the way. So a select group of party leaders meets in a "smoke-filled room" and decides that the way to break the deadlock is through a "neutral" third figure, perhaps a political unknown or one who was not an avowed candidate before the convention got underway. The figure is produced, and the weary convention delegates wheeled into line to make him the party's Presidential candidate.

But a glance at the actual history of nominating conventions shows that "dark horse" candidates were few and far between; and of the few, most were on the grey instead of the dark side. For example, only two men who won Presidential nominations were not avowed candidates before the convention met. They were Horatio Seymour, Democrat (1868), and James Garfield, Republican (1880). See *The Great Decliners.* Only seven other men who won Presidential nominations were given little more than an outside chance in advance of a convention. They were James K. Polk, Democrat (1844); Franklin Pierce, Democrat (1852); Rutherford B. Hayes, Republican (1876); William Jennings Bryan, Democrat (1896); Warren G. Harding, Republican (1920); John W. Davis, Democrat (1924) and Wendell Willkie, Republican (1940).

The count and spacing here is significant. Add the names up and they come to eight men in all. But add the total number of men our major parties have nominated for the Presidency since the convention system matured in the 1840's, and it is somewhere in the neighborhood of sixty-four. So the historical odds against the dark horse are 55-9.

Yet a 55-9 possibility becomes still more unfavorable when a further detail is taken into account. In the case of the Democratic party, every "dark horse" candidate emerged during the period when the two-thirds rule for nominations was in force—a rule that was eliminated in 1936. Under that rule, no Democrat could win a Presidential nomination unless he polled two-thirds of all delegates who voted. Now, however, the Democrats like the Republicans nominate by a simple majority. A nomination by a simple majority vote does not, of course, eliminate the possibility of a hopelessly deadlocked convention. But it markedly reduces the possibility— and with it, the chances for the emergence of a dark horse.

A further detail of importance comes to light in the mere listing of the dark horse candidates of the past. All except two held major public offices at the time they were chosen and enjoyed a certain degree of celebrity because of that fact. It may have been the sort of celebrity that led a New Hampshire innkeeper to say of his neighbor, Franklin Pierce: "Waal, up here, he's a right smart sort of fella, but spread him over the whole nation and I'm afeerd he will be very thin in spots." Yet all did spread, at least to a degree that led to a pre-convention listing of their names among a party's possible candidates.

Here are some examples:

James Polk, a Democrat, had been a Congressman, Speaker of the House, Governor of Tennessee and an aspirant for the Vice-Presidency — all before he became in 1844 the original "dark horse" in our history. These facts alone made him more of a grey than a "dark horse." Yet he approached the color of an albino when his grooming was taken into account. It was supervised by no less a master than Ex-President Andrew Jackson and other like-minded men who turned away from the front-running Martin Van Buren when the latter came out against the annexation of Texas.

At the 1844 Democratic convention proper, the fate of Martin Van Buren, who had a majority of the delegates, was doomed from the start by the adoption of the two-thirds rule of Southerners. Lewis Cass, the only other candidate who started the race, favored the annexation of Texas —a fact that led to his overtaking Van Buren on the fifth ballot and increasing his lead on the two that followed. But at this point, when Cass was still short of the two-thirds that were required to nominate, he made a fateful blunder. He allowed the delegates to adjourn for the night.

Now the Jackson forces went to work. They argued that Van Buren and Cass had split the party; that a peace-and-harmony man was needed; that he should be a border-state man oriented to the southwest horizon; and that this man should be James Polk, since he was already acceptable to almost everyone as a Vice-Presidential choice. Furthermore, said the Jackson lieutenants acting in Polk's interest, there was a place where the freeholders of the North could expand to offset the expansion of the slave power toward the Southwest. The place was an enlarged Oregon Territory—if necessary, through war with Great Britain. (Hence the 1844 Democratic war cry: "Oregon and Texas!") Polk's name was placed in nomination for the Presidency when the convention reconvened the next morning. Seemingly out of nowhere, he received forty-nine votes on the opening ballot, on the next, the stampede to him began and the nomination was his.

"We Polked you in 1844 and we shall Pierce you in 1852," cried the Democrats to the Whigs when they came up with their second "dark horse." Franklin Pierce had been a Congressman for four years, and a Senator for an added five before he resigned to get away from Washington and for a variety of reasons. Thereafter, he served in the Mexican War as a Brigadier General, and still later, had the good fortune to have as a friend the very great American novelist, Nathaniel Hawthorne, who stood by to write his campaign biography.

Though a New Hampshire man, he nevertheless expressed sentiment favorable to the South on the slavery issue. Thus he was "available" as a person who could surmount the barrier of the two-thirds rule. In any case, while many persons were active on his behalf well in advance of the convention, he emerged as a "dark horse" candidate because during a deadlock between the front runners, the managers for one of the front runners, James Buchanan, erred in their judgment. As part of a complicated strategy, they threw a few votes to Pierce just to show that nobody could really break the deadlock and that Buchanan would have to be the Democratic Presidential nominee if there was to be any at all.

With the sudden appearance of Pierce's name—it was on the forty-seventh ballot—the stampede to him began two ballots later. "Sir," he said to a friend, "you are looking at the most surprised man that ever lived!" His Vice-Presidential running mate, meanwhile, complained bitterly against the tendency of the convention system to choose men for the Presidency who are unfit for the job! Yet the men who had expected Buchanan to win, were not too disgruntled. They knew they had an identical twin in Pierce.

In Democratic party annals, the dark horse nomination of William Jennings Bryan in 1896 was unusual because it was not the result of a deadlock. Bryan literally rose on the wings of words. At 36, his only political qualification was the two terms he served as a Congressman from Nebraska. It would have been highly presumptuous for the "boy orator" to have to open a pre-convention headquarters and to announce his candidacy. In any case, the nomination appeared to be sewed up for "Silver Dick" Bland, a veteran congressman from Missouri. Yet Bryan labored through most of the night before he was to give his now famous "cross of gold" speech, working over his old material, and picking out the most effective phrases in his repertoire. Years later a young page boy who was in the convention hall, named Harry S. Truman, recalled how Bryan's "bell-like" voice reached out to the 17,000 people in the audience, and electrified it with its final words: "You shall not press down upon the brows of labor this crown of thorns, you shall not crucify mankind upon a cross of gold." This performance "stole" the nomination of the fifth ballot.

The deadlock between Al Smith and William Gibbs McAdoo in 1924 that led to the nomination of John W. Davis on the 103rd ballot after the two leaders withdrew in his favor, and need not be gone into, except to identify Davis. He had been an able Congressman, a gifted Solicitor General of the United States, an effective Ambassador to England, and a lawyer whose clientele embraced the radical world of the United Mine Workers and the coupon-clipping world of Wall Street firms like J. P. Morgan & Co. Furthermore, he had been widely boomed for the Democratic nomination as early as 1920. By any test, therefore, he qualified as a gray-to-albino "dark horse" when his name at the 1924 Democratic Convention was placed in nomination as West Virginia's favorite son. With one foot in the North and one in the South by virtue of his West Virginia origin, he was a logical choice to heal the wounds the party had inflicted on itself in the Smith-McAdoo deadlock, caused by bitter differences over the Ku Klux Klan, prohibition and the League of Nations issues.

Among "dark horse" candidates, Wendell Willkie, Republican (1940) stands in a class all by himself. Prior to his nomination, he had never before sought or held public office. And in his identity as a Wall Street lawyer and utility executive, he ran against the grain of a key rule of availability, which places party leadership beyond the reach of any man who is conspicuously identified with a special economic interest. He was an avowed candidate for the Republican Presidential nomination in advance of the convention, but was not thought of as a serious contender. The "front-runners" at the time were Senators Arthur Vandenberg and Robert Taft, and Governor Thomas E. Dewey.

It is true that Willkie was supported by a combination of zealous amateurs, shrewd publicists, and what the politicians call "Eastern big business." Yet these alone would not have been powerful enough to win the nomination for Willkie had it not been for a further fact. The Republican convention in that year met at a time when American opinion was jolted by the sudden eruption of the Nazi forces into the Low Countries, by the imminent fall of France and the prospective isolation of Great Britain. Vandenberg, Taft and Dewey had previously been cool to the idea of "aid to the allies" and critical of Roosevelt's attempts to extend that aid. Caught in their "institutional position," they could not shift quickly enough to catch the new tide of opinion in the United States. Willkie, on the other hand, was more favorably placed. He had been active all along in the "aid-to-the-allies" movement. The Republican convention therefore reached over the heads of its "old pros" whose position on international questions promised to be a source of embarrassment in a campaign. They settled on Willkie as the man who could appeal to the growing sentiment for helping the beleaguered allies.

A final word. When foreign affairs now loom so large in American life, it is hard to imagine why any future nominating convention would want to give its Presidential nomination to any man inexperienced in them. That in turn means that it is hard to imagine a Presidential nomination going to any man who has not lived and worked at the very center of American politics where foreign and domestic questions converge. If so, it is hard to imagine how the legend of the "dark horse" candidate, of questionable truth even in generations past, can have any more life left in it in the generations ahead.

Television's hottest new news team will take you right down to the wire in the 1964 Presidential race

RON COCHRAN BADEN LANGTON
BOB YOUNG BILL DOWNS BILL LAWRENCE BOB FLEMING
JOHN SCALI RICHARD BATE JOHN CASSERLY LISA HOWARD
BOB CLARK JOHN ROLFSON PAUL GOOD AL MANN

HOWARD K. SMITH, EDWARD P. MORGAN

You'll discover an exciting new kind of television journalism in the ABC News coverage of the 1964 campaigns and elections.

Right now, Senator Hubert Humphrey, Senator Sam Ervin and Arthur Schlesinger, Jr. are covering the Democratic National Convention as special on-the-air consultants for ABC News.

During the Republican Convention General Dwight D. Eisenhower discussed San Francisco trends and developments exclusively for ABC News.

And in Howard K. Smith and Edward P. Morgan—anchormen for all political coverage—ABC News has the hottest new news team in the industry.

Harriet Van Horne (New York World-Telegram & Sun) wrote, "...in all TV election coverage this year, the most interesting talk, factual and philosophical, came from ABC's silver-haired men of distinction."

Terry Turner (Chicago Daily News) says that "...it is impossible to listen to either...without learning something...or seeing something in a more clear perspective."

With Bill Lawrence, Ron Cochran, Bob Young, Lisa Howard and a full team of top reporters, ABC News will take you right down to the wire in the 1964 Presidential race.

ABC Television Network

"More power to the party of the great presidents. The true party of the people." *Bart Lytton*

Bart Lytton, President and Chairman of the Board, Lytton Financial Corporation.

LYTTON
FINANCIAL CORPORATION
ASSETS OVER ONE/HALF BILLION DOLLARS

OUR SAVINGS SUBSIDIARIES CORDIALLY INVITE YOUR ACCOUNT BY MAIL

LYTTON
SAVINGS AND LOAN ASSOCIATION
FOUNDED 1906
8150 SUNSET BOULEVARD
HOLLYWOOD 46, CALIFORNIA

LYTTON
SAVINGS AND LOAN ASSOCIATION
OF NORTHERN CALIFORNIA · FOUNDED 1925
UNIVERSITY AT EMERSON
PALO ALTO, CALIFORNIA

Hardly an hour goes by...that we don't hang our shingle in a new location

In our business it is a symbol of status. As a matter of fact, we have been building our status since 1953, serving the needs of the Washington, D. C. Metropolitan Area in residential and commercial real estate.

(Complimentary Sales — Rental Bulletin available upon request)

OFFERED
Routh Robbins
REAL ESTATE CORP.
836·6200

ROUTH M. ROBBINS, *President* / DONALD E. McNARY, *Vice President*

ROUTH ROBBINS REAL ESTATE CORP., 400 NORTH WASHINGTON STREET, ALEXANDRIA, VIRGINIA 22313

7A is in Hollywood

and around the world producing outstanding motion pictures. Now in release, Tennessee Williams' THE NIGHT OF THE IGUANA, starring Richard Burton, Ava Gardner, Deborah Kerr and Sue Lyon; SEVEN DAYS IN MAY, which stars Burt Lancaster, Kirk Douglas, Fredric March and Ava Gardner; W. Somerset Maugham's OF HUMAN BONDAGE, starring Kim Novak and Laurence Harvey. Forthcoming productions include THIS PROPERTY IS CONDEMNED, the Tennessee Williams' drama which will star Elizabeth Taylor and will be directed by Richard Burton; REFLECTIONS IN A GOLDEN EYE, from the Carson McCullers' novella which will be directed by Tony Richardson; THE HILL, a story of World War II, which will star Sean Connery; H. Rider Haggard's SHE, the classic adventure story which will star Ursula Andress; Rudyard Kipling's adventure story, THE MAN WHO WOULD BE KING, with John Huston directing.

7A is on Broadway

The lights of Broadway glitter that much more with musical events like Ray Stark's FUNNY GIRL, starring Barbra Streisand. The 1964-'65 season will be worth several trips to Broadway with such Seven Arts stage projects now being developed as MRS. 'ARRIS GOES TO PARIS, a musical based on Paul Gallico's novel; Georgia Brown, star of the hit musical "Oliver," will make her dramatic debut in FRENCH STREET by Norman Krasna and directed by Jose Quintero; FILM OF MEMORY, by Paul Osborn, will be produced in association with Leland Hayward; IT'S BEEN WONDERFUL, a comedy-drama by John Patrick, which Fred Coe will direct.

7A is on Television

With its "Films of the 50's" from the major Hollywood studios, including Warner Bros., 20th Century-Fox and Universal, among the Seven Arts' releases currently being telecast throughout the U.S. are such great films as MAGNIFICENT OBSESSION, THE GLENN MILLER STORY, WILL SUCCESS SPOIL ROCK HUNTER?, A HATFUL OF RAIN, AUNTIE MAME, SAYONARA and MISTER ROBERTS. In addition to feature films, Seven Arts also distributes other television programs, including the BOSTON SYMPHONY ORCHESTRA Concert Specials; EN FRANCE, a series of half-hour French language entertainment-instruction films starring Dawn Addams; CHURCHILL, THE MAN; THE EMMETT KELLY SHOW and MAHALIA JACKSON SINGS.

7A is entertainment

Seven Arts
200 Park Avenue, New York
Beverly Hills · Toronto · London · Paris

OFFICIAL PROCEEDINGS OF THE DEMOCRATIC NATIONAL CONVENTION 1960

"The Democratic Party has endured and prospered because it rested on the belief that a party exists to advance the freedom and the welfare of all the people." —Lyndon B. Johnson

NATIONAL DOCUMENT PUBLISHERS, INC.

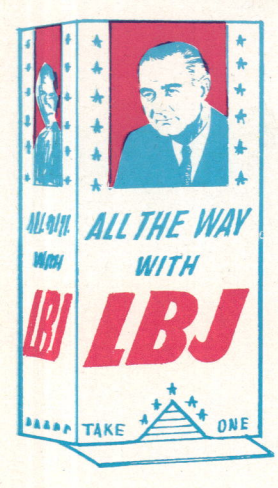

WASHINGTON REPRESENTATIVES OF ROSE PRINTING COMPANY, developers of the *MULTI-PURPOSE, DISPENSER-PACKAGE*, for distribution of booklets and pamphlets on a self-service basis, dispensed from the same colorful and attractive package in which they were shipped. Eliminates waste, saves time, stays clean, ships safely, stores easily, saves space and *attracts customers!*

PATENT PENDING

FOR THE FIRST TIME

For the first time, the Democratic Party is making available to the public a special collector's edition of THE OFFICIAL PROCEEDINGS OF THE DEMOCRATIC NATIONAL CONVENTION 1960. For your enjoyment—and for the education of your children—this significant volume should become a permanent addition to your library.

Review and remember all the excitement, the tension, the historical drama of the Convention that offered our Nation the leadership of JOHN F. KENNEDY and LYNDON B. JOHNSON. Relive this event in your own home today and forever.

In addition to its record of convention proceedings, this valuable reference work contains *facts about the Democratic Party; list of all convention delegates and alternates; color and black-and-white photographs.*

TAKE ADVANTAGE OF THIS SPECIAL OFFER NOW!

Clip and mail coupon today.

NATIONAL DOCUMENT PUBLISHERS, INC.
P.O. Box 90, Ben Franklin Station
Washington, D. C.

Gentlemen:
Please send me at $8.95 each, _____ copies of the Collector's Edition of "THE OFFICIAL PROCEEDINGS OF THE DEMOCRATIC NATIONAL CONVENTION 1960." I understand that delivery will be made on or before September 1, 1964.

NAME: _____
STREET OR P. O. _____
CITY _____
STATE _____ ZIP_____
CHECK ENCLOSED.

It was rugged, mates. *33 days in a lifeboat and worst of all no Schlitz!*

real gusto

in a great light beer

Schlitz

The Beer that made Milwaukee Famous
...simply because it tastes so good.

MUSCULAR DYSTROPHY ASSOCIATIONS OF AMERICA, INC.
1790 Broadway • New York, New York 10019

Ambassadors of Goodwill...

ROBBIE AND KERRIE WHITAKER are too young to know that their very lives depend on the success of the vast scientific offensive which has been mounted by MDAA. But they realize that, as National Poster Children, they are the Association's ambassadors to the people of America. "We've got to tell everybody about the work MDAA is doing." Kerrie nods and smiles that devastating smile. "But we love it," she says. "We love airplanes and people and everything we do."

MUSCULAR DYSTROPHY ASSOCIATIONS OF AMERICA, INC., is dedicated to the scientific conquest of neuromuscular diseases through basic and applied research into nerve, muscle and metabolism... assisting patients through therapy, service programs and clinics. Also supporting the Institute for Muscle Disease a unique research center — the first anywhere devoted exclusively to the study of muscle and its pathologies — was built by and receives support from Muscular Dystrophy Associations of America, one of the country's leading health agencies. Research data from the hundreds of MDAA sponsored clinics and grantees across the country is transmitted to the Institute, which serves as a clearing house for information on muscle pathology. The findings of IMD's staff is made available to scientists in other institutions who, in turn, send records of their experiments to the Institute.

MRS. LYNDON JOHNSON, *Honorary Chairman*

JERRY LEWIS, *National Chairman*

"...to the lasting benefit of our nation's health."

JOHN F. KENNEDY

This advertisement represents the contribution of the undersigned companies to the public informational activities of the Muscular Dystrophy Associations of America.

Chemical Leaman Tank Lines, Downingtown, Pa.
Cooper Jarrett, Inc., Orange, New Jersey.
W. F. Crossett, Inc., Warren, Pennsylvania.
Keystone-Lawrence Transfer & Storage Co., Newcastle, Pa.
Masten Transportation, Milford, Delaware.
Matlack, Inc., Philadelphia, Pennsylvania.
Rand Express Freight Lines, Lyndhurst, New Jersey.

We make some odds and ends really perform.

We took a syringe and invented a new way to remove excess solder—saved $25,000 a year in labor costs. A shrink-sleeving technique using a plain induction coil saved $50,000. Clothespins to hold coaxial cable marking tags—another $20,000. Cardboard + masking tape + perforated metal strips—presto!—an inexpensive electrical wiring harness board saving $70,000 annually in direct costs. But the performance has just begun. Sperry Rand divisions, through a concerted economy drive, last year attained remarkable savings both large and small, totaling many, many millions of dollars of benefits to our customers. Such cost reduction techniques are being applied to such things as guidance and control systems, computers and business machines, hydraulics, farm equipment and electric shavers, to bring each Sperry Rand customer technically excellent products at the lowest possible cost.

SPERRY RAND CORPORATION

Good government is the concern of everyone. It is the duty as well as the privilege of each citizen to be alert, to study all available information and to support the candidates, the parties and the principles which he believes are best for all.

E. W. Axe Co., Inc.
R. H. Axe, President
Tarrytown, New York

HOTEL SAHARA
LAS VEGAS

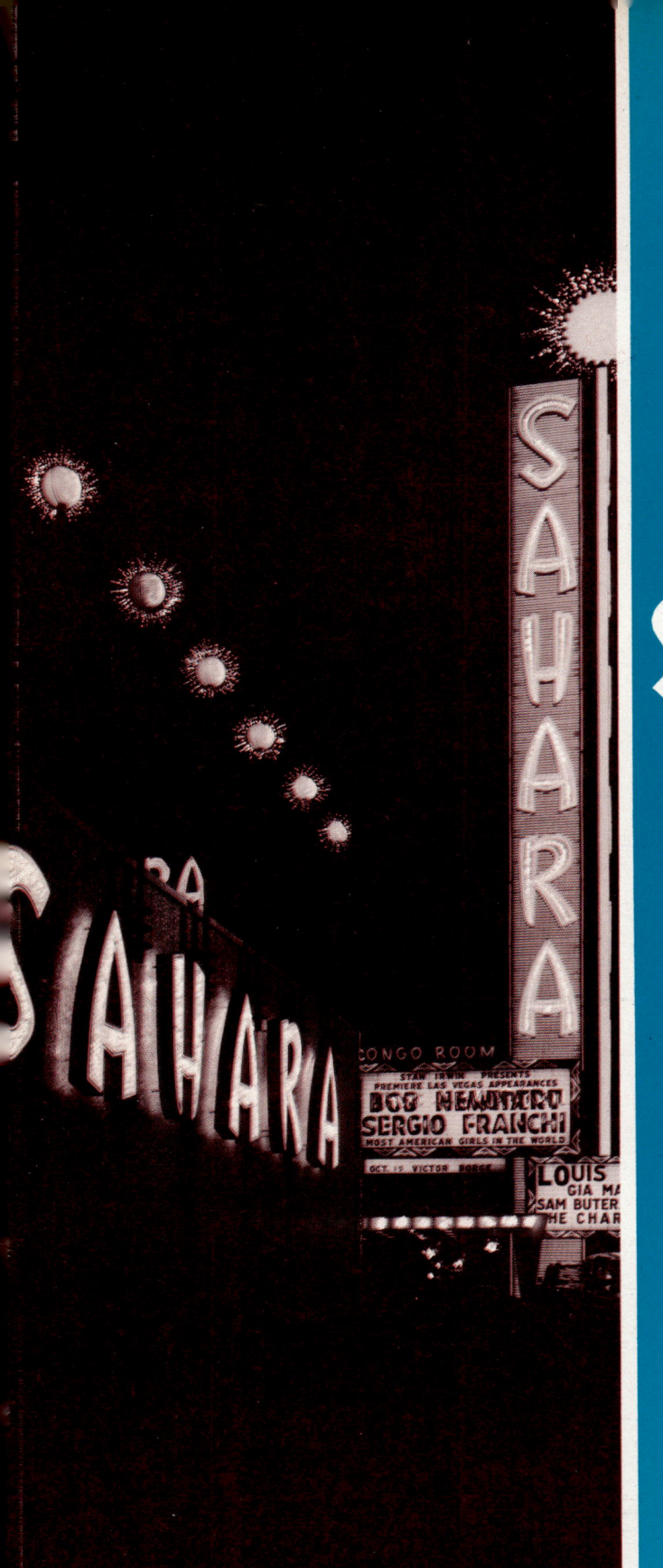

one of the wonders of the resort world

[ENJOY A GOLDEN WEBB OF HOSPITALITY]

In Las Vegas one hotel stands above the rest . . . It's the Spectacular Hotel Sahara . . . flagship of the Webb Hotels . . . the vacation wonder in the world's wonder city . . . now with 1,000 rooms and room for everybody! All this luxurious leisure . . . fun . . . relaxation . . . available at rates anyone can afford. Sun-swimming in three spacious pools . . . dining in three famous restaurants . . . star studded entertainment in two great showrooms. Shops, buffets, health club, golfing, riding, convention facilities for 10 to 1,600 persons — a real "Treasure of Pleasure" PLUS a visit downtown to the magnificent Mint and the Lucky Casino! It's the vacation visit of a lifetime!

PROPERTIES OF A DEL E. WEBB CORPORATION SUBSIDIARY

For fifty-eight years, C and H Sugar has had a major role in the economic growth and development of California and Hawaii ...two great western states.

California and Hawaiian Sugar Refining Corporation, Ltd.
and the 26 Cane Sugar Companies of Hawaii

DECISION
the conflicts of Harry Truman

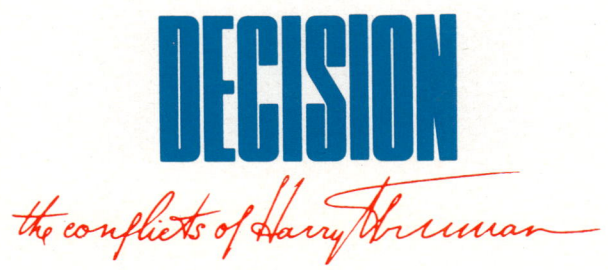

The major dramatic series of the 1964-65 television season.

In this series of dramatic half-hours, Mr. Truman becomes
the first President ever to participate in a series of television
dramatizations, disclosing his innermost thoughts
and conflicts at the time he made the most critical decisions of
his administration. This series, scheduled for
telecasting in cities from coast-to-coast commencing
November 10, 1964, is destined to make television history.

SCREEN GEMS

Why Do Tigers Wag Their Tails?

When you see a Flying Tiger Swing-tail-44 with its tail out of joint, you see the biggest cargo-loading threshold in captivity. Tiger's straight-in loading swallows your freight safely, economically, speedily. We call it "one-gulp" loading.

The Tiger's 6'9" high cargo hold is over two boxcar-lengths deep. If we can't get your outsize shipment on board, nobody can. Sideloaders just aren't of the same stripe when it comes to handling single units of large size.

Flying Tigers is the Airfreight Specialist that gets whatever you've got — or want — in, up, down and off according to your schedule.

For big, or little, airfreight shipments, track us down. This is the way your problems end, not with a whimper but a roar.

the airfreight specialist **FLYING TIGER LINE**

General Precision offers its established capabilities in research, development, systems management, and manufacturing around the world in the following major product categories: **navigation, guidance and control systems, simulators, computers, data processors, industrial controls.**

General Precision supports these operations from 15 plant locations in the United States and the network of facilities and licenses throughout the British Isles, Continental Europe and the Far East. General Precision, Inc., Tarrytown, New York — the principal operating subsidiary of General Precision Equipment Corporation.

GENERAL PRECISION AROUND THE WORLD

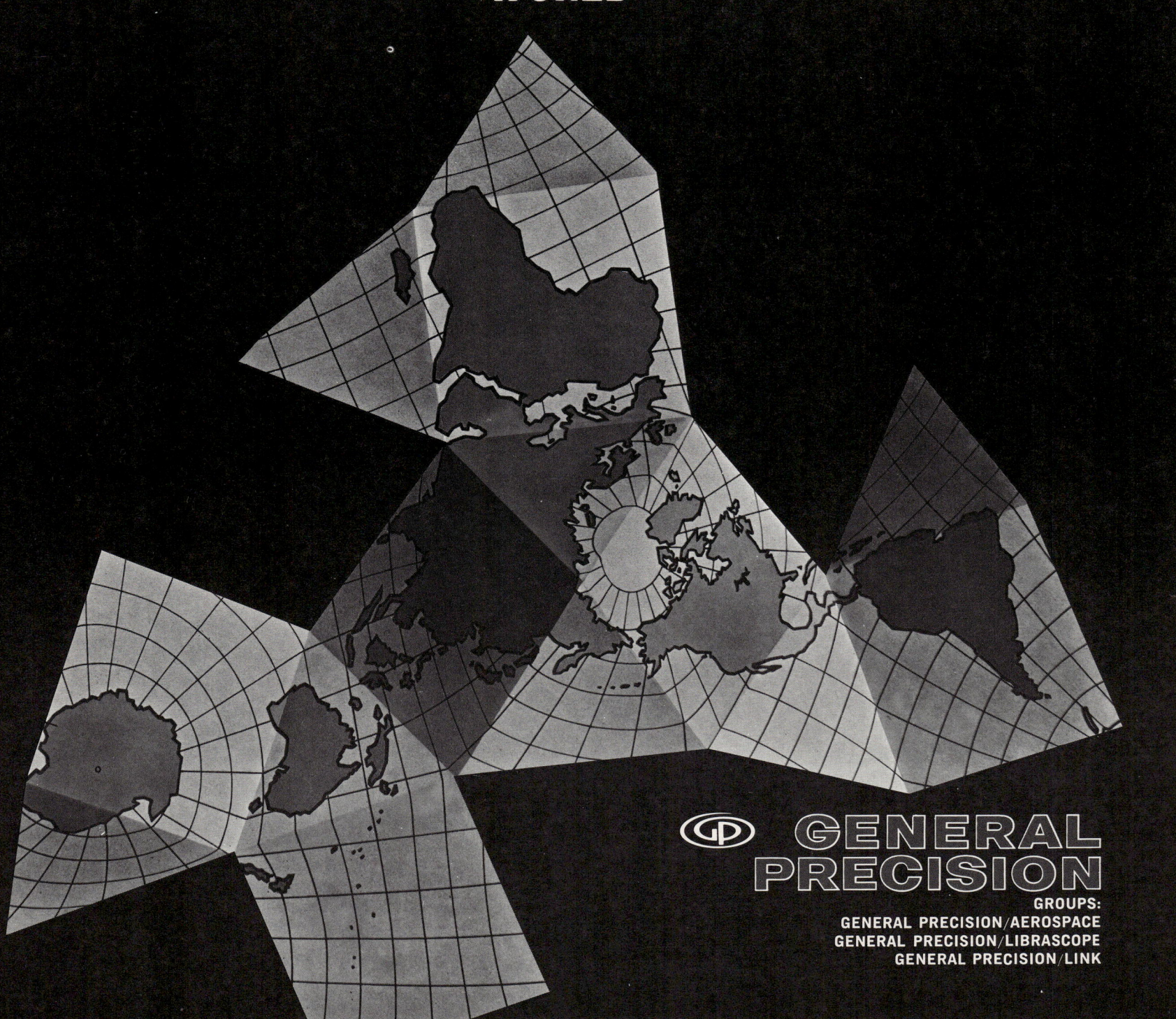

GENERAL PRECISION

GROUPS:
GENERAL PRECISION/AEROSPACE
GENERAL PRECISION/LIBRASCOPE
GENERAL PRECISION/LINK

What links an electronic systems company with a wire and cable firm, a beryllium fabricator, an instrument company, a packaging specialist, a components producer and distributor, and a toy manufacturer?

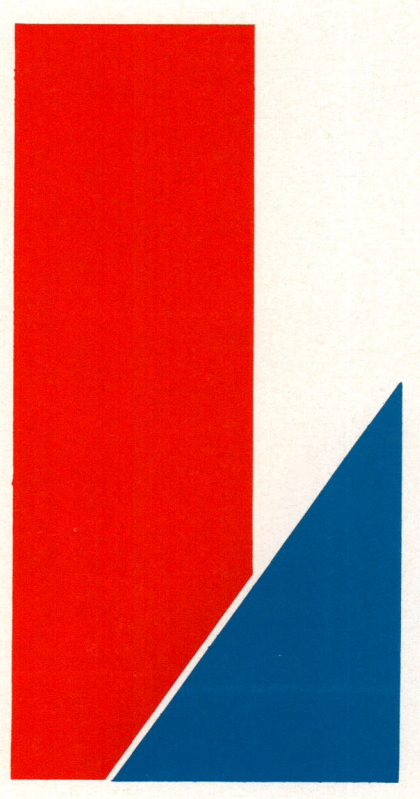

An efficient corporate management group with an eye for growth.

Loral Electronics Corporation CORPORATE HEADQUARTERS: 688 WHITE PLAINS ROAD, SCARSDALE, NEW YORK 10583

OPERATING ACTIVITIES: A&M INSTRUMENT: Long Island City, N. Y.; Englewood, N. J.; Chicago, Ill. (Electrical measuring instruments); ALPHA WIRE: New York, N. Y.; Holbrook, N. Y.; Union, N. J.; Torrance, Calif. (Wire, cable, and tubing; heat-shrinkable plastics); AMERICAN BERYLLIUM: Sarasota, Fla.; Inglewood, Calif. (Fabricated beryllium); AMERICAN METALS & CERAMICS: Bradenton, Fla.; The Bronx, N. Y. (Industrial ceramics); ARCO ELECTRONICS: Great Neck, N. Y.; Dallas, Texas; Los Angeles, Calif. (Electronic circuit elements: capacitors, connectors, transformers, diodes, relays); LERMER PACKAGING: Garwood, N. J. (Flexible and rigid plastic packaging products); LORAL ELECTRONIC SYSTEMS: The Bronx, N. Y. (Electronic systems for anti-submarine warfare, electronic warfare, navigation and display; oceanographic vehicles and equipment; microwave components); MULTIPLE PRODUCTS: The Bronx, N. Y. (Thermoformed, blow-moulded and injection-moulded plastic toys and playsets).

GILBERT SYSTEMS, INC.

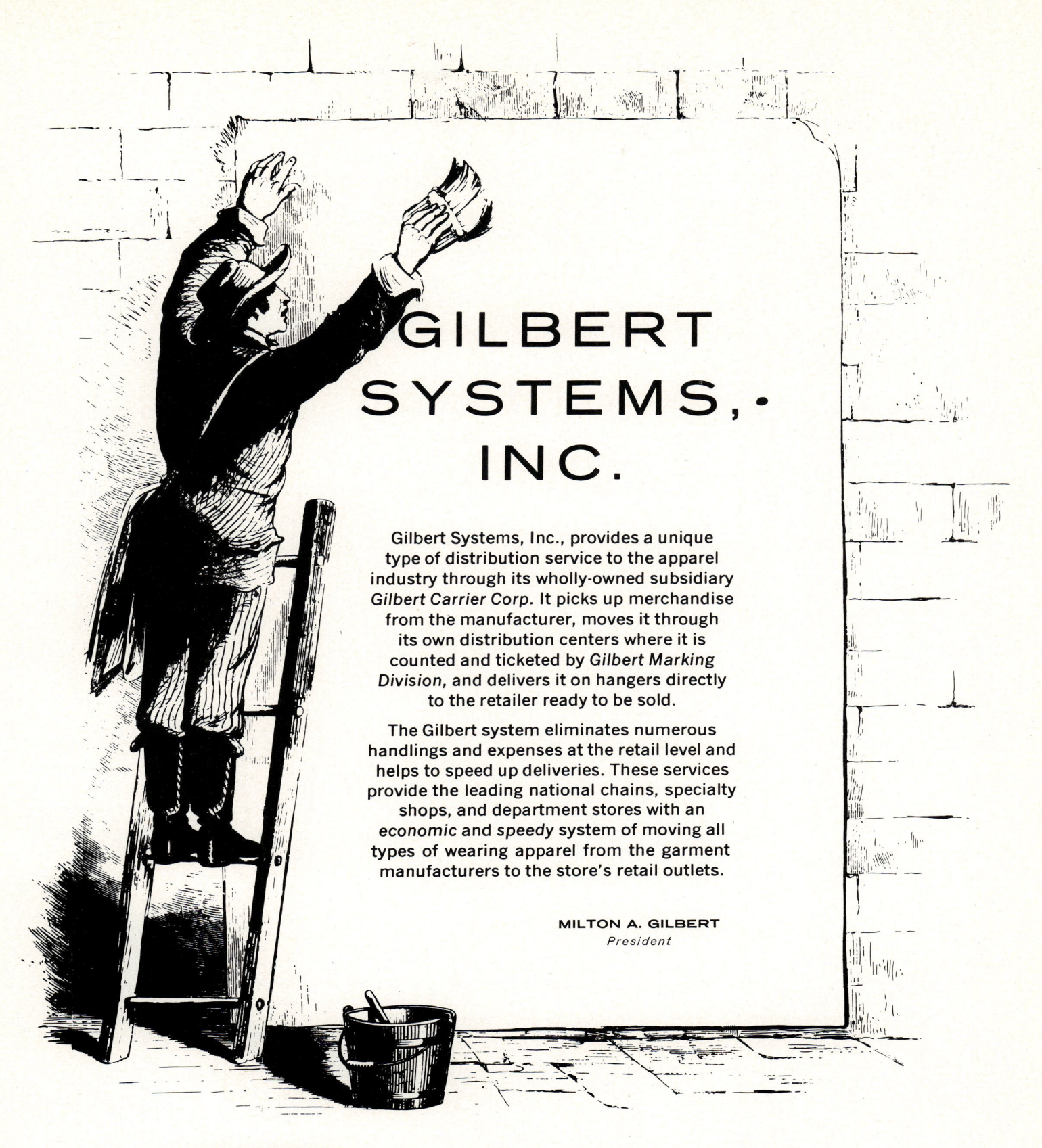

Gilbert Systems, Inc., provides a unique type of distribution service to the apparel industry through its wholly-owned subsidiary *Gilbert Carrier Corp.* It picks up merchandise from the manufacturer, moves it through its own distribution centers where it is counted and ticketed by *Gilbert Marking Division*, and delivers it on hangers directly to the retailer ready to be sold.

The Gilbert system eliminates numerous handlings and expenses at the retail level and helps to speed up deliveries. These services provide the leading national chains, specialty shops, and department stores with an *economic* and *speedy* system of moving all types of wearing apparel from the garment manufacturers to the store's retail outlets.

MILTON A. GILBERT
President

441 Ninth Avenue / New York, N.Y.
DISTRIBUTION CENTERS:
Cleveland-Akron, Ohio • Detroit-Grand Rapids, Mich. Chicago, Ill. • Milwaukee, Wis. • Minneapolis-St. Paul, Minn. • Los Angeles-San Diego, Calif. • Rochester, N.Y. San Francisco-Sacramento, Calif. • Atlanta, Ga. • Denver, Colo. • Dallas, Texas (To be opened December 1964)

Subsidiaries and Divisions: Gilbert Carrier Corp., New York Haulage Corp., Nelson Trucking Service, Inc., Gilbert Property Corp., Gilbert Marking Division, Gilbert Data Processing Division.

To The Delegates:

We salute this convention as an American institution—an offspring of our political genius.

In the development of its program and pageantry, our convention system has produced a succession of Chiefs of State, whose dedication, vision, and talent for national leadership is unsurpassed in the history of nations.

This is not to say that every American president has been a statesman of the first rank.

We have from time to time seated commonplace men in what is now the mightiest public office in the world.

But measured against the dire needs of our country in years of momentous crisis—domestic and international—the American system of selecting candidates for the highest office in the land has stood the test of internal change and world upheaval.

From the candidates presented to the people by the two great parties, the voters have chosen for their Presidents men who have achieved paramount influence in global affairs and won the affection of millions in the far corners of the earth.

Now we have come to a date in the annals of mankind when practically any important decision —any switch in policy—by the President of the United States is reflected in the world capitals—friendly or hostile—in both hemispheres.

It is apparent therefore that the delegates, whether they realize it or not, are carrying a somewhat awesome responsibility.

Tomorrow's history is an unwritten book. But any thoughtful American knows that unknown perils haunt the future and that his President has at his command a concentration of power never before in the hands of one man.

In contrast the delegate's power is transitory. His importance temporary. His moment of service brief. But he is a maker of history. In those few hectic hours at the convention, he shares in a decision which may write indelible pages in the chronicles of the greatest nation yet born and himself be a living witness to the effectiveness of the democratic process.

Call these times the Electronic Epoch, the Space Age or the Automation Era, yet they are but the creations of the minds of men.

Our delegates to the nominating conventions, many of them humble men in humble occupations, may also rendezvous with destiny. Each delegate may well ask himself: "By my vote for the party nominee, will I be launching a personality on the road to greatness and at the same time be maintaining the blessings of liberty for myself and my descendants?"

S. H. FABIAN
President

STANLEY WARNER CORPORATION
Presented as a public service

playtex — STANLEY WARNER THEATRES — TYLAC — Southern Latex — Isodine

sarong — WAST television — Morning Star Paisley — PHYSICIANS PRODUCTS

Executive Offices   1585 Broadway, New York 36; N. Y.

GROWTH COMPANY

The giant Redwood and the Douglas Fir are among the fastest-growing things on earth. Their seedlings will be 60 feet high in 20 years. So don't make the mistake of some newcomers and plant one in your front yard—a tree like this can literally grow you out of house and home.

But we at Georgia-Pacific are in the business of growing giant Redwoods and Firs as well as Pine, Hardwoods and other important kinds of timber. Today we plant 5 trees for every one we cut, and Georgia-Pacific's annual growth is considerably greater than its harvest.

This is great news for conservationists. It is equally great news for our stockholders. For example, Georgia-Pacific's total assets have grown from $205 million to $565 million in 7 years. And our growth program has already resulted in ownership of 2½ million acres of timber worth many, many times its cost.

This remarkable growth in our resources stems from sun, soil, water, time and management—magnificent business instruments when you know how to use them!

GEORGIA–PACIFIC / THE GROWTH COMPANY
Plywood · Paper · Chemicals · Natural Gas · Metallurgical Coal · Wood Products

"...ask not what your country can do for you...ask what you can do for your country."

You can help build a living memorial to John F. Kennedy

If you have been wishing there were some way you could pay a personal tribute to the memory of the late President, here is your opportunity. The American people are completing the project he was planning when he died, the John F. Kennedy Library, in Boston, Massachusetts.

The goal is $10,000,000. Thousands of donations, large and small, have already brought in $5,000,000. A national magazine gave the $75,000 profit from their memorial issue. A girl in Cincinnati sent Caroline $1 for her daddy's library which she had saved from her lunch money.

MORE THAN A LIBRARY. Presidential libraries were built by public or private subscription for Hoover, Roosevelt, Truman and Eisenhower. The priceless documents of each administration are collected there, and the libraries turned over to the American people for their use. John F. Kennedy wanted his library to be more than a museum, however. *As he envisioned it, it will also be a place where young people, scholars and administrators, will be inspired and trained to bring to public service the highest ideals and practical skills.*

If you want to help keep alive this dream for America that was John F. Kennedy's, you will want to give.

PUBLISHED AS A PUBLIC SERVICE BY: KEN RINKE and SID LEIKEN OF OREGON

Contributions will be acknowledged by Mrs. Kennedy. Your name will be recorded in the Great Book of Contributions, which will be on permanent display in the Library.

Honorary Chairman: LYNDON B. JOHNSON • Chairman: EUGENE BLACK • President: ROBERT F. KENNEDY • Vice President: MRS. JOHN F. KENNEDY

HOW TO GIVE. If you wish to contribute to the memorial building fund for the John F. Kennedy Library, fill out the coupon below and mail it with your donation. *All contributions are tax deductible.*

THE KENNEDY LIBRARY, Box 2500, Boston, Mass.

NAME_____

ADDRESS_____
_____
_____

DONATION_____

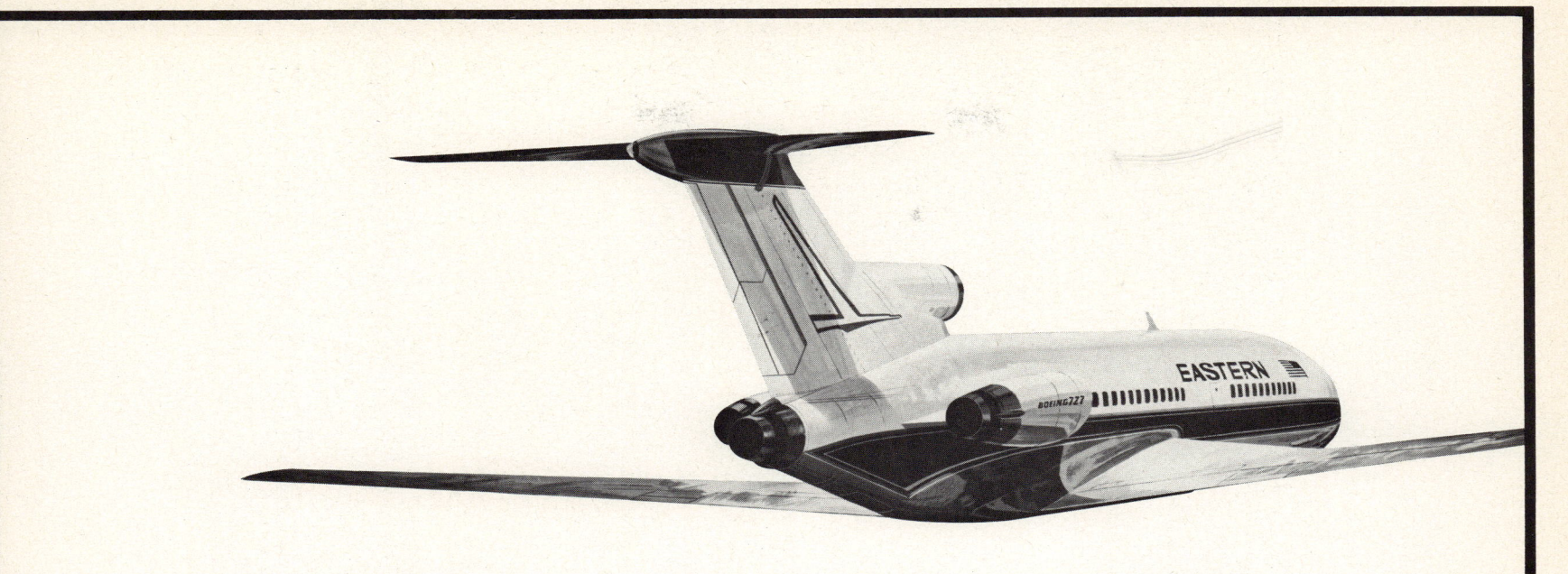

Shhh... there goes one of Eastern's new Whisperjets.

Whisperjet is a service mark of Eastern Air Lines, Inc.

Ever been aboard a plane like this? Gets off the ground quicker, back softer, is quieter than any other kind of jet airliner. It belongs to Eastern Air Lines.

Eastern

Shell's Dave Berry and Fred Schuette drove this highly modified 1924 coupe to a Mileage Marathon record.

How a Shell research team got 168.47 miles per gallon in an off-hours experiment

Some years ago a group of Shell scientists decided to see how many miles they could really get out of a gallon of gasoline. From their informal competition the first Shell Mileage Marathon grew. The all-time winner of this event was the team of Dave Berry and Fred Schuette. Their record: an astonishing 168.47 miles per gallon.

Berry and Schuette used a lot of tricks to set this record. Oversized wheels that drove them 9½ feet per revolution. Tires worn smooth and overinflated to cut friction. An "engine-on, engine-off" driving technique, accelerating to 20 miles an hour, cutting the engine and then re-starting when the speed dropped back to 5 miles an hour.

Of course, all these tricks are highly impractical or downright dangerous on public highways. Definitely *not* recommended.

One thing you can do for good mileage is to try Super Shell gasoline. One of Super Shell's ingredients is noted for good mileage. It is called Platformate. Platformate can release more energy per gallon than the finest 100 octane aviation gasoline. In your car this energy becomes good mileage. It's a good thing to remember next time you need gasoline.

At work and after hours, Shell scientists are forever learning more about cars and gasoline. And how to make them work better together—for you.

SEE AMERICA BEST—BY CAR

GIIIIID

AIRCRAFT
SPACE VEHICLES
SUBMARINES
MISSILES
ELECTRONICS
NUCLEAR REACTORS
INDUSTRIAL EQUIPMENT

GENERAL DYNAMICS CORPORATION

AMERICANS EVERYWHERE CAN ENJOY THE GOOD LIFE

AND SAVE TIME, MONEY AND ENERGY WITH

SPIEGEL CATALOGS

*it takes top candidates
and top issues...
it also takes money!*

POLITICAL SUCCESS BEGINS AT THE GRASS ROOTS...

Aerojet-General has pioneered a Good Citizenship Program that brings results and we recommend it to other companies and to the leaders of both political parties.

The Aerojet program is simplicity itself—we just ask *all* our employees to voluntarily contribute to the party or candidates of their choice. This is how they have answered the call:

	1958	1960	1962
Total Employee Contributions	$25,000	$60,000	$97,000
Average Per Employee	$2.30	$3.20	$4.00
Employees Contributing	(11,000 out of 16,000)	(21,000 out of 27,000)	(25,000 out of 33,000)
Percentage of Employee Participation	70%	81%	74%

During each of the last two campaigns, approximately 5000 employees were registered as voters by Deputy Registrars working at our plants and major candidates for State and National offices appeared at rallies held after hours in our plant cafeterias.

We have prepared a booklet and a 10-minute sound film on the Aerojet program. Both are available on application to Public Relations Department, Aerojet-General Corp., El Monte, California.

AEROJET-GENERAL CORPORATION

A Subsidiary of The General Tire & Rubber Co.

Six space-age projects at Republic Aviation
(190,000,000 Americans get the fringe benefits)

Among hundreds underway at Republic, here are just six projects, in the biggest scientific push the world has ever seen. Each has a specific goal. And each is also generating an unsought bounty of new ideas and products and by-products and facts. In short: the scientific "fallout" of the space effort is certainly going to make life easier—and longer—for every one of us. And it may even change our fundamental notions about such things as food, clothing and shelter.

Example. The general goal of our Life Science Labs at Republic is to find ways of maintaining life in outer space. (A recent task: materials evaluation and ventilation tests on pressure suits to provide information for development of the Apollo Space Suit, under contract to International Latex Corp., developer, and Hamilton Standard, NASA's prime contractor. The glove suggests the suit's construction; the gesture indicates the tests' results.)

Our life-science people are also developing a vest system to provide medical information on pilots during flight. The same principle, and similar equipment, is already being used in hospitals, to permit nurses to monitor patients from a central location.

Monitoring a celestial body—the sun—is the goal of another current Republic project. We're doing development work on AOSO (Advanced Orbiting Solar Observatory), a satellite that will go outside the earth's atmosphere, study the sun, and move us closer to the day when we can predict the sun's effects on our weather, our communications, our expeditions into outer space. There will be expeditions into hydrospace, too: by U.S.S. Dolphin, among others. She will be the Navy's newest and deepest-diving experimental sub. And when she goes deep, Dolphin will be controlled by a steering and diving system designed and built by Republic's Hydrospace Division. Her goal: to probe the vast, and largely unknown, oceans...a virtually untapped source of energy and mineral wealth.

For those who travel on the surface (amphibious troops, for example) we are working on a remarkable craft that sails above the bounding main. It's an air-cushion vehicle, developed by Vickers of Great Britain. A future craft may look something like this, and be capable of carrying 90 passengers at speeds above 60 knots. Air cushion vehicles have already been licensed for passenger service in England. Fast commute, anyone?

Faster and even more versatile vehicles may soon emerge from our Advanced Development Objective-12 study contract for V/STOL weapon systems. V/STOL planes take off and land vertically like helicopters but can fly at supersonic speeds. Variable-geometry wings fold out for slow speeds, fold back for the supersonic ranges. Combined, they could mean new military versatility... and could be the precursor of some extraordinary jetliners (and probably some very small jetports!)

Finally, our "care" packages. They contain parts for NASA's Saturn Booster, and they're handled with speed, as well as care. On these and other space-vehicle projects, we've occasionally had to develop completely new materials, and then work out new techniques for machining them. You may see these materials some day in lightweight auto engines, or in furniture, or building materials...right here on Earth...or somewhere else...

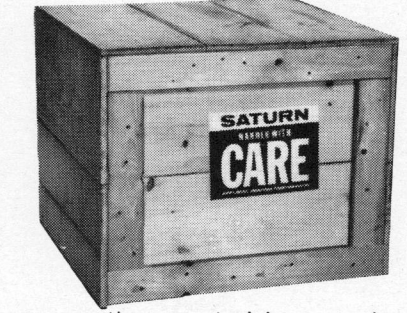

REPUBLIC AVIATION CORPORATION.
Farmingdale, L. I., New York.

The secret is out...
(about oil...and how to get more)

The exciting facts about Thermo-Flood® are now spreading throughout the oil industry to majors and independents alike. Thermo-Flood®...the most superior equipment ever built for steam injection secondary oil recovery.

Struthers Wells, leaders in oil field equipment developments for over a hundred years, is now ready to deliver in eight weeks.

Write or call Mr. A. M. Michell today for a brochure and details about delivery... consultation services...and portable equipment.

Struthers Wells Corporation

International Sales Agent: Struthers Scientific and International Corporation

Corporate offices: 630 Fifth Avenue, New York 20, N.Y.

In the fields of · Petroleum · Chemicals · Power · Petro-chemicals

Producers of · Nuclear Marine Propulsion Components · Nuclear Power Generation Equipment · Steam Generating Equipment · Heat Recovery Equipment · High Pressure Vessels · Heat Exchangers · Distillation Equipment · Sea water conversion · Freeze concentration of foods · Crystallizers and Evaporators

> See how desalination of sea water can help solve the world's water shortage problems. Visit a working model of a Struthers-Umano Freeze Desalination plant at the American Chemical Society Exhibit in the Hall of Science at the New York World's Fair.

UNIVERSITY NURSING HOME / Washington, D. C.

WESTHAMPTON NURSING HOME / Westhampton, L.I., N.Y.

Ross Nursing Home—Sands Point Nursing Home
Westhampton Nursing Home
University Nursing Home
Mosholu Parkway Nursing Home

Forest Green Park Cemeteries /

EXECUTIVE OFFICES:
515 Madison Ave.
New York 22, New York

NEW YORK TELEPHONE NUMBER
212 Plaza 9-5223

How many times will you vote today?

Under our American *political* system you get a chance to vote in our national elections every two years. Under our American *economic* system you vote many times *each day* — every time you make a purchase.

No one can calculate the number of individual purchases—from groceries to gasoline—that are made in this country each day. But we know they must far exceed 700 million. (By contrast, even an election as vital as our presidential election is expected to draw less than 70 million votes this year.)

This infinitely complex process of voting — by buying or not buying the goods and services offered in our free market — is a wonderfully democratic mechanism. It continually registers the ever-changing needs and wishes of all the people in the country — directing what should be produced, at what price, and in what quantities.

The curling iron gives way to the home permanent; the celluloid collar is replaced by the wash-and-wear shirt; not because of any governmental edict, but simply because the American people "vote" them in and out of existence.

Ironically, communism and socialism — which purport to be "economic systems of the masses"— are the least democratic of all. The people have little opportunity to "vote" on what they want. Instead, a central authority determines for them what shall be produced, how much, and where it will be distributed.

In this country the "private segment" of our economy (which accounts for 4/5 of our Gross National Product) is literally and truly directed by the "votes" of the people. For that reason U.S. capitalism is the most democratic institution the world has ever known.

UNION OIL COMPANY OF CALIFORNIA 76

MANUFACTURERS OF SUPER-ROYAL TRITON, THE AMAZING PURPLE MOTOR OIL

FPE

growth through creative energy

A COMPLETE LINE OF
ELECTRICAL CONTROL,
DISTRIBUTION, AND
POWER EQUIPMENT

FOR HOMES, INDUSTRIAL PLANTS,
UTILITY SYSTEMS, AND COMMERCIAL
OR INSTITUTIONAL BUILDINGS

FEDERAL PACIFIC ELECTRIC COMPANY
General Headquarters: Fifty Paris Street, Newark, New Jersey

STAB-LOK® CIRCUIT BREAKER LOAD CENTERS • FUSIBLE SERVICE EQUIPMENT • FUSES
SAFETY SWITCHES • ELECTRICAL HEATING EQUIPMENT • INDUSTRIAL CIRCUIT BREAKERS
PANELBOARDS • SWITCHBOARDS • MOTOR CONTROLS • MOTOR CONTROL CENTERS
CAPACITORS • BUS DUCT • SWITCHGEAR • SUBSTATIONS • TRANSFORMERS

BUSINESS PLANES (ABOVE) DEPEND ON RELIABLE LYCOMING ENGINES (BELOW)

Offices in the air

More than 40,000 aircraft are now used for business flying in this country. Engines from Avco's Lycoming Division today power more twin-engined planes for executive and utility uses than those of any other manufacturer. Leading executive aircraft manufacturers depend on Lycoming engines for reliability, operating economy, and lower maintenance.

Avco

UNUSUAL CAREER OPPORTUNITIES FOR QUALIFIED SCIENTISTS AND ENGINEERS...REGARDLESS OF RACE, CREED, COLOR OR NATIONAL ORIGIN...WRITE AVCO TODAY. AVCO CORPORATION, 750 THIRD AVENUE, NEW YORK 17, NEW YORK

Meet your friends at the Coca-Cola Tower at the World's Fair

COPYRIGHT © 1964, THE COCA-COLA COMPANY. "COCA-COLA" AND "COKE" ARE REGISTERED TRADE-MARKS WHICH IDENTIFY ONLY THE PRODUCT OF THE COCA-COLA COMPANY.

You'll go better refreshed. Coca-Cola, cold and crisp...gives that special zing...refreshes best.

things go better with Coke

Drink Coca-Cola

1964 Democratic National Convention Program

August 24-27
Convention Hall
Atlantic City, New Jersey

DEMOCRATIC NATIONAL COMMITTEE OFFICERS

John M. Bailey,
Chairman
Mrs. Margaret Price,
Vice-Chairman
Richard Maguire,
Treasurer
Mrs. Dorothy Vredenburgh Bush,
Secretary

1964 CONVENTION STAFF

J. Leonard Reinsch,
Executive Director
Samuel C. Brightman,
Publicity Director
Jack F. Christie,
Radio-Television Coordinator
George O'Gorman,
Transportation Director
Marvin Watson,
Housing Director
Gloria Cee Klein,
Assistant to Convention Director
Frank McCue,
Manager
Convention Hall
John Pitale,
Assistant to Manager,
Convention Hall
Miss Mary Kerey,
Convention Hall Manager's office

DEMOCRATIC CONGRESSIONAL CAMPAIGN COMMITTEE OFFICERS

Hon. Michael J. Kirwan,
Chairman
Kenneth R. Harding,
Assistant to the Chairman
Edmund L. Henshaw,
Research Director

DEMOCRATIC SENATORIAL CAMPAIGN COMMITTEE OFFICERS

Hon. Warren G. Magnuson,
Chairman
Hon. Hubert H. Humphrey,
Vice-Chairman
Frederick J. Lordan,
Secretary
Alwyn F. Matthews,
Executive Director
Isabelle M. Peterson,
Executive Secretary

YOUNG DEMOCRATIC CLUBS OF AMERICA
Official Youth Organization of the Democratic Party

J. Albert House, Jr.,
National President
Roanoke Rapids, North Carolina
Ed Rosewell,
First Vice-President
Northfield, Ohio
Alice McMahon,
Vice-President
Maitland, Florida

Ken Lester,
College Vice-President
Washington, D.C.
Edwin Kruse,
Secretary
Chatham, New Jersey
Mary Kennedy,
Treasurer
Hartford, Connecticut

Allen Hoffard,
Chairman of Board,
Regional Directors
Washington, D.C.
Don Hamilton,
General Counsel
Oklahoma City, Oklahoma
Frederick A. Ricci,
Executive Secretary
Washington, D.C.

NEW JERSEY DEMOCRATIC STATE COMMITTEE

ATLANTIC
Irving L. Jacobs
Mrs. Janet Perrella
BERGEN
Carmine T. Perrapato
Mrs. Marie N. Buxton
BURLINGTON
Dr. Charles H. Ehrlich
Mrs. Eleanor M. Pall
CAMDEN
Alexander Feinberg
Mrs. Cecelia L. Jackson
CAPE MAY
Carlton E. Mason
Mrs. Frances E. Goetz
CUMBERLAND
Allie J. Fralinger
Mrs. Thelma P. Sharp
ESSEX
Harry Lerner
Mrs. Mae Mead Mazza

GLOUCESTER
Joseph L. Bowe
Mrs. Jennie LaPorta
HUDSON
John M. Deegan
Mrs. Alice M. Dolan
HUNTERDON
Rudolph Wishy
Mrs. Eva Kostik
MERCER
Walter A. Schoeller
Miss Margaret B. Holmes
MIDDLESEX
Christian J. Jorgenson
Mrs. Catherine K. Jamieson
MONMOUTH
Paul Kiernan, Sr.
Mrs. Katherine E. White
MORRIS
E. Marco Stirone
Miss Agnes L. Glaab

OCEAN
James W. Farrell
Mrs. Mary C. Lee
PASSAIC
Joseph V. McGuire
Mrs. Helen Casey Rodgers
SALEM
Henry Young
Mrs. Alice M. Diamond
SOMERSET
Charles W. Engelhard
Mrs. Matilda E. Woerner
SUSSEX
Al Richard
Mrs. Laura Ward
UNION
William G. Dowd, Jr.
Mrs. Jean Krulish
WARREN
William H. Blackton
Mrs. Lillie B. Frankenfield

THORN LORD
Chairman
EDWARD G. WILMS
Executive Director
JUSTUS C. HIGHAM
Secretary

COOPERATING INDUSTRIES

Associated Railroads of New Jersey
Newark, New Jersey

Atlantic City Racing Commission
Atlantic City, New Jersey

Bamberger's
Newark, New Jersey

Bankers National Life
Insurance Company
Montclair, New Jersey

Beneficial Finance Company
Morristown, New Jersey

Bristol-Myers Company
New York, New York

Broad Street National Bank
Trenton, New Jersey

California Oil Co.
Perth Amboy, New Jersey

Central Home Trust Company
Elizabeth, New Jersey

CIBA Pharmaceutical Co.
Summit, New Jersey

E. I. Du Pont de Nemours and Co.
Wilmington, Delaware

Elastic Stop Nut Corp.
Union, New Jersey

First Trenton National Bank
Trenton, New Jersey

Ford Motor Co.
Detroit, Michigan

Garden State Race Track
Camden, New Jersey

Grand Union Company
East Paterson, New Jersey

Gulf Oil Corp.
Pittsburgh, Pennsylvania

Hoffmann-LaRoche, Inc.
Nutley, New Jersey

ITT Federal Laboratories
Nutley, New Jersey

Monmouth Park Jockey Club
Oceanport, New Jersey

Mutual Benefit Life Insurance Co.
Newark, New Jersey

National Newark and Essex Bank
Newark, New Jersey

New Jersey Brewers Assn.
Newark, New Jersey

New Jersey Manufacturing Corp.
Trenton, New Jersey

New Jersey Natural Gas Company
Asbury Park, New Jersey

New Jersey Wine & Spirits
Wholesale Association
Newark, New Jersey

Phelps Dodge Corporation
New York, New York

Ronson Corporation
Woodbridge, New Jersey

Schering Corporation
Bloomfield, Illinois

Sealand Services, Inc.
Elizabeth, New Jersey

Socony-Mobil Oil Co., Inc.
New York, New York

E. R. Squibb
New Brunswick, New Jersey

Standard Oil Company (New Jersey)
New York, New York

Suburban Propane Gas Company
Whippany, New Jersey

Sun Oil Company
Philadelphia, Pennsylvania

Transcontinental Gas Pipe Line Corp.
Houston, Texas

United States Steel Corporation
Washington, D.C.

Warner-Lambert Pharmaceutical Co.
Morris Plains, New Jersey

Wigton-Abbott Corporation
Plainfield, New Jersey

Worthington Corporation
Harrison, New Jersey

WOMEN'S ACTIVITIES
Mrs. Richard J. Hughes
Mrs. Thelma P. Sharp

HOSPITALITY
Richard V. Mulligan

PRESIDENT'S BIRTHDAY PARTY
St. John Terrell
Mrs. Richard Switlik

HEALTH & WELFARE
Dr. Gene Shrader

YOUNG DEMOCRATS
John F. Geaney, Jr.

JERSEY JOHNSON GIRLS
Janet Perrella

NEW JERSEY HOST COMMITTEE

Honorary Chairman
Honorable Richard J. Hughes,
Governor of New Jersey
Trenton, New Jersey

Chairman
Charles W. Engelhard,
Chairman and President
Engelhard Industries, Inc.
Newark, New Jersey

Treasurer
James C. Kellogg, III,
Spear, Leeds and Kellogg
New York, New York

Executive Director
Robert J. Burkhardt,
Secretary of State
Trenton, New Jersey

John Adams,
President-Publisher
Press Publishing Company
Atlantic City, New Jersey

Joseph Altman,
Mayor of Atlantic City
Atlantic City, New Jersey

Carl W. Badenhausen,
President
P. Ballantine & Sons
Newark, New Jersey

Alfred H. Beadleston,
Speaker, New Jersey State Assembly
Red Bank, New Jersey

Orville E. Beal,
President
The Prudential Insurance Company
 of America
Newark, New Jersey

William S. Beinecke,
President
The Sperry & Hutchinson Company
New York, New York

T. Roland Berner,
Chairman and President
Curtiss-Wright Corporation
Wood-Ridge, New Jersey

Robert G. Clarkson,
President
Carteret Savings and Loan Association
Newark, New Jersey

Robert S. Conahay, III,
"Stagmont"
Hackettstown, New Jersey

John T. Connor,
President
Merck & Co., Inc.
Rahway, New Jersey

Bishop Fred Pierce Corson,
President
World Methodist Council,
The Methodist Church
Philadelphia, Pennsylvania

J. Edward Crabiel,
Minority Leader, New Jersey
State Assembly
Milltown, New Jersey

H. Joseph Curry,
Vice President
New Jersey Bankers Association
The Phillipsburg National Bank & Trust Co.
Phillipsburg, New Jersey

C. Malcolm Davis,
President
The Fidelity Union Trust Company
Newark, New Jersey

J. H. Davis,
President
Stevens Institute of Technology
Hoboken, New Jersey

Fairleigh S. Dickinson, Jr.,
President
Becton, Dickinson & Company
East Rutherford, New Jersey

Most Reverend John J. Dougherty,
President
Seton Hall University
South Orange, New Jersey

Alfred E. Driscoll,
President
Warner-Lambert Pharmaceutical Company
Morris Plains, New Jersey

Mrs. Walter E. Edge,
Princeton, New Jersey

Frank S. Farley,
New Jersey State Senator, Atlantic County
Atlantic City, New Jersey

Malcolm S. Forbes,
Editor-in-Chief & Publisher
Forbes, Inc.
New York, New York

Robert F. Goheen,
President
Princeton University
Princeton, New Jersey

Frederick H. Groel,
President
New Jersey State Chamber of Commerce
Newark, New Jersey

Mason W. Gross,
President
Rutgers—The State University
New Brunswick, New Jersey

Anthony J. Grossi,
Minority Leader, New Jersey State Senate
Paterson, New Jersey

James P. Hayward,
President
Atlantic City Electric Company
Atlantic City, New Jersey

Carlton E. Heritage,
President
New Jersey Farm Bureau
Trenton, New Jersey

Leon Hess,
President
Hess Oil & Chemical Corp.
Perth Amboy, New Jersey

Joel R. Jacobson,
President
New Jersey Independent Union Council,
AFL-CIO
Newark, New Jersey

Leonard C. Johnson,
President
New Jersey Manufacturers Association
Trenton, New Jersey

Robert W. Johnson,
Johnson & Johnson
New Brunswick, New Jersey

Theodore H. Kendall,
President
South Jersey Gas Company
Atlantic City, New Jersey

Elwood F. Kirkman,
President
The Boardwalk National Bank
Atlantic City, New Jersey

Kenneth H. Klipstein,
President
American Cyanamid Company
Wayne, New Jersey

John W. Kress,
President
The Howard Savings Institution
Newark, New Jersey

Mrs. Morgan F. Larson,
Metuchen, New Jersey

Philip J. Levin,
President
Philip J. Levin & Affiliated Companies
North Plainfield, New Jersey

Thorn Lord,
State Chairman
New Jersey Democratic State Committee
Trenton, New Jersey

Donald C. Luce,
President
Public Service Electric and Gas Company
Newark, New Jersey

William H. McElwain,
President
New Jersey Power & Light Company
Morristown, New Jersey

Robert B. Meyner,
Former Governor of New Jersey
Newark, New Jersey

Charles J. Milton,
Milton, Keane & DeBona
Jersey City, New Jersey

Mrs. A. Harry Moore,
Jersey City, New Jersey

Franklin C. Nixon,
Master
New Jersey State Grange
Vincentown, New Jersey

Rabbi Joachim Prinz,
President
American Jewish Congress
Newark, New Jersey

Robert A. Roe,
Commissioner of Conservation and
 Economic Development
Trenton, New Jersey

Mrs. Mary G. Roebling,
President
Trenton Trust Company
Trenton, New Jersey

Vincent Salierno, President
Victory Optical Manufacturing Company
Newark, New Jersey

Peter Sammartino,
President
Fairleigh Dickinson University
Rutherford, New Jersey

Charles W. Sandman, Jr.,
President, New Jersey State Senate
Cape May, New Jersey

1964 Democratic National Convention Program

August 24-27 Convention Hall Atlantic City, New Jersey

DEMOCRATIC NATIONAL COMMITTEE OFFICERS

John M. Bailey,
Chairman
Mrs. Margaret Price,
Vice-Chairman
Richard Maguire,
Treasurer
Mrs. Dorothy Vredenburgh Bush,
Secretary

1964 CONVENTION STAFF

J. Leonard Reinsch,
Executive Director
Samuel C. Brightman,
Publicity Director
Jack F. Christie,
Radio-Television Coordinator
George O'Gorman,
Transportation Director
Marvin Watson,
Housing Director
Gloria Cee Klein,
Assistant to Convention Director
Frank McCue,
Manager
Convention Hall
John Pitale,
Assistant to Manager,
Convention Hall
Miss Mary Kerey,
Convention Hall Manager's office

DEMOCRATIC CONGRESSIONAL CAMPAIGN COMMITTEE OFFICERS

Hon. Michael J. Kirwan,
Chairman
Kenneth R. Harding,
Assistant to the Chairman
Edmund L. Henshaw,
Research Director

DEMOCRATIC SENATORIAL CAMPAIGN COMMITTEE OFFICERS

Hon. Warren G. Magnuson,
Chairman
Hon. Hubert H. Humphrey,
Vice-Chairman
Frederick J. Lordan,
Secretary
Alwyn F. Matthews,
Executive Director
Isabelle M. Peterson,
Executive Secretary

YOUNG DEMOCRATIC CLUBS OF AMERICA
Official Youth Organization of the Democratic Party

J. Albert House, Jr.,
National President
Roanoke Rapids, North Carolina

Ed Rosewell,
First Vice-President
Northfield, Ohio

Alice McMahon,
Vice-President
Maitland, Florida

Ken Lester,
College Vice-President
Washington, D.C.

Edwin Kruse,
Secretary
Chatham, New Jersey

Mary Kennedy,
Treasurer
Hartford, Connecticut

Allen Hoffard,
Chairman of Board,
Regional Directors
Washington, D.C.

Don Hamilton,
General Counsel
Oklahoma City, Oklahoma

Frederick A. Ricci,
Executive Secretary
Washington, D.C.

NEW JERSEY DEMOCRATIC STATE COMMITTEE

ATLANTIC
Irving L. Jacobs
Mrs. Janet Perrella

BERGEN
Carmine T. Perrapato
Mrs. Marie N. Buxton

BURLINGTON
Dr. Charles H. Ehrlich
Mrs. Eleanor M. Pall

CAMDEN
Alexander Feinberg
Mrs. Cecelia L. Jackson

CAPE MAY
Carlton E. Mason
Mrs. Frances E. Goetz

CUMBERLAND
Allie J. Fralinger
Mrs. Thelma P. Sharp

ESSEX
Harry Lerner
Mrs. Mae Mead Mazza

GLOUCESTER
Joseph L. Bowe
Mrs. Jennie LaPorta

HUDSON
John M. Deegan
Mrs. Alice M. Dolan

HUNTERDON
Rudolph Wishy
Mrs. Eva Kostik

MERCER
Walter A. Schoeller
Miss Margaret B. Holmes

MIDDLESEX
Christian J. Jorgenson
Mrs. Catherine K. Jamieson

MONMOUTH
Paul Kiernan, Sr.
Mrs. Katherine E. White

MORRIS
E. Marco Stirone
Miss Agnes L. Glaab

OCEAN
James W. Farrell
Mrs. Mary C. Lee

PASSAIC
Joseph V. McGuire
Mrs. Helen Casey Rodgers

SALEM
Henry Young
Mrs. Alice M. Diamond

SOMERSET
Charles W. Engelhard
Mrs. Matilda E. Woerner

SUSSEX
Al Richard
Mrs. Laura Ward

UNION
William G. Dowd, Jr.
Mrs. Jean Krulish

WARREN
William H. Blackton
Mrs. Lillie B. Frankenfield

THORN LORD
Chairman

EDWARD G. WILMS
Executive Director

JUSTUS C. HIGHAM
Secretary

COOPERATING INDUSTRIES

Associated Railroads of New Jersey
Newark, New Jersey

Atlantic City Racing Commission
Atlantic City, New Jersey

Bamberger's
Newark, New Jersey

Bankers National Life
Insurance Company
Montclair, New Jersey

Beneficial Finance Company
Morristown, New Jersey

Bristol-Myers Company
New York, New York

Broad Street National Bank
Trenton, New Jersey

California Oil Co.
Perth Amboy, New Jersey

Central Home Trust Company
Elizabeth, New Jersey

CIBA Pharmaceutical Co.
Summit, New Jersey

E. I. Du Pont de Nemours and Co.
Wilmington, Delaware

Elastic Stop Nut Corp.
Union, New Jersey

First Trenton National Bank
Trenton, New Jersey

Ford Motor Co.
Detroit, Michigan

Garden State Race Track
Camden, New Jersey

Grand Union Company
East Paterson, New Jersey

Gulf Oil Corp.
Pittsburgh, Pennsylvania

Hoffmann-LaRoche, Inc.
Nutley, New Jersey

ITT Federal Laboratories
Nutley, New Jersey

Monmouth Park Jockey Club
Oceanport, New Jersey

Mutual Benefit Life Insurance Co.
Newark, New Jersey

National Newark and Essex Bank
Newark, New Jersey

New Jersey Brewers Assn.
Newark, New Jersey

New Jersey Manufacturing Corp.
Trenton, New Jersey

New Jersey Natural Gas Company
Asbury Park, New Jersey

New Jersey Wine & Spirits
Wholesale Association
Newark, New Jersey

Phelps Dodge Corporation
New York, New York

Ronson Corporation
Woodbridge, New Jersey

Schering Corporation
Bloomfield, Illinois

Sealand Services, Inc.
Elizabeth, New Jersey

Socony-Mobil Oil Co., Inc.
New York, New York

E. R. Squibb
New Brunswick, New Jersey

Standard Oil Company (New Jersey)
New York, New York

Suburban Propane Gas Company
Whippany, New Jersey

Sun Oil Company
Philadelphia, Pennsylvania

Transcontinental Gas Pipe Line Corp.
Houston, Texas

United States Steel Corporation
Washington, D.C.

Warner-Lambert Pharmaceutical Co.
Morris Plains, New Jersey

Wigton-Abbott Corporation
Plainfield, New Jersey

Worthington Corporation
Harrison, New Jersey

WOMEN'S ACTIVITIES
Mrs. Richard J. Hughes
Mrs. Thelma P. Sharp

HOSPITALITY
Richard V. Mulligan

PRESIDENT'S BIRTHDAY PARTY
St. John Terrell
Mrs. Richard Switlik

HEALTH & WELFARE
Dr. Gene Shrader

YOUNG DEMOCRATS
John F. Geaney, Jr.

JERSEY JOHNSON GIRLS
Janet Perrella

NEW JERSEY HOST COMMITTEE

Honorary Chairman
Honorable Richard J. Hughes,
Governor of New Jersey
Trenton, New Jersey

Chairman
Charles W. Engelhard,
Chairman and President
Engelhard Industries, Inc.
Newark, New Jersey

Treasurer
James C. Kellogg, III,
Spear, Leeds and Kellogg
New York, New York

Executive Director
Robert J. Burkhardt,
Secretary of State
Trenton, New Jersey

John Adams,
President-Publisher
Press Publishing Company
Atlantic City, New Jersey

Joseph Altman,
Mayor of Atlantic City
Atlantic City, New Jersey

Carl W. Badenhausen,
President
P. Ballantine & Sons
Newark, New Jersey

Alfred H. Beadleston,
Speaker, New Jersey State Assembly
Red Bank, New Jersey

Orville E. Beal,
President
The Prudential Insurance Company
  of America
Newark, New Jersey

William S. Beinecke,
President
The Sperry & Hutchinson Company
New York, New York

T. Roland Berner,
Chairman and President
Curtiss-Wright Corporation
Wood-Ridge, New Jersey

Robert G. Clarkson,
President
Carteret Savings and Loan Association
Newark, New Jersey

Robert S. Conahay, III,
"Stagmont"
Hackettstown, New Jersey

John T. Connor,
President
Merck & Co., Inc.
Rahway, New Jersey

Bishop Fred Pierce Corson,
President
World Methodist Council,
The Methodist Church
Philadelphia, Pennsylvania

J. Edward Crabiel,
Minority Leader, New Jersey
State Assembly
Milltown, New Jersey

H. Joseph Curry,
Vice President
New Jersey Bankers Association
The Phillipsburg National Bank & Trust Co.
Phillipsburg, New Jersey

C. Malcolm Davis,
President
The Fidelity Union Trust Company
Newark, New Jersey

J. H. Davis,
President
Stevens Institute of Technology
Hoboken, New Jersey

Fairleigh S. Dickinson, Jr.,
President
Becton, Dickinson & Company
East Rutherford, New Jersey

Most Reverend John J. Dougherty,
President
Seton Hall University
South Orange, New Jersey

Alfred E. Driscoll,
President
Warner-Lambert Pharmaceutical Company
Morris Plains, New Jersey

Mrs. Walter E. Edge,
Princeton, New Jersey

Frank S. Farley,
New Jersey State Senator, Atlantic County
Atlantic City, New Jersey

Malcolm S. Forbes,
Editor-in-Chief & Publisher
Forbes, Inc.
New York, New York

Robert F. Goheen,
President
Princeton University
Princeton, New Jersey

Frederick H. Groel,
President
New Jersey State Chamber of Commerce
Newark, New Jersey

Mason W. Gross,
President
Rutgers—The State University
New Brunswick, New Jersey

Anthony J. Grossi,
Minority Leader, New Jersey State Senate
Paterson, New Jersey

James P. Hayward,
President
Atlantic City Electric Company
Atlantic City, New Jersey

Carlton E. Heritage,
President
New Jersey Farm Bureau
Trenton, New Jersey

Leon Hess,
President
Hess Oil & Chemical Corp.
Perth Amboy, New Jersey

Joel R. Jacobson,
President
New Jersey Independent Union Council,
AFL-CIO
Newark, New Jersey

Leonard C. Johnson,
President
New Jersey Manufacturers Association
Trenton, New Jersey

Robert W. Johnson,
Johnson & Johnson
New Brunswick, New Jersey

Theodore H. Kendall,
President
South Jersey Gas Company
Atlantic City, New Jersey

Elwood F. Kirkman,
President
The Boardwalk National Bank
Atlantic City, New Jersey

Kenneth H. Klipstein,
President
American Cyanamid Company
Wayne, New Jersey

John W. Kress,
President
The Howard Savings Institution
Newark, New Jersey

Mrs. Morgan F. Larson,
Metuchen, New Jersey

Philip J. Levin,
President
Philip J. Levin & Affiliated Companies
North Plainfield, New Jersey

Thorn Lord,
State Chairman
New Jersey Democratic State Committee
Trenton, New Jersey

Donald C. Luce,
President
Public Service Electric and Gas Company
Newark, New Jersey

William H. McElwain,
President
New Jersey Power & Light Company
Morristown, New Jersey

Robert B. Meyner,
Former Governor of New Jersey
Newark, New Jersey

Charles J. Milton,
Milton, Keane & DeBona
Jersey City, New Jersey

Mrs. A. Harry Moore,
Jersey City, New Jersey

Franklin C. Nixon,
Master
New Jersey State Grange
Vincentown, New Jersey

Rabbi Joachim Prinz,
President
American Jewish Congress
Newark, New Jersey

Robert A. Roe,
Commissioner of Conservation and
  Economic Development
Trenton, New Jersey

Mrs. Mary G. Roebling,
President
Trenton Trust Company
Trenton, New Jersey

Vincent Salierno, President
Victory Optical Manufacturing Company
Newark, New Jersey

Peter Sammartino,
President
Fairleigh Dickinson University
Rutherford, New Jersey

Charles W. Sandman, Jr.,
President, New Jersey State Senate
Cape May, New Jersey

Joseph A. Santangelo, M.D.,
President, Medical Staff
Columbus Hospital
Newark, New Jersey

David Sarnoff,
Chairman of the Board
Radio Corporation of America
New York, New York

Stuart T. Saunders,
Chairman of the Board
The Pennsylvania Railroad Company
Philadelphia, Pennsylvania

Mrs. Thelma Parkinson Sharp,
Democratic National Committeewoman
  from New Jersey
Vineland, New Jersey

Sylvester C. Smith, Jr.,
Carpenter, Bennett & Morrissey
Newark, New Jersey

Louis Stein,
President
Food Fair, Inc.
Philadelphia, Pennsylvania

W. Paul Stillman,
Chairman of the Board
National State Bank of Newark
Newark, New Jersey

Mrs. Richard Switlik,
Allentown, New Jersey

Paul L. Troast,
President
Mahoney-Troast Construction Co.
Clifton, New Jersey

E. Hornsby Wasson,
President
New Jersey Bell Telephone Company
Newark, New Jersey

Mrs. Katharine Elkus White,
United States Ambassador to Denmark
Copenhagen, Denmark

David T. Wilentz,
Democratic National Committeeman
  from New Jersey
Perth Amboy, New Jersey

Reverend S. Howard Woodson,
Pastor
Shiloh Baptist Church
Trenton, New Jersey

1964 Democratic National Convention Program

First Session
Monday, August 24

Convention convenes at 8:30 p.m.

Invocation—The Most Reverend
  Celestine J. Damiano

Presentation of Colors

Pledge of Allegiance—
  The Hon. Daniel Inouye,
  United States Senator, Hawaii

National Anthem—Robert Merrill

Official Call of the Convention—
  Mrs. Dorothy Vredenburgh Bush,
  Secretary, Democratic National Committee

Address of Welcome—
  The Hon. Richard J. Hughes,
  Governor, State of New Jersey

Election of Temporary Officers
  of the Convention

"The People Speak"—Democratic progress
  in domestic affairs (Film)

Keynote Address—The Hon. John Pastore,
  United States Senator, Rhode Island

Report of Committee on Rules and Order
  of Business—The Hon. Carl Sanders,
  Governor, State of Georgia

Remarks by Mr. J. Albert House, Jr.,
  National President, Young Democratic
  Clubs of America

Address—Mr. David Bruce Marth, Winner of
  1964 American Legion Oratorical Contest

Report of Committee on Credentials—
  The Hon. David Lawrence, Pennsylvania

Benediction—The Rev. Franklin Clark Fry

Adjournment

Second Session
Tuesday, August 25

Convention convenes at 8 p.m.

Invocation—Rabbi Joachim Prinz

Pledge of Allegiance

National Anthem—Mace Barrett

Report of Committee on Permanent
  Organization—Norman Stahl,
  National Committeeman, Oregon

Address by Permanent Chairman—
  The Hon. John McCormack, Speaker,
  United States House of Representatives

Address—The Hon. Charles Weltner,
  Congressman, State of Georgia

"The Quest for Peace"—Democratic
  progress in foreign affairs (Film)

Report on Nomination of National
  Committeeman and Committeewomen

Report of Committee on Resolutions and
  Platform—Representative Democrats

"The Two Platforms"—Address by the
  Hon. Birch Bayh, United States Senator,
  Indiana

Benediction—The Rev. Frank A. P. Pehrson

Third Session
Wednesday, August 26

Convention convenes at 8:30 p.m.

Invocation—Rt. Rev. Leland J. Stark

Pledge of Allegiance

National Anthem—Miss Mahalia Jackson

Roll Call of the States for Nominations for the
  Office of the President of the United States

Balloting on the Nominees

"The Road to Leadership"—A biography of
  President Lyndon B. Johnson (Film)

Roll Call of the States for Nominations
  for the Office of the Vice-President
  of the United States

Balloting of the Nominees

Acceptance Speech by the Democratic
  Nominee for the Office of the
  Vice-President of the United States

Benediction—Bishop Prince A. Taylor, Jr.

Adjournment

Fourth Session
Thursday, August 27

Convention convenes at 8:30 p.m.

Invocation—
  His Eminence Archbishop Iakovos

Pledge of Allegiance

National Anthem—Enzo Stuarti

Memorial Program

"A Thousand Days": A tribute to
  President John F. Kennedy (Film)
  Tribute to Mrs. Eleanor Roosevelt
  Tribute to Speaker Sam Rayburn

Recess

Acceptance Speech by the
Democratic Nominee for the Office
of the President of the United States

Benediction—Rev. John Barclay

Adjournment *sine die*

Map No.	HOTEL
8	ABBEY
65	AMBASSADOR
1	BREAKERS
19	CAROLINA CREST
13	CHALFONTE-HADDON HALL
45	CLARIDGE
9	COLTON MANOR
29	COLUMBUS
67	DEAUVILLE
53	DENNIS
48	EASTBOURNE
28	FLANDERS
7	HOLMHURST
36	JEFFERSON
37	KENTUCKY
74	LaCONCHA
31	LEXINGTON
40	MADISON
52	MARLBOROUGH-BLENHEIM
26	MAYFLOWER
3	MORTON
23	NEW BELMONT
22	PENN-ATLANTIC
83	PRESIDENT
32	RICHFIELD-BOSCOBEL
60	RITZ CARLTON
49	RUNNYMEDE
4	SEASIDE
55	SHELBURNE-EMPRESS
35	STERLING
41	TRAYMORE

Map No.	MOTEL
33	ACAPULCO
69	ALGIERS
76	ALOHA
61	ASCOT
42	BALA
18	BARBIZON
15	BARCLAY
71	BARONET
80	BLAIR
21	BURGUNDY
59	CALIFORNIAN
75	CARIBE
20	CAROLINA CREST
70-A	CASTLE ROC
17	CATALINA
43	COLONY
10	COLTON MANOR
39	CONTINENTAL
14	CORONET
46	CRILLON
12	CROWN
68	DEAUVILLE & DEAUVILLE WEST
54	DENNIS
63	DIPLOMAT
66	DUNES
47	EASTBOURNE
62	ELDORADO
30	ENVOY
25	FIESTA
64	GALAXIE
16	LaFAYETTE
85	LINCOLN-ROOSEVELT BEACH
34	LOMBARDY
77	MALIBU
70	MARDI GRAS
51	MARLBOROUGH-BLENHEIM
73	MARTINIQUE
27	MAYFLOWER
44	MIDTOWN
82	MONTE CARLO BEACH
11	MONTEREY
50	MT. ROYAL
81	NAUTILUS
2	OCEAN VIEW
58	PAGEANT
84	PRESIDENT
57	SAXONY
5	SEASIDE
56	SHELBURNE-EMPRESS
38	SORRENTO
79	STRAND
72	TEPLITZKY'S
6	TERRACE
24	TRINIDAD
78	TROPICANA

Hotel Assignments for State Delegations

DELEGATION	HOTEL
Alabama	Chalfonte
Alaska	Aloha
Arizona	Siesta
Arkansas	Haddon Hall
California	Ambassador
Colorado	Barbizon
Connecticut	Dennis and Empress
Delaware	Marlborough-Blenheim
Florida	Caribe and La Concha
Georgia	Traymore and Madison
Hawaii	St. Lo
Idaho	Richfield-Boscobel
Illinois	Continental, Madison, Sorrento and Traymore
Indiana	Morton and Seaside
Iowa	Ambassador
Kansas	Mt. Royal
Kentucky	Mayflower
Louisiana	Algiers and Mardi Gras
Maine	Malibu
Maryland	Marlborough-Blenheim
Massachusetts	Lafayette
Michigan	President
Minnesota	Shelburne and Saxony
Mississippi	Chalfonte
Missouri	Traymore
Montana	Acapulco
Nebraska	Fiesta and Penn-Atlantic
Nevada	Barclay
New Hampshire	Coronet
New Jersey	Colony
New Mexico	Deauville
New York	Ritz-Carlton, Ascot, El Dorado, Castle Roc and Dunes
North Carolina	Marlborough-Blenheim
North Dakota	Jefferson
Ohio	Seaside Terrace
Oklahoma	Shelburne and Saxony
Oregon	Bala
Pennsylvania	Dennis and Empress
Rhode Island	Trinidad
South Carolina	Mayflower
South Dakota	Abbey
Tennessee	Colton
Texas	Haddon Hall
Utah	Strand
Vermont	Traymore
Virginia	Monte Carlo Beach
Washington	Lombardy
West Virginia	Carolina Crest and Burgundy
Wisconsin	Jefferson
Wyoming	Sterling
District of Columbia	Tropicana
Canal Zone	Morton
Guam	St. Lo
Puerto Rico	Mt. Royal
Virgin Islands	Acapulco

(another delegation at Lincoln)

Special Events

Thursday, August 20
5-7 p.m.
Joint reception for women members of Platform Committee Terrace Suite, Claridge Hotel
Hostesses: Mrs. Richard J. Hughes, Mrs. Margaret Price (By invitation only)

Friday, August 21
Opening sessions, National Committee Meeting, Young Democratic Clubs of America, Jefferson Hotel

Saturday, August 22
8 a.m.
YDCA National Officers Meeting—Jefferson Hotel
12 Noon
YDCA Luncheon—Guest speaker: Franklin D. Roosevelt, Jr.
6 p.m.
YDCA Reception (Guests of honor)
7 p.m.
YDCA Banquet—Speaker: Sen. Hubert Humphrey

Sunday, August 23
9 a.m.
YDCA Breakfast, Hotel Jefferson
11 a.m.
Brunch for National Committeewomen and newly-elected National Committeewomen. Smithville Inn, Absecon, New Jersey (Bus transportation provided)
Hostesses: Mrs. Margaret Price, Mrs. John M. Bailey (By invitation only)
3 p.m.
Reception for New Jersey Delegation
Host: Sen. Harrison A. Williams, Jr.
Zaberers Restaurant
6 p.m.
Meet the Press, Convention Hall Studio
8 p.m.
Young Citizens for Johnson—Young Democrats Orientation
Atlantic City High School Auditorium
Speakers: Sen. Birch Bayh, Gov. Richard J. Hughes, Robert J. Burkhardt

Monday, August 24
7-9 a.m.
Today Show, Claridge Hotel
9-10 a.m.*
First of three TV programs on "Women's Challenge in The Great Society." Program producer: Mrs. Constance D. Casey
Today's subject: "Peace"
Moderator: Hon. Frank Church

10 a.m.-5 p.m.
Cumberland County Agriculture Tour (Buses leave Columbus Plaza)
1:30 p.m.
Golf Match—Tony Lema and Sam Snead Mays Landing Country Club, Admission, $5.
2-6 p.m.
Guided Tours to Renault Winery (Buses leave at 2 p.m. and 3 p.m., returning at 6 p.m.)
3 p.m.
"Salute to Women Doers"—A reception for women delegates, and alternates, wives of delegates, National Committeewomen and wives of National Committeemen. Grand Ballroom-Kerry Hall, Shelburne Hotel (By invitation only)
5-7 p.m.
Reception honoring Majority Leader and Majority Whip of Senate
Host: Charles W. Engelhard
Shelburne Hotel Penthouse
(By invitation only)

Tuesday, August 25
7-9 a.m.
Today Show, Claridge Hotel
9-10 a.m.
Second TV Program on "Women's Challenge in the Great Society."
Today's subject: "Prosperity"
Moderator: Hon. W. Willard Wirtz
9:30 a.m.
Young Citizens for Johnson
Campaign Seminar
Atlantic City High School Auditorium
10 a.m.-5 p.m.
Cumberland County Agricultural Tour
11:30 a.m.
"Ladies Day" at the Races:
Atlantic City Race Track
Transportation, admission, luncheon on the dining terrace and fashion show. Tickets, $5.75. Buses leave Convention Hall at 11:30 a.m., return after last race.
11:30 a.m.
Tour of Lenox China Showroom at Pomona. Smorgasbord luncheon at Zaberers. Tour divided into two sections: #1-tour and luncheon, #2-luncheon and tour. Buses leave Convention Hall at 11:30 a.m. and return no later than 3 p.m.
12 Noon
Luncheon—State YDCA Presidents
2-3 p.m.
Guided Tour, Renault Winery. Buses leave at 2 and 3 p.m., return at 6 p.m.
5:30-7 p.m.
Reception for New Jersey Host Committee and New Jersey delegates and alternates. Shelburne Hotel Penthouse
Host: Gov. Hughes and Charles W. Engelhard
(By invitation only)

Wednesday, August 26

7-9 a.m.
Today Show, Claridge Hotel
9-10 a.m.
Third TV Program on "Women's Challenge in the Great Society."
Today's subject: "Political Participation"
Moderator: Pierre Salinger
9:30 a.m.
Young Citizens for Johnson
Campaign Seminar
Atlantic City High School Auditorium
10 a.m.-12 Noon
Gala Fashion Show
Ballroom, Shelburne Hotel. Free admission
(More than 500 door prizes)
Hostess: Mrs. Richard J. Hughes
10 a.m.-5 p.m.
Cumberland County Agricultural Tour
1:30 p.m.
Day at the Races
Atlantic City Race Track
2-3 p.m.
Guided Tour, Renault Winery. Buses leave at 2 and 3 p.m., return at 6 p.m.
3-5 p.m.
Tea for National Committeewomen, New Jersey State Committeewomen and New Jersey Vice Chairmen
St. Denis Room, Dennis Hotel
Hostess: Mrs. Thelma Parkinson Sharp
(By invitation only)

Thursday, August 27

7-9 a.m.
Today Show, Claridge Hotel
10 a.m.
Tour of historic Batsto, restored area of Wharton Tract. Visit to Renault Winery. Luncheon at Smithville Inn.
10 a.m.-2 p.m.
Splash Party for Children. Colony Motel Pool. No child under 7 admitted without an adult. Entertainment, games, prizes, outdoor lunch available at nominal cost. Beach for bathing. Wear beach attire. Admission free.
10 a.m.-5 p.m.
Cumberland County Agricultural Tour
11 a.m.-1 p.m.
Young Citizens Convention Rally
Convention Hall
An historic first convention session for young people featuring some of the nation's outstanding entertainment groups and political leaders. Rally Director: Mike Nichols. Admission by ticket only. Tickets available at Young Citizens for Johnson Headquarters, Crane Building.
4-7 p.m.
California Delegation Dinner Party
Shelburne Hotel
9 p.m.-midnight
President's Birthday Party. Boardwalk
11 p.m.-midnight
President's Birthday Party.
Ballroom, Convention Hall
Midnight
Midnight Supper in honor of Presidential and Vice-Presidential Candidates.
Shelburne Hotel.

*TELEVISION CHANNEL 5 IN ATLANTIC CITY WILL BROADCAST EXCLUSIVELY PROGRAMS OF INTEREST TO CONVENTION DELEGATES AND GUESTS FROM 3 P.M.—11 P.M. SUNDAY AND—8 A.M. TO MIDNIGHT MONDAY-THURSDAY. WATCH CHANNEL 5 FOR CONVENTION PROGRAM CHANGES, ANNOUNCEMENTS OF MEETINGS AND SPECIAL EVENTS FOR CONVENTION DELEGATES AND GUESTS.